D1157583

Little Words

WITHDRAWAL

Georgetown University Round Table on Languages and Linguistics series
Selected Titles

Crosslinguistic Research in Syntax and Semantics:
Negation Tense and Clausal Architecture
RAFFAELLA ZANUTTINI, HÉCTOR CAMPOS, ELENA HERBURGER,
AND PAUL H. PORTNER, EDITORS

Discourse and Technology: Multimodal Discourse Analysis
PHILIP LEVINE AND RON SCOLLON, EDITORS

Educating for Advanced Foreign Language Capacities
HEIDI BYRNES, HEATHER D. WEGER-GUNTHARP, KATHERINE SPRANG, EDITORS

Language in Our Time: Bilingual Education and Official English, Ebonics
and Standard English, Immigration and Unz Initiative
JAMES E. ALATIS AND AI-HUI TAN, EDITORS

Language in Use: Cognitive and Discourse Perspectives
on Language and Language Learning
ANDREA E. TYLER, MARI TAKADA, YIYOUNG KIM, AND
DIANA MARINOVA, EDITORS

Linguistics, Language, and the Professions: Education, Journalism,
Law, Medicine, and Technology
JAMES E. ALATIS, HEIDI E. HAMILTON, AND AI-HUI TAN, EDITORS

Linguistics, Language, and the Real World: Discourse and Beyond
DEBORAH TANNEN AND JAMES E. ALATIS, EDITORS

Little Words: Their History, Phonology, Syntax, Semantics,
Pragmatics, and Acquisition
RONALD P. LEOW, HÉCTOR CAMPOS, AND DONNA LARDIERE, EDITORS

Sustaining Linguistic Diversity: Endangered and Minority Languages
and Language Varieties
KENDALL A. KING, NATALIE SCHILLING-ESTES, LYN FOGLE, JIA JACKIE LOU,
AND BARBARA SOUKOUP, EDITORS

▓ Contents

Illustrations

Tableaux

Preface

The Georgetown University Round Table of Languages and Linguistics (GURT) is an annual conference with a long-standing tradition—Georgetown University has hosted GURT since 1949. The conference began as a gathering for discussion of issues in all fields of language studies; over time it has developed into a nationally and internationally known forum for the in-depth treatment of special topics.

The 2007 Georgetown University Round Table on Languages and Linguistics (GURT 2007) was cohosted by the Department of Spanish and Portuguese and the Department of Linguistics and was held March 8–11. GURT 2007 focused on "little words"—items such as clitics, pronouns, determiners, conjunctions, discourse particles, auxiliary/light verbs, prepositions, and so on—including their phonology, morphology, syntax, semantics, pragmatics, discourse function, historical development, variation, and acquisition (by children or adults). The plenary speakers, representing the broad scope of the theme of the conference, were Jonathan D. Bobaljik (University of Connecticut), Thomas Cravens (University of Wisconsin–Madison), Katherine Demuth (Brown University), Kai von Fintel (Massachusetts Institute of Technology), and Claire Lefebvre (Université du Québec à Montréal). The conference drew more than two hundred attendees from local, national, and international institutions that included representatives from Asia, Europe, and Canada. There were seventy-four paper presentations, twelve poster presentations, and one colloquium.

To address the broad disciplinary scope of the conference's focus on little words and provide a relatively balanced representation from the different areas of research disseminated during the conference, we had the difficult task of accepting only a small number of manuscripts for each research area from the many high-quality submissions we received. To this end, the following chapters address each of the six areas of research that were well presented and discussed during this event, which may be the first professional conference devoted to little words from a multidisciplinary perspective.

We are very grateful to the Faculty of Languages and Linguistics (FLL), the Department of Linguistics, and the Department of Spanish and Portuguese for financially supporting GURT 2007 and to all the reviewers who shared their expertise in helping us select a representative number of high-quality papers to be presented and published. We would also like to express our deepest appreciation to all the graduate students who assisted in one way or another to make this conference a success, especially Mika Hama, our graduate organizer who spent countless hours participating in the planning and implementation of many of the aspects of the conference, displaying her remarkable organizational abilities and sharing her magnetic enthusiasm while undertaking these heavy responsibilities. Finally, we would like to sincerely thank our colleague, Dr. Maite Camblor-Portilla, who not only served as our webmaster and GURT contact person throughout the conference but also assisted with the preparation of this volume.

1

▩ Introduction

RONALD P. LEOW, HÉCTOR CAMPOS, AND DONNA LARDIERE
Georgetown University

▩ "LITTLE WORDS"—items such as clitics, pronouns, determiners, conjunctions, discourse particles, auxiliary/light verbs, prepositions, and so on—have been the focus of investigation in many research areas that include phonology, morphology, syntax, semantics, pragmatics, discourse function, historical development, variation, and acquisition. The unique purpose of GURT 2007 was to bring these different research areas into one professional conference that would promote discussion, both cross-disciplinary and within a single discipline, during the course of the event. To reflect the broad disciplinary scope of GURT 2007, *Little Words: Their History, Phonology, Syntax, Semantics, Pragmatics, and Acquisition* is divided into six parts that address each of these research areas.

Part I: History

In chapter 2 Łazorczyk and Pancheva make the novel observation that Old Church Slavonic (OCS) *oba,* the historical counterpart of the modern Slavic "both," was not a distributive quantifier (like Modern Slavic and English "both") but simply a numeral "two," although it differed from another numeral *dъva* "two" in that it was associated with a definiteness presupposition. They propose an account of the syntactic and semantic reanalysis of *oba* where it changes from a numeral, merged as a specifier of number phrase inside a [+] definite-marked determiner phrase (DP), to a quantifier merged as a specifier of a functional projection higher than the DP, headed by a null distributive operator. In this chapter they discuss the motivation for this historical change and the larger implications of their findings.

Elsman and Holt discuss in chapter 3 the phenomenon of the grammaticalization of lexical words into function words that has received much attention in various fields of linguistics. They point out that while grammaticalization usually results in the phonological reduction of the words in question, this reduction does not usually result in the loss of semantic recoverability. However, given that function words are inherently phonologically short, any reduction resulting from grammaticalization would incur a proportionally greater loss to the surface realization of their meaning. To support this phenomenon, they provide a close analysis of data from Medieval Leonese, which suggests that as function words are grammaticalized and undergo phonological reduction, individual features take on a correspondingly greater role in distinguishing meaning that was previously represented by entire segments. In this chapter, the authors show how the burden of morphological representation shifts from the segmental to the featural level to prevent the complete loss of surface forms that are already short.

Part II: Phonology
In chapter 4 Lord, Berdan, and Fender analyze the prosodic differences between function words and content words in English. Adults reading aloud showed reduced stress on function words, as measured by acoustic correlates including length, intensity, pitch, and vowel quality. Compared with proficient readers, nonproficient children showed less distinction between function words and content words. This difference appears to be a major contributor to the impression of word-by-word nonfluent reading. Fluent readers look ahead in the text in order to construct appropriate phrasal word groups and assign prosodic contours. In contrast, many of the nonfluent readers are looking only as far as the next word; their cognitive resources are focused on next-word recognition, and there are too few words in the look-ahead queue to assign phrasal groupings. The authors suggest that acoustic analysis and eye tracking can contribute to our understanding of the development of reading fluency.

Rochman addresses the motivation for using floating quantifiers in chapter 5. In contrast to other research on floating quantifiers that focuses on the syntax of how the quantifier comes to occur in the position it does, she looks at why speakers opt to use the floated word order. Rochman shows that floating quantifiers are used preceding *foci,* a type of focus marker. Interpretively, the floating quantifiers result in a contrastive interpretation of the focus (producing a contrastive focus). She then briefly discusses how the floating quantifier comes to occur in the position that it does in the linear string and concludes with a possible phonological account for why in natural speech floating quantifiers only occur in one of the several possible positions.

Part III: Syntax
In chapter 6 Sáez discusses how third-person accusative clitics of Spanish verbs like *ayudar* trigger *me-lui* constraint effects. Because they are accusative (not dative) and third-person (not first-/second-person) clitics, their offending status escapes standard formulations of such constraint, including Ormazábal and Romero's (1998a, 1998b) one. Sáez proposes that those accusative clitics can find easy accommodation if they are actually generated in the specifier of an applicative phrase (as goals). He provides several pieces of evidence to support his claim: impossibility of a dative clitic, inherent interpretation for adverbs like *mucho,* and unavailability of depictives. The complement of the applicative phrase (the theme) is a cognate object undergoing conflation, and its covertness explains the goal accusative makeup as resulting from a case assignment principle (a variant of the one in Alsina [1997]). Finally, adopting Ormazábal and Romero's (2007) approach to *me-lui* constraint effects, he proposes that they are triggered in these cases not by the clitic itself (a determiner undergoing cliticization) but by the (silent) applicative object agreement.

Gergel analyzes in chapter 7 the Romanian little word *de* as it occurs with adjectives. The claim is that the word under scrutiny serves as an exponent in degree constructions. He discusses the pertinent morphosyntactic properties found in the language together with the paradox arising from a positive setting for degrees as far as the basic morphological and syntactic facts of the language are concerned, on the one hand, and some apparent negative tests (e.g., in questions and subcomparatives), on the other. To resolve this paradox, Gergel proposes that *de* is inserted in the relevant degree constructions under a functional degree—and in general also movement-sensitive head. In addition the chapter analyzes new evidence from an independent domain involving the little word *de*, namely as it is attested in (adjectival) doubling constructions.

In chapter 8 Taylor discusses comparative correlatives in English that consist of two clauses, both of which obligatorily begin with the word *the*. She points out that if this *the* is analyzed as a determiner, it must be concluded that the expressions consist of two DPs, perhaps similar to an equative expression. However, Taylor states that there is evidence against such an equative-like analysis—the verb in the second clause is the main verb, contrasting with the verb in the first clause, which never shows these properties. In order to account for these facts, Taylor proposes that the obligatory *the* at the start of both clauses be treated as a complementizer (C0), the head of its clause. This analysis of *the* is extended to another English expression, nominal extraposition.

Progovac's goal in chapter 9 is to provide a theoretical argument, using the tools of the syntactic framework of minimalism (e.g., Chomsky 1995), that certain small clauses (syntactic objects with no or few little words), which can be found in root contexts as well as in other unexpected uses, may represent "living fossils" from a root small-clause stage in language evolution. In addition to the root small-clause stage, the clausal development may have also gone through a proto-coordination stage, on its way to developing specific functional categories. According to Progovac, these claims are consistent (a) with a syntactic analysis of what counts as an increase in complexity, (b) with well-known grammaticalization processes, (c) with "living fossil" evidence, and (d) with stages in language acquisition. Progovac argues that not only does this approach help situate syntax in an evolutionary framework, but it also sheds light on some crucial aspects of syntax itself.

In chapter 10 Velázquez-Mendoza and Aranovich analyze the distribution of Spanish personal *a* in ditransitives. They observe that the kind of direct objects that are normally marked by personal *a* in monotransitives (human, definite) occur without *a* in ditransitives. To account for this, they suggest that personal *a* cannot occur on secondary objects. These are defined as the direct object of a ditransitive in which the goal immediately follows the verb. A consequence of their analysis is that in ditransitives with pronominal themes the only possible word order is V-Theme-Goal, because object pronouns must be marked by personal *a*. Their analysis receives further support from evidence based on relativization of Spanish ditransitives. The conclusion of their study is that little word *a* reveals that Spanish is in the process of becoming, or has already become, a primary object/secondary object (PO/SO) language.

Part IV: Semantics

In chapter 11 Beavers examines the role of adposition semantics in the realization of oblique arguments. Contra recent approaches in which either the verb or the adposition carries the core predicational force of a clause and thus solely determines how arguments within the clause are realized, Beavers suggests that both verbs and adpositions assign thematic roles to oblique arguments, albeit subject to a compatibility constraint: the role assigned by the verb must crucially subsume the role assigned by the adposition. He then shows how various typological parameters (including motion encoding and the presence of dative shift) can be reduced on this approach to cross-linguistic variation in adposition inventories. Finally, Beavers reexamines the notion of semantically vacuous "default" adpositions and suggests that such adpositions do not exist, further supporting the idea that argument-marking adpositions are semantically contentful.

In chapter 12 Thomas and Michaelis argue that Krifka's (1998) path-based analysis of temporal measure adverbials can be extended to aspectual adverbials that denote time points, in particular *by* temporal adverbials (e.g., *That should happen by today*). Using data from the *Wall Street Journal* corpus they demonstrate that *by* temporal adverbials presuppose a path schema that, subject to the demands of context, might represent a schedule or a process. In all contexts, they claim, the *by* adverbial denotes the first point at which some observer—whether the author or a participant—got, expects to get, or hopes to get a positive answer to the question "Is state x in force?" In some contexts, they argue, this sampling point represents an earlier than expected point of eventuation (as in, e.g., *By 8 a.m. [the traffic] already had thinned out*), in others it represents a deadline (as in, e.g., *Mr. Bush has called for an agreement by next September at the latest*), and in still others it simply represents the first point at which the relevant state is evident (as in, e.g., *U.S. oil supplies [. . .] had peaked in 1970 and 1971 and by 1973 were declining*). Because the sampling-point schema is compatible with a number of more specific ones, they suggest that the *by* temporal adverbial is a contextual operator in the sense of Kay (1990): It instructs the interpreter to retrieve an appropriate semantic frame and place the situation denoted by the predication into that frame.

Park's main goal in chapter 13 is to provide the generalized patterns of interpretations of distributivity, which are drawn from the non-nominal plural marker (NNM) *–tul* and its interactions with different types of predicates. In particular, Park shows that there are two distinct types of distributive effects, an argument and an event distributive reading, and that only the latter is due to the presence of the NNM plural marker *–tul*, while the former is due to the distributive operator introduced by a plural subject. In order to explain the generalized patterns, Park proposes the eclectic approach under the neo-Davidsonian event semantics, which combines both the syntactic agreement approach and the semantic approach.

Part V: Pragmatics

In chapter 14 Pellet examines the use of French discourse markers (DMs) *donc* and *alors* (both equivalent to English "so") in native speaker conversational discourse to argue that the two DMs are not functionally equivalent: *donc* and *alors* occur in complementary distribution. *Donc* asserts the validity of the speaker's viewpoint and occurs within turn, whereas *alors* is used to preface a reaction to just-heard information and occurs at the beginning of a turn. A discourse analysis of the occurrences of these markers demonstrates that there is no functional overlap between the two. Pellet concludes with a justification of exclusive uses of the two markers (instances where only one marker is possible) with what each of them indexes respectively ([logical] continuity for *donc,* change of orientation for *alors*), hence reinforcing the argument that they are not functional equivalents. She ends with a discussion of the possible compound *alors donc* and the unacceptability of *donc alors.*

Alba-Juez reports in chapter 15 on the qualitative and quantitative results of her analysis of the little words *macho/a* and *tío/a* in Spanish and *man* in English. Following Fraser's (1996, 2006) taxonomy, she categorizes these expressions as parallel pragmatic markers that appear in the form of vocatives and are characteristic of oral, colloquial language, mainly found in the corpora used within the framework of the so-called small talk. She analyzes the strategies used by "small talkers" when employing these markers, as well as the main discourse functions they fulfil, namely their function as markers of (im)politeness, interaction regulators, and as alerters (focusing function). Alba comments on the issues of solidarity and gender with respect to these little words and especially about the uses of the Spanish marker *macha.*

Biesenbach-Lucas, in chapter 16, examines the impact of faculty's higher status and relative social distance on the use of greetings and closings in student–professor e-mail communication. She conducts an analysis of linguistic realizations of greetings and closings, examines closings for sequenced moves, and compares the linguistic patterns and moves used by native and nonnative speakers of English. Her findings indicate that two distinct e-mail formats set native speakers (NSs) apart from non-native speakers (NNSs): unlike NNSs, NSs produce brief openings and closings that are nevertheless appropriately status congruent given the faculty addressee. In contrast, NNSs inappropriately blend formal business letter formulae with informal, often oral, expressions. Biesenbach-Lucas's study suggests that e-mail from students to professors in an academic context is developing toward brevity and ritual formulae that differ from conventional business letters but adhere to status-appropriate social protocol.

Part VI: Acquisition

In chapter 17, Bowles and Montrul investigate the efficacy of form-focused instruction involving explicit rule presentation and practice with explicit corrective feedback. Specifically their instruction focuses on intermediate-level second-language (L2) learners of Spanish and differential object marking in Spanish. Results show positive effects for the instruction, with significant improvements in the learners' ability to distinguish between grammatical and ungrammatical uses of the target structure (as measured by a grammaticality judgment test) and increased ability to produce the target structure in obligatory contexts (as measured by a controlled written production test). Results provide support for Schwartz and Sprouse's (1996) claim that learners can overcome the structure imposed by their first language (L1) and restructure their interlanguages accordingly. The authors present implications for future research and pedagogy.

In chapter 18 de la Fuente addresses the field of instructed discourse language development of advanced L2 learners. In particular, her study examines the effect of type of focus on form task (explicit, i.e., consciousness-raising [C-R] vs. implicit, i.e., input enrichment that is meaning [content] focused) on the acquisition of discourse markers, and some of the processes that take place when students orally produce the language in these pedagogical tasks. Participants were twenty-four adult college learners of Spanish randomly assigned to pairs in one of the two experimental conditions. The quantitative analyses reveal that the C-R task was more effective at promoting attention to and noticing of discourse markers, as shown by the higher levels of both comprehension (meaning, function) and production (form) of the items. This superior performance is supported by the results of the qualitative analyses: They reveal that although input enrichment tasks seem to promote some level of effective attention to and noticing of discourse markers in the L2 input, C-R tasks seem more effective by focusing learners' attention on their forms, meanings, and uses and consequently raising learners' awareness of such forms. In addition, during C-R tasks, learners negotiate meaning of L2 forms by formulating hypotheses and testing them. De la Fuente concludes that, given the lack of salience of L2 discourse markers, explicit learning (via C-R tasks) and metalinguistic awareness may be necessary cognitive steps to learn such linguistic items in the input.

Kupisch et al. discuss in chapter 19 different approaches to the omission of articles in early child speech: the nominal mapping parameter and prosodic accounts. She analyzes data from the four Germanic languages—English, German, Norwegian, and Swedish—showing that children acquiring the Scandinavian languages omit fewer articles in obligatory contexts than mean length of utterances (MLU)-matched children acquiring English or German. Kupisch and colleagues conclude that the nominal mapping parameter does not predict these results while they can be accommodated in prosodic models of article omission.

In chapter 20 Dye investigates the status of functional elements in first language acquisition by focusing on the status of auxiliaries in child French. Based on analyses of a new child French corpus including cross-sectional speech samples from eighteen normally developing monolingual children (ages 1;11–2;11), which reveal a continuum in the surface realization of auxiliary forms, Dye argues that early productions are not as impoverished as typically assumed and that children may have greater grammatical knowledge than previously thought.

References

Alsina, Alex. 1997. Causatives in Bantu and Romance. In *Complex predicates,* ed. Alex Alsina, Joan Bresnan, and Peter Sells, 203–46. Stanford, CA: CSLI Publications.

Chomsky, Noam. 1995. *The Minimalist Program.* Cambridge, MA: The MIT Press.

Fraser, Bruce. 1996. Pragmatic markers. *Pragmatics* 6 (2): 167–90.

———. 2006. Towards a theory of discourse markers. In *Approaches to discourse particles,* ed. K. Fischer. Bremen: Elsevier.

Kay, Paul, 1990. Even. *Linguistics and Philosophy* 13:59–111.

Krifka, Manfred. 1998. The origins of telicity. In *Events and grammar,* ed. Susan Rothstein, 197–235. Dordrecht: Kluwer Academic.

Ormazábal, Javier, and Juan Romero. 1998a. Attract-F. A case against case. Paper presented at the 21st GLOW Colloquium, Tillburg, April 16.

———. 1998b. On the syntactic nature of the *me-lui* and the person-case constraints. *Anuario del Seminario de Filologia Vasca Julio de Urquijo* 32:415–34.

———. 2007. The object agreement constraint. *Natural Language and Linguistic Theory* 25:315–47.

Schwartz, B., and R. Sprouse. 1996. L2 cognitive states and the Full Transfer/Full Access model. *Second Language Research* 12:40–72.

History

2

From "Two" to "Both"

Historical Changes in the Syntax and Meaning of *Oba* in Slavic

AGNIESZKA ŁAZORCZYK AND ROUMYANA PANCHEVA
University of Southern California

WE MAKE THE NOVEL OBSERVATION that Old Church Slavonic (OCS) *oba,* the historical counterpart of the modern Slavic "both," meant simply "two." We propose an account of the syntactic reanalysis of *oba* and the accompanying change in its meaning and discuss the broader implications of our findings.

Old Church Slavonic

The grammatical descriptions of OCS (e.g., Huntley 1993; Lunt 2001) as well as dictionaries and glossaries consistently give the meaning of *oba* as "both."[1] This is probably so for two reasons: *oba* does mean "both" in the modern Slavic languages, and the meanings of "both" and "two" overlap and are difficult to distinguish in definite contexts that allow a distributive interpretation. Thus, whereas the contrast between *The two girls sang together* and **Both girls sang together* shows that *both* is necessarily distributive, predicates that are not obligatorily collective can mask the semantic distinction between *both* and *the two,* for example, *The two girls sang* and *Both girls sang.*

OCS *oba,* however, could not have meant "both." First, *oba* could be used to form complex numerals, as shown in (1).[2] Clearly, the only semantic contribution *oba* can have in such cases is its cardinality of 2. It was no different than the other numerals from 1 to 9, which similarly participated in the formation of complex numerals, for example, *četyre na desęte,* "*fourteen,*" literally "four on ten," and *sedmь na desęte,* "seventeen," literally "seven on ten."

(1) siję <u>oba na desęte</u> posъla isъ. zapovědavъ imъ glę.

   these two on ten   sent   Jesus having-ordered them saying . . .

   "These twelve Jesus sent out with the following instructions . . ." (Matt. 10:5)

Second, *oba* could be used with collective predicates, as exemplified in (2), which is also an environment where *both* is prohibited.

(2) I prilěpitъ sę ženě svoei . I bǫdete <u>oba</u> vъ plъtь edinǫ.

   and will-cling REFL wife self's and will-be two in body one

"And he will cling to his wife, and the two will become one flesh." (Matt. 19:5) cf. *English* And he will cling to his wife, and *both/the two will become one flesh.

Finally, *oba* could be the complement of a partitive preposition, as shown in (3). Again, this is not an environment where *both* is acceptable.

(3) ky   otъ <u>obojǫ</u> sъtvori voljǫ otьčǫ?
     which of   two   did   will   of-the-father
     "Which of the two did what his father wanted?"   (Matt. 21:31)
     cf. *English* Which of *both/the two (of them) did what his father wanted?

These examples show clearly that the OCS *oba* must have been simply a numeral "two." In Codex Marianus there are forty-one cases of the use of *oba* in environments such as (1)–(3), where it clearly did not mean "both." The remaining thirteen occurrences did not distinguish between a "both" and a "two" interpretation.

In addition to the semantic arguments for treating OCS *oba* as a numeral, there is also evidence from word order pointing to the same conclusion. *Oba* could co-occur with demonstratives (OCS did not have a definite article), and in such cases it followed the demonstrative, as in (4):

(4) vъ seju   <u>oboju</u> zapovědiju .   vesь zakon ъ i   proroci   visętь .
     in these two   commandments all   law   and prophets hang
     "All the Law and the Prophets hang on these two commandments." (Matt. 12:24)

In English *both* appears before determiners, as in *both these commandments* or in Brisson's (1998, 18) example *Both the girls went to the gym*.[3]

In sum, both semantic and syntactic arguments suggest that *oba* was a numeral. Interestingly, it was restricted to definite contexts.[4] Even when *oba* appeared without a determiner, its nominal phrase was interpreted as definite. Another numeral, *dъva*, also meaning "two," was used in both definite and indefinite contexts, though it was more typically found in indefinite ones (ninety-seven out of one hundred uses in Codex Marianus).

The Modern Slavic Languages

The situation with *oba* in the modern Slavic languages is markedly different from OCS. *Oba* is found in all the modern languages in the family except Bulgarian and some dialects of Macedonian, and in all the languages that have it, *oba* means "both." In that function, *oba* unambiguously marks distributive readings.

As a distributive marker, *oba* is no longer found in complex numerals in modern Slavic. This is shown in (5). The only possible numeral in this context is *dva*. (Examples are from a representative language from the west, east, and south branches of the Slavic family, respectively.)

(5) a. Polish
     I   usiadłszy,   przywołał <u>dwunastu</u> i   rzekł im . . .
     and having-sat-down called   two-on-ten and said   them

b. Russian

I   sev,   on pozval <u>dvenadtsat'</u> i   skazal im . . .

and having-sat-down he called two-on-ten and said   them

c. Serbian

Seo je i   pozvao <u>dvanaestoricu</u> i rekao im . . .

sat is and call   two-on-ten   and said   them

"And having sat down, he called the twelve and said to them . . ."

In the modern languages, *oba* cannot be used with collective predicates, as exemplified in (6) and (7). Again, in this respect, modern *oba* differs from its OCS predecessor.

(6) a. Polish

połączy się   z   żoną swoją, i   będą   ci   <u>dwoje/*oboje</u> jednym

*will-join REFL with wife self's and will-be these two/*both   one*

ciałem

body

b. Russian

soedenitsa   so svoej ženoi, i   <u>dvoe/*oba</u> stanut   odnoi plot'iu.

*will-join-REFL with self's wife   and two /*both will-become one   flesh*

c. Serbian

sjediniti se   sa   zenom svojom i   biće   njih <u>dvoje/*oboje</u> jedno

*will-join REFL with wife   self's   and will-be these two /*both   one*

telo

body

"(For this reason a man will leave his father and mother and be united to his wife,) and the two will become one flesh."

(7) a. Polish

<u>Obie</u> kobiety przyszły (*razem).

both women came   together

b. Russian

<u>Obe</u> zhenshchiny prishli (*vmeste).

both women   came together

c. Serbian

<u>Obe</u> žene   su došle (*zajedno).

both women are came together

"(*Both) women came together."

Last, just like *both, oba* cannot be a complement of a partitive preposition, as exemplified in (8). Again, recall that in this syntactic context OCS *oba* was acceptable.

(8) a. Polish

Który z   tych <u>dwóch/*obu</u> wypełnił wolę ojcowską?

*which from these two /*both   fulfilled   will   of-father*

b. Russian

Kto iz   etikh <u>dvoikh/*oboikh</u> sdelal to,   chto khotel   otets?

*who from these two /*both   did   this what wanted father*

c. Serbian

Koji od njih   <u>dvojice/*obojice/*oba</u> je učinio   šta

*which from these two /*both   is fulfilled what*

je njegov otac   želeo?

is his   father wanted.

"Which of these two did what his father wanted?"

As these examples show, in the languages that have preserved *oba,* it no longer functions as the numeral 2. Instead, it is a distributive quantifier corresponding to English "both."[5] The question arises how this historical change from a numeral to a distributive quantifier came to be and what factors contributed to it.

An additional question stems from the fact that, in Bulgarian and certain dialects of Macedonian, *oba* was lost as a lexical item. The function of "both" is fulfilled by the phrase "and the two," as exemplified in (9).

(9) Bulgarian

I   <u>dvamata</u> studenti dojdoha (*zaedno)

and the-two   students arrived   together

"Both students arrived (*together)."

A distributive-marking syntactic construction is a cross-linguistically available alternative for languages that do not have a lexicalized *both,* for example, Greek, French, Turkish, and, of course, OCS. Moreover, it is available for any numeral, not just "two." The exact syntactic structure used may differ from language to language, though a definite article and an additive particle, as in (9), are common elements. It is of interest to find out whether there is a principled reason behind the different history between the two groups of Slavic languages—Polish, Russian, Serbian, and others versus Bulgarian and dialects of Macedonian.

The Semantics and Syntax of "Both"

Before we present our analysis of the historical change in the meaning and syntax of *oba,* let us review briefly the accounts of the semantic and syntactic function of *both* as they have been proposed for English.

An important early account can be found in Barwise and Cooper (1981), who propose that *both* is a determiner with the same meaning as "the two." However, we already know that these two expressions are not equivalent. This is also indicated by examples such as **One of both children sneezed* and *One of the two children sneezed,* which have been used to criticize Barwise and Cooper's account.

In response to this problem Ladusaw (1982) proposes that *both* has a distributive component, which makes it impossible inside partitives and incompatible with collective predicates, as in **Both students are a happy couple* and *The two students are a happy couple*. This idea is further developed in Roberts (1987) and Landman (1989), who argue that *both* is equivalent to the distributive universal quantifier *each/every* but with the addition of a cardinality presupposition of 2. Brisson (1998) does not analyze *both* as a quantifier but rather as a modifier to nominal phrases. It is licensed in the presence of a distributive operator and has the semantic function of a maximizer—it picks up the maximal individual denoted by (the rest of) the nominal phrase and disallows exceptions

With respect to the syntax of *both,* it has been analyzed by Sportiche (1988), Schwarzschild (1996), and others as an adjunct to determiner phrases (DPs) that can be stranded after the DP moves, for example, *The children have both seen the movie.* An analysis along the lines of Shlonsky (1991) puts *both* in the head of a functional projection that selects the DP as a complement, while still allowing stranding after the DP moves. Doetjes (1997) and Fitzpatrick (2006) do not adopt a stranding analysis of floating *both* but analyze it as a VP-adverbial, composed of an adnominal *both* either adjoined to a null DP or in a functional projection selecting a null DP. Another type of analysis treats *both* as a cross-categorial modifier in the nominal and verbal domain, that is, a DP-adjunct or a VP-adjunct (e.g., Brisson 1998; Bobaljik 2003; Dowty and Brodie 1984).

Last, it should be mentioned that, as many authors have pointed out (e.g., Brisson 1998; Edmondson 1978; Progovac 1999; Schwarzschild 1996; Stockwell, Schachter, and Partee 1973), the word *both* in English also functions as a conjunction-reduction marker, whose presence signals strictly distributive, multiple event readings, for example, *Adam both acts and directs = Adam acts and Adam directs; The idea is both new and clever = The idea is new and the idea is clever; Both Peter and Paul read the book = Peter read the book and Paul read the book.*

While the floated quantifier *both* may be amenable to a uniform adnominal analysis, in one of its various instantiations as a stranded DP-adjunct (Sportiche 1988), or a stranded Q-head (Shlonsky 1991), or an adjunct/specifier/higher head with a null DP (Doetjes 1997; Fitzpatrick 2006), the function of *both* as a conjunction-reduction marker is not easily given such an analysis. Rather this use of *both* is a strong motivation to treat it as a cross-categorial adjunct and to extend that analysis to the use of *both* with nonconjoined nominals. We can conclude that *both* is uniformly an adjunct, to DPs or to conjunctions of various categories, and that it is associated with (a) distributivity, (b) cardinality of 2 (of individuals or events), and (c), in the case of DP-adjoined *both,* definiteness.

Historical Changes in the Syntax and Semantics of *Oba*

Returning to the previous discussion of Slavic, we can assume the structure as in (10) for OCS, where *oba* is a numeral with a definiteness presupposition, merging in the specifier of the number phrase (NumP). The specifier position is adopted for uniformity with complex numerals, which, we assume, have phrasal syntax. *Oba* lacks quantificational force of its own; it is a cardinality expression. The grammar of *dъva,* the other numeral 2, is the same, except for the fact that D^0 can be specified [definite] or not.

(10)

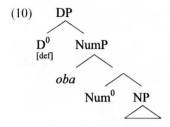

   In Polish, Russian, Serbian, and the other languages, apart from Bulgarian and dialects of Macedonian, *oba* was reanalyzed from a numeral, a nonquantificational cardinality expression, to a quantifier associated with distributivity. Syntactically, that meant that *oba* would no longer merge as a specifier of the NumP. But does it merge as an adjunct to the DP, as posited for English, or does it appear in a functional projection selecting the DP as a complement? It needs to be noted that Slavic *oba* cannot be used in conjunction reduction structures. Rather the conjunction *i*, "and," is used to introduce conjunction reduction in Slavic (cf. Progovac 1999). The example in (11) shows that this construction was already available in OCS.

(11) boite že sę   pače . mogǫščaago i   dšǫ i   tělo pogubiti v ъ Ge(enně
     OCS
     fear but REFL more being-able   and soul and body kill   in hell
     "Rather, be afraid of the one who can kill both soul and body in hell."
                                                                      (Matt.10:28b)

Because *oba* is not used with conjunctions, we propose to treat it as a specifier of a quantifier phrase (QP) head in the extended nominal projection, but we acknowledge that the alternative, adjunct-to-DP analysis, is also possible. The head of QP has a null distributive operator, a justified move, as distributive readings are possible without any overt marking. We cannot offer here a complete theory of the grammatical representation of distributivity (see, e.g., Brisson 1998; Schwarzschild 1996). Nor do we have an explanation for why *oba* had to be associated with a distributive interpretation. The syntactic reanalysis of *oba* yielded the present-day situation as represented in (12).

(12) The Modern Grammar of *Oba*

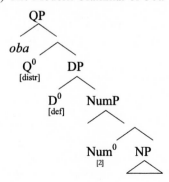

In (12) [*def*] D is null in all the modern languages, except for the dialects of Macedonian that have *oba,* where it is expressed with an overt definite article.

The fact that *oba* was promoted to a higher projection, freeing up the numeral position within the NumP, is evidenced by the fact that some modern Slavic languages allow the numeral *dva* to co-occur with *oba.* Examples of that are given in (13). Examples like this suggest that modern *oba* is directly merged as a Spec, QP, rather than first being merged as a numeral in Spec, NumP. It agrees with a Num^0 specified for a cardinality of 2.

(13) a. Polish

> <u>Obaj/obydwaj</u> chcieli   zapłacić za bilet.
>
> *both /both-two wanted to-pay   for ticket*
>
> "Both (men) wanted to pay for the ticket."

b. Serbian

> <u>Oba/obadva</u>   dečaka su želela   da plate kartu.
>
> *both/both-two boys   are wanted to pay   ticket*
>
> "Both boys wanted to pay for the ticket."

The position of demonstrative pronouns with respect to *oba* also indicates that *oba* is merged higher than the NumP. As the examples in (14) show, *oba* must precede the demonstrative pronoun.

(14) a. Polish

> <u>Obaj ci/*ci obaj</u>   chłopcy chcieli zapłacić za bilet.
>
> *both these/these both boys   wanted to-pay   for ticket*

b. Russian

> <u>Oba eti/??eti oba</u>   mal'chika khoteli zaplatit' za bilet.
>
> *both these/these both boys   wanted to-pay   for ticket*

c. Serbian

> <u>Oba ta/*ta oba</u>   dečaka su   zelela   da plate kartu.
>
> *both these/these both boys   are wanted to pay   ticket*
>
> "Both these boys wanted to-pay for ticket."

This contrasts with the position of the numerals, which must follow the demonstrative pronoun:

(15) a. Polish

> *<u>Dwaj ci/ci dwaj</u>   chłopcy chcieli zapłacić za bilet.
>
> *two these/these two boys   wanted to-pay   for ticket*

b. Serbian

> *<u>Dva ta/ta dva</u>   dečaka su   zelela   da plate kartu.
>
> *two   these/these two boys   are wanted to pay   ticket*
>
> "These two boys wanted to pay for the ticket."

These examples show clearly that *oba* has undergone a change: the original numeral *oba,* which at first merged in the NumP, was moved higher up. The syntactic change was accompanied by a semantic change into a distributive quantifier.

The Motivation for the Changes

Oba had a marked status in the system of numerals in OCS. It had a counterpart, *dъva,* with the same meaning (cardinality of 2), the difference being only that *oba* could be used in a subset of the syntactic environments in which *dъva* could be used (recall that although *dъva* occurred most often in indefinite DPs, it could also be found in definite DPs). Furthermore, *oba* was the only numeral with a definiteness requirement. All other numerals were like *dъva,* neutral with respect to (in)definiteness of the DP in which they appeared. Thus *oba* simultaneously stood apart in the system of numerals and was in competition with a numeral that was an unexceptional member of the system. As such, *oba* was a likely candidate for reanalysis or loss. Both of these developments occurred in the history of Slavic.

Oba was lost in Bulgarian and in the dialects of Macedonian in contact with Bulgarian and Greek. This path of development likely occurred due to the emergence of the definite article.[6] With an overt article present, a definite DP could be marked unambiguously even with the numeral *dъva,* something which was not possible earlier, since the use of bare (article-less) *dъva* could not distinguish between definite and indefinite DPs. In other words, whereas previously *oba* was competing with a lexical item *dъva* for use in syntactic structures such as [definite]-specified DP as in (10), and it had the advantage of unambiguously signaling a definite DP, now it no longer had that advantage. This ultimately led to the disappearance of *oba* in the relevant language.

Oba was reanalyzed in the rest of the Slavic languages. None of these languages have developed a definite article, so *oba* remained the only way to unambiguously mark a DP as definite. This presumably precluded the outright loss of *oba.* A reanalysis of *oba* as a distributive quantifier was not inevitable; after all, OCS managed to do without such a quantifier. But the change fulfilled a double function—it apparently met a need, common cross-linguistically, for a distributive dual quantifier and also resolved the marked status of *oba* in the grammar.

If languages have a need for a distributive dual quantifier, then why did Bulgarian and dialects of Macedonian not develop one, reanalyzing the otherwise not needed *oba?* The answer must lie in the fact that a syntactic alternative was available to the lexical item strategy. The use of *i,* "and," as a distributive marker was already present in South Slavic, as seen in (11) in the conjunction reduction strategy. With a definite article present, all the individual pieces of the meaning of *both* were at hand.

(16) and   + the   + two
    (DISTRIBUTIVITY marker, as seen also   [DEFINITENESS]   [DUALITY]
    in conjunction reduction structures)

The *and the n* strategy is cross-linguistically attested, and it is a general one, as it could be used with any numeral, not just 2. So, in the presence of a syntactic construction expressing exactly the same meaning, and with a wider applicability (i.e., not restricted to cardinality of 2), a distributive dual quantifier, a lexical item, was not developed. This state of affairs may also have been reinforced through influence from Greek, which lacked a lexical item meaning "both" but had the syntactic means of expressing this meaning through the *and the n* construction.

Implications for Other Indo-European Languages

The fact that OCS *oba* was originally a numeral and that it became a marker of distributivity later, in the process of historical change, is of consequence not only to Slavic but also to the larger Indo-European (IE) language family. The lexical item *oba* derives from the Proto-Indo-European (PIE) word **ambho:,* with its other descendants being *both* (English), *beide* (German, Dutch), *ambos* (Spanish), and so on. Given that in other languages the cognates of *oba* are commonly understood to be distributive, the OCS facts suggest two paths of development from **ambho:* to *both, beide, oba, ambos,* and so forth.

(17) a. distributive **ambho:*   →   distributivity lost in OCS, distributivity
    regained & kept in other IE languages in Modern Slavic
   b. nondistributive **ambho:*   →   parallel developments in the meaning of
    both, beide, oba, ambos, and so on.

In order to decide which of the two pathways represents the actual development of **ambho:*, we must naturally look beyond Slavic. More concretely, we need to look for the use of the cognates of *oba* in the numeral function in other IE languages, including the ancient ones. While careful investigation into non-Slavic IE languages is beyond the scope of this work, some preliminary evidence in favor of (17-b) can be found in Modern German and Dutch. In both these languages, as it turns out, the meaning of *beide* alternates between the distributive "both" reading and a numeral 2 reading. The latter reading is found whenever *beide* is preceded by a definite article (D. Büring, B. Schwarz [pc]):

(18) German
    Welcher von ?(die) beiden hat gewonnen?
    which   of   (the) both   has won
    "Which of the two won?"

(19) Einer von ?(die) beiden wird gewinnen.
    one   of (the) both   will win
    "One of the two will win."

(20) Die beiden Männer haben diese zwei Frauen geheiratet.
    the both   men   have these two women married
    "The two men married the two women." (collective reading possible)
cf.

(21) Beide Männer haben diese zwei Frauen geheiratet.
    both men   have these two   women married
    "Both men married the two women."   (distributive reading only)

These German examples in conjunction with the OCS data indicate that the ancestor of *oba* and *beide,* that is, **ambho:* was in fact not a distributive quantifier but meant something like "the two" and that the distributive function of *both, beide,* modern *oba,* and so on was a later, parallel development in the individual languages. In other words, our finding that OCS did not have a distributive dual quantifier may in fact be a more general finding about some of the early IE languages. If this is indeed so, it will suggest that a change from "two" to "both" is a natural development for grammars.

Summary

The OCS word *oba,* a relative of *both, beide,* and so forth, was a numeral with a definiteness presupposition, not a distributive quantifier. That numeral has been either reanalyzed or lost in all modern Slavic languages. In those languages where it has been preserved, it acquired a distributive quantifier function. In languages where it was lost, it was replaced by a periphrastic construction with a more general functionality.

These findings are of importance for more than just the history of *oba* in Slavic. They show the primacy of grammar, in the structures it generates and the system of relationships it determines, over lexical items (*oba* was lost when the syntactic means of expressing its meaning became available). They also show that marked elements are susceptible to change (*oba* did not replace *dъva,* but rather *dъva* replaced *oba* in its definite use, making *oba* redundant and therefore subject to reanalysis).

The history of Slavic "both" also suggests that the meaning of the PIE word **ambho:,* from which *oba, both,* and other corresponding words in different IE languages are derived, may not have had a distributive component and that the distributive-marking function of such words observed in the modern IE languages was a later development.

NOTES

This work was supported by a National Science Foundation grant on "The Historical Syntax of Medieval South Slavic" (BCS 0418581) to Roumyana Pancheva. We would like to thank the following people for helpful comments, suggestions, and language data: Daniel Büring, Tania Ionin, Jelena Krivokapic, Ljiljana Progovac, Don Ringe, Joseph Salmons, Barry Schein, and Bernard Schwarz. Any remaining errors are naturally ours.

1. OCS is the oldest recorded Slavic language. Although it belongs to the South Slavic branch of the family, it is thought to be sufficiently similar to, and thus a good representative of, Common Slavic, the common predecessor of all the Slavic languages (e.g., Lunt 2001, 1; Schenker 1995, 71, 185–86).
2. The data are from Codex Marianus, an eleventh century AD text of the four Gospels. We used the annotated text of the Codex in Pancheva et al. (2007), which in turn is based on the electronic edition of Codex Marianus in Jouko Lindstedt's *Corpus Cyrillo-Methodianum Helsingiense: An Electronic Corpus of Old Church Slavonic Texts.*
3. The alternate order appears to be possible only in very restricted cases, perhaps dialectal, such as *the both of us.*
4. Morphosyntax does not distinguish between determiners and numerals. They all inflect like adjectives, agreeing in number, gender, and case with the head noun. Thus demonstrative *t ъ* "this'" had the same inflectional affixes in the dual as did *oba.*
5. The term "quantifier" is used rather descriptively here. English adnominal *both* has been argued to be either a quantificational determiner with a generalized quantifier meaning or, alternatively, a modifier that eliminates exceptions to the maximality interpretation of plural definites.

6. We assume here that the definite article was introduced before the reanalysis of *oba*. The completed development of the article is dated rather early, in the twelfth to thirteenth centuries (Duridanov et al. 1993, 555), whereas the OCS texts are from the eleventh century, so this is not an implausible assumption.

REFERENCES

Barwise, Jon, and Robin Cooper. 1981. Generalized quantifiers and natural language. *Linguistics and Philosophy* 4:159–219.

Bobaljik, Jonathan. 2003. Floating quantifiers: Handle with care (revision of 1998 Glot article). In *The second Glot international state-of-the-article book,* ed. Lisa Cheng and Rint Sybesma, 107–48. Berlin: Mouton de Gruyter.

Brisson, Christine. 1998. *Distributivity, maximality and floating quantifiers*. PhD diss., Rutgers University.

Doetjes, Jenny. 1997. Quantifiers and selection: On the distribution of quantifying expressions in French, Dutch, and English. HIL diss., The Hague.

Dowty, David, and Belinda Brodie. 1984. The semantics of floated quantifiers in a transformational grammar. In *Proceedings of WCCFL III*, ed. Susannah MacKaye, Mark Cobler, and Michael Wescoat, 75–90. Stanford, CA: Stanford Linguistic Association.

Duridanov, Ivan, et al. 1993. *Gramatika na starobulgarskija ezik*. [Grammar of Old Bulgarian]. Sofia: Izdatelstvo na Bălgarskata akademija na naukite.

Edmondson, Jerold A. 1978. On how to get both in categorial grammar. *Studies in Language* 2 (3): 295–312.

Fitzpatrick, Justin. 2006. The syntactic and semantic roots of floating quantification. PhD thesis, Massachusetts Institute of Technology.

Huntley, David. 1993. Old Church Slavonic. In *The Slavonic languages, ed.* Bernard Comrie and Greville Corbett, 125–87. London: Routledge.

Ladusaw, William. 1982. Semantic constraints on the English partitive construction. *Proceedings of WCCFL I*, ed. Susannah MacKaye, Mark Cobler, and Michael Wescoat, 231–42. Stanford, CA: Stanford Linguistic Association..

Landman, Fred. 1989. Groups, I. *Linguistics and Philosophy* 12:559–605.

Lunt, Horace. 2001. *Old Church Slavonic grammar.* 7th rev. ed. Berlin: Mouton de Gruyter.

Pancheva, Roumyana, Agnieszka Łazorczyk, Jelena Krivokapic, and Yulia Minkova. 2007. *Codex Marianus.* In *USC parsed corpus of Old South Slavic* (an electronic resource).

Progovac, Ljiljana. 1999. Events and economy of coordination. *Syntax: A Journal of Theoretical, Experimental and Interdisciplinary Research* 2 (2): 141–59.

Roberts, Craige. 1987. *Modal subordination, anaphora and distributivity*. PhD diss., University of Massachusetts, Amherst.

Schenker, Alexander M. 1995. *The dawn of Slavic: An introduction to Slavic philology.* New Haven, CT: Yale University Press.

Schwarzschild, Roger. 1996. *Pluralities*. Dordrecht: Kluwer Academic.

Shlonsky, Ur. 1991. Quantifiers as functional heads: A study of quantifier float in Hebrew. *Lingua* 84:159–80.

Sportiche, Dominique. 1988. A theory of floating quantifiers and its corollaries for constituent structure. *Linguistic Inquiry* 19 (3): 425–49.

Stockwell, Robert, Paul Schachter, and Barbara Partee. 1973. *The major structures of English.* New York: Holt, Rinehart and Wilson.

3

When Small Words Collide

Morphological Reduction and Phonological Compensation in Old Leonese Contractions

MINTA ELSMAN AND D. ERIC HOLT
University of South Carolina

THE PHENOMENON of the grammaticalization of lexical words into function words has received much attention in various fields of linguistics (Hopper and Traugott 1993, among numerous works). While grammaticalization usually results in the phonological reduction of the words in question, this reduction does not usually lead to the loss of semantic recoverability. However, function words are inherently phonologically short, so any reduction resulting from grammaticalization would incur a proportionally greater loss to the surface realization of their meaning. An example of such grammaticalization comes from Medieval Leonese, and a close analysis of this data suggests that, as function words are grammaticalized and undergo phonological reduction, individual features take on a correspondingly greater role in distinguishing meaning that was previously represented by entire segments.

The following section presents the Leonese preposition + article contraction data that motivate the theoretical claims of the article, subsequent sections lay out our formal assumptions and present tableaux and explications of the varying success of the competing candidates across related forms and dialects, and the final section offers a summary and concluding remarks and discusses avenues for further research.

Leonese Preposition + Article Combinations and Grammaticalization

Tuten (2003) discusses the contraction of preposition + article sequences into single words in various regions of Medieval Spain, and here we focus our attention on Leonese, which we have decomposed for expository purposes into palatalizing and nonpalatalizing varieties.[1] (Data adapted from Tuten 2003, 115–17, based mainly on Menéndez-Pidal 1964, 330–39, and Staaff 1907, 253–58. Note that *nn* = [ɲ]; *ll* = [ʎ].)[2]

In the contractions listed above, the preposition and article form a single word that is in some instances phonologically distinct from either of its components; for example, despite the existence of the contraction *connas* (table 3.1) there exists no preposition *conn* or article *nnas* or *as*.

The data by Tuten represent a unique case of grammaticalization of function words into even smaller morphemic units, and the phonological reduction that results

Table 3.1
"Palatalizing" Leonese

	Basic Forms	por + Article	de + Article	a + Article	con + Article	en + Article
m. sg.	*llo*	*pollo*	*del*	*al*	*conno, collo*	*enno, enne*
f. sg.	*lla*	*polla*	*de la*	*a la*	*conna, colla*	*enna*
m. pl.	*llos*	*pollos*	*de los*	*a los*	*connos, collos*	*ennos*
f. pl.	*llas*	*pollas*	*de las*	*a las*	*connas, collas*	*ennas*

Table 3.2
"Nonpalatalizing" Leonese

	Basic Forms	por + Article	de + Article	a + Article	con + Article	en + Article
m. sg.	*elo, lo*	*polo*	*del*	*al*	*cono*	*eno, ene, no*
f. sg.	*ela*	*pola*	*de la*	*a la*	*cona*	*ena, na*
m. pl.	*elos*	*polos*	*de los*	*a los*	*conos*	*enos, nos*
f. pl.	*elas*	*polas*	*de las*	*a las*	*conas*	*enas, nas*

threatens the surface representation of these forms. In what follows, we show how the burden of morphological representation shifts from the segmental to the featural level to prevent the complete loss of surface forms that are already short.

Theoretical Preliminaries/Constraints

The phonological changes that resulted from preposition + article contraction suggest that the underlying forms of these contractions violated certain highly-ranked markedness constraints that mandated phonological simplification of the surface form.

(1) **#l: no word initial [l]; initial *l-* tends to palatalize in Leonese (Menéndez-Pidal 1962, 64–68).

**#nn: no word-initial palatal [ɲ]: word-initial palatal [ɲ] is rare in modern Spanish, appearing much less frequently than palatal [ʎ] or nonpalatal [n].

*PAL: Palatal consonants are marked (Baković 2001; Zubritskaya 1997).

SYLCON: Sonority may not rise across a syllable boundary (Gouskova 2001; Hooper 1976; Murray and Vennemann 1983).

In the case of grammaticalization of "little words" to bound morphemes presented here, phonological changes that might satisfy the above markedness constraints threaten the adequate representation of meaning, as the deletion or alteration of a single segment severely reduces the surface forms of morphemes that are already quite small. Thus faithfulness constraints are required to ensure that meaning is represented in the output via the preservation of entire segments [by the constraints in (2)] or individual features [by the constraints in (3)].

(2) MAX: Input segments must have output correspondents (McCarthy 1995).

DEP: Output segments must have input correspondents (McCarthy 1995).

COALESCE: No element of the output has multiple correspondents in the input (McCarthy 1995, "UNIFORMITY").

CONTIGSTEM: Stem morphemes contiguous in the input must be contiguous in the output ("No epenthesis between stems").

(3) MAX-FMS: The input features of a monosegmental morpheme must be preserved in the output (adapted from Casali 1997).

MAX-[C-Place]: C-Place nodes in the input must be present in the output (see Lombardi 2001 for Max-F constraints).

The features relevant to the analysis here are [nasal], which distinguishes palatal nasals from palatal laterals, [DOR], which distinguishes between nasals, and [cont], which distinguishes between rhotics. Also relevant is the number of C-Place nodes, which distinguishes palatal from alveolar nasals and laterals. (Features that distinguish pairs of segments are indicated in bold.)

By focusing on the featural level, faithfulness constraints such as MAX-FMS and MAX-[C-Place] may preserve some surface representation of a meaningful segment, even when the segment itself is deleted. In addition, the selection of the morpheme to be preserved may be determined based on its function, as formalized in the following constraint.

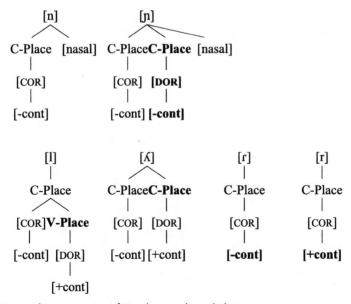

Figure 3.1 Structural Representation of Nasals, Laterals, and Rhotics

(4) MAX-FMORPHSYN: Input features of syntactic morphemes must be preserved in the output.

This constraint is consistent with the fact that functional morphemes are often shorter than lexical morphemes and therefore subject to proportionately greater loss at the level of phonological representation. In the contractions examined here, the gender (*o/a*) and number (*s*) affixes found on the definite articles are considered "syntactic" morphemes, as they link constituents within a clause by marking agreement between nouns and their articles. The prepositions are similarly syntactic, in that they act as case markers (Penny 1991, 194) for determiner phrases and noun phrases, linking them with a verb in the clause. In contrast, the definiteness morpheme (*l*) of the articles does not link syntactic constituents but rather serves a discourse/pragmatic function of marking specificity. The distinction between syntactic versus nonsyntactic morphemes plays a crucial role in the selection of the optimal forms, as explained in the following section.

Tableaux and Explications

The constraint ranking proposed for Palatalizing Leonese (PL) is as follows:

#l,#nn, SYLCON, *ContigStem, MAX-[C-Place] »
Max-FSynMorph, Max-FMS, Coalesce » Dep » *Pal

Although the proposed constraints are ranked within groups, two constraint relations uniquely distinguish the PL dialect. First, MAX-[C-Place] » *PAL determines that, all other things being equal, palatalization, though marked, is permitted if it preserves a C-Place node that is deleted in all nonpalatalized candidates. Second, the lack of a relative ranking between MAX-FSYNMORPH and MAX-FMS gives equal priority to the preservation of the features of syntactic morphemes and those of all monosegmental morphemes, syntactic or not. The effects of both of these relationships can be seen in the output form of the contraction /con + la/.[3]

When *con* and *la* come together, the abutting segments violate syllable contact restrictions, ruling out [conla]. All other candidates avoid this violation, either by

Tableau 3.1 *con + la > colla, conna*

/con + la/	*#l	*#nn	SYLCON	CONTIG STEM	MAX-[C-Place]	MAX-F SYNMORPH	MAX-FMS	COALESCE	DEP	*PAL
conla			*!							
conela				*!					*	
cona					*!		*	*		
cola					*!	*		*		
☞colla [ʎ]						*		*		*
☞conna [ɲ]							*	*		*

[n]   +   [l]   →   [ʎ]

C-Place [n̶a̶s̶a̶l̶]   C-Place   C-Place C-Place

   | /\ | |

[COR]   [COR] V-P̶l̶a̶c̶e̶   [COR]   [DOR]

   | | / | |

[-cont]   [-cont] [DOR]   [-cont] [+cont]

                      [+cont]

Figure 3.2 Structural Blending of *con* + *la* > *colla*

epenthesis ([conela]), loss ([cona], [cola]), or coalescence-cum-palatalization ([colla], [conna]). The latter are evaluated as optimal because they violate no high-ranking constraints, and the palatalized output best preserves the input features of both the syntactic morpheme *con* and the definiteness morpheme *l*. [colla] violates MAX-FSYNMORPH, because [nasal] is part of the syntactic (case-marking) preposition but does not violate MAX-FMS, as the features of the monosegmental definiteness morpheme *l* are present in surface *ll* [ʎ]. [conna] violates MAX-FMS, because the [+cont] feature of *l* is lost but does not violate MAX-FSYNMORPH, as the [nasal] feature of /n/, part of the syntactic (case-marking) *con,* remains intact. Figures 3.2 and 3.3 illustrate this.[4]

Because MAX-FSYNMORPH and MAX-FMS are unranked relative to each other, and because *colla* and *conna* each violates only one of these constraints while violating none of the higher-ranked constraints, either output is possible. (For variation in optimality theory [OT], see Anttila 2002.) These forms are also preferred to [cona] and [cola], because *cona* and *cola* fail to preserve the C-Place of both the preposition and article consonants, which *conna* and *colla* do, due to the low ranking of *PAL.[5]

Given the *conna~colla* variation, it is reasonable to expect similar patterns for *en* + *la* and *por* + *la,* yet each of these contractions has only one optimal form. First, *en* + *la* is expected to yield both [enna]~[ella], yet only the former is grammatical. We propose that the underlying form of the preposition *en* in the PL preposition + article

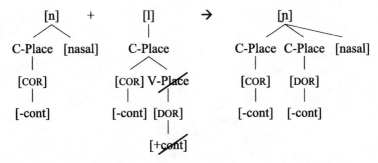

Figure 3.3 Structural Blending of *con* + *la* > *conna*

Tableau 3.2 *(e)n + la > enna*

/n + la/	*#l	*#nn	SylCon	Contig Stem	Max-[C-Place]	Max-F SynMorph	Max-FMS	Coalesce	Dep	*Pal
nla			*!							
nela				*!					*	
na					*!		*	*		
la	*!				*!	*	*	*		
nna		*!					*	*		*
lla						*(!)	*	*		*
ella						*(!)	*	*	*	*
☞enna							*	*	*	*

contractions is not /en/ but /n/ (a hypothesis that receives further support from the non-palatalizing dialect, which shows *na*).

The realization of /n + la/ as [nla] violates SylCon, which the other candidates avoid, through epenthesis ([nela]), deletion ([na], [la]), or coalescence via palatalization ([nna], [lla]). Candidate [lla] is less optimal than [nna], as it violates both Max-FSynMorph and Max-FMS by deleting the [nasal] feature of [n], which is both a syntactic and monosegmental morpheme; likewise for [ella]. Although [nna] avoids these violations, it violates highly ranked *#nn, which is resolved via word-initial epenthesis, yielding the winning candidate *enna*.

For /poɾ + la/, despite the fact that [ɾ] and [l] are both liquids, the consonant sequence in [poɾla] is marked (tableau 3.3). Note that in figure 3.1, [l] is characterized by a V-Place node that is [+cont], a property that contributes to sonority and that [ɾ]

Tableau 3.3 *por + la > polla*

/poɾ + la/	*#l	*#nn	SylCon	Contig Stem	Max-[C-Place]	Max-F SynMorph	Max-FMS	Coalesce	Dep	*Pal
poɾla			*!							
poɾela				*!			ʔ		*	
poɾa					*!		*	*		
pola					*!	*	*			
poɾa					*!	*	*	*		
☞polla [ʎ]								*		*

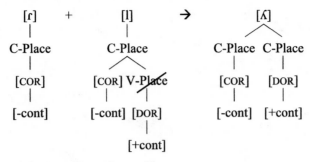

Figure 3.4 Structural Blending of *por* + *la* > *polla*

lacks. Therefore contracting *por* + *la* results in a rise of sonority across a syllable boundary, violating SYLCON. The remaining candidates avoid this violation, again by epenthesis ([porela]), loss ([pola], [pora]), or coalescence via palatalization ([polla]), and this latter form wins, as it alone preserves the C-Place of each input segment (figure 3.4) without violating any of the highly-ranked constraints. Given the *conna~colla* alternation observed for [con + la], one might expect an analogous alternation of [porra]~[polla] for *por* + *la*. However, figure 3.5 illustrates that *colla:conna :: polla:porra* is not an accurate analogy: while both *ll* and *nn* are palatal sounds, characterized by dual C-Place articulations, *rr* is simply the [+cont] correlate of singly articulated tap *r*.

The remaining contractions, *de* + *la* and *a* + *la,* are unproblematic, as the fully faithful output forms (*dela* and *ala*) do not violate SylCon and are therefore optimal.[6]

Finally, the surface form of the bare article itself remains to be explained, given that its underlying form is posited as /la/.

The form *la* is ruled out by top-ranking *#l. Although [ela] and [ella] avoid this violation via epenthesis, this results in violations of DEP not incurred by [lla].[7] The remaining competitor, [a], is ruled out by MAX-FMS, since it deletes the entire monosegmental definiteness morpheme *l*.

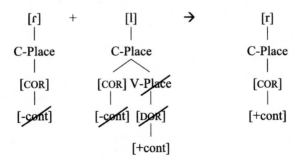

Figure 3.5 Structural Blending of *por* + *la* > *porra* Disallowed

Tableau 3.4 *la* > *lla*

/la/	*#l	*#nn	SylCon	Contig Stem	Max-[C-Place]	Max-F SynMorph	Max-FMS	Coalesce	Dep	*Pal
la	*!									
☞lla										*
a					*!		*			
ela									*!	
ella									*!	*

"Nonpalatalizing" Leonese

The constraints operating in "Nonpalatalizing" Leonese (NPL) are identical to those operating in PL; however, the differing ranking of the constraints in NPL yields different output forms.

#l,*#nn, SylCon, *ContigStem, *Pal, Max-FSynMorph »

Max-F MS, Max-[C-Place], Coalesce » Dep

The most obvious difference is the undominated ranking of *Pal, which disallows palatalization, even when it otherwise would preserve a specific feature. The second unique characteristic of NPL is that it ranks Max-FSynMorph above Max-FMS, which allows (potentially complete) deletion of a nonsyntactic morpheme's features, if such deletion results in an output form that satisfies higher-ranked markedness constraints and preserves the features of a syntactic morpheme, as illustrated in tableau 3.5.[8]

As in PL, the contraction of *con* + *la* results in a violation of SylCon, which is resolved in the remaining candidates via epenthesis ([conela]), deletion ([cona],

Tableau 3.5 *con* + *la* > *cona*

/con + la/	*#l	*#nn	SylCon	Contig Stem	*Pal	Max-F SynMorph	Max-FMS	Max-[C-Place]	Coalesce	Dep
conla			*!							
conela				*!						*
☞cona							*	*	*	
cola					*!			*	*	
colla			*!		*!				*	
conna					*!		*		*	

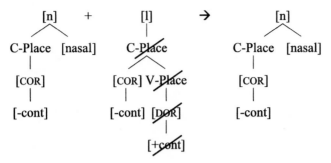

※ Figure 3.6 Structural Simplification of con + la > cona

[cola]), and coalescence resulting in palatalization ([colla], [conna]). The high ranking of *PAL in this dialect rules out the palatalized forms, while the high ranking of *CONTIGMORPH rules out *conela*. Of the remaining candidates, [cona] is preferred to [cola] because the latter deletes the [nasal] feature from the syntactic morpheme *con,* fatally violating MAX-FSYNMORPH.

The output form of *en + la* ([ena]) is selected as that of the output form for *con + la* ([cona]).[9]

For the contraction of *por + la,* it is reasonable to predict that the contraction will yield **pora*, as both *con + la* and *en + la* yield simplified *cona* and *ena∼na,* where SYLCON is resolved by deleting the definiteness morpheme. However, the optimal form is in fact *pola.* Recall that in PL the maximum number of features is preserved via the coalescence that results in palatalization, an option not available in NPL due to the undominated ranking of *PAL. However, there is no undominated constraint prohibiting other types of coalescence. The realization of the [r + l] sequence as [l], though different from palatalization, still constitutes a case of coalescence, because [l] preserves all of the input features of [r] (figure 3.8 and tableau 3.6).

While realizing /r + l/ as [l] constitutes an additive process, realizing /r + l/ as [r] is a subtractive one, as [l] loses both its [DOR] and its [+cont] features (figure 3.9), making [pora] suboptimal to *pola,* which preserves all of the input features.

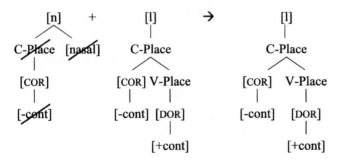

※ Figure 3.7 Structural Simplification of con + la > *cola Disallowed

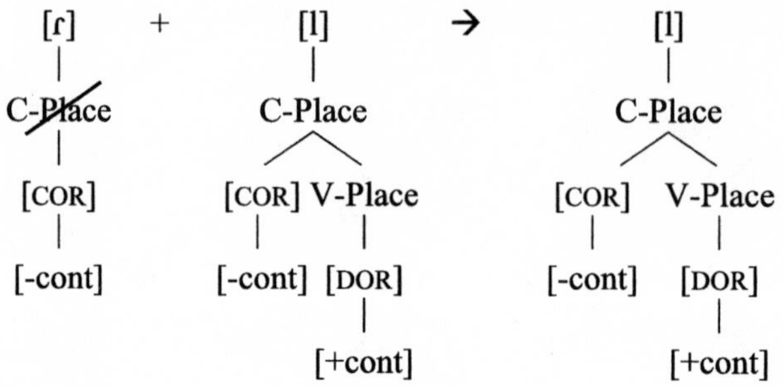

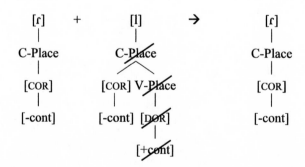

Figure 3.8 Structural Blending of *por* + *la* > *pola*

Tableau 3.6 *por* + *la* > *pola*

/por + la/	*#|	*#nm	SylCon	Contig Stem	*Pal	Max-F SynMorph	Max-FMS	Max-[C-Place]	Coalesce	Dep
poɾla			*!							
poɾela				*!						*
☞pola								*	*	
poɾa							*!	*	*	
polla				*!					*	
poɾa						*!		*	*	

Figure 3.9 Structural Simplification of *por* + *la* > **pora* Disallowed

Tableau 3.7 *la > ela*

/la/	*#l	*#nn	SylCon	Contig Stem	*Pal	Max-F-SynMorph	Max-FMS	Max-[C-Place]	Coalesce	Dep
la	*!									
lla					*!					
a						*!	*!			
☞ ela										*
ella					*!					*

The realization of the contractions /de + la/ and /a + la/ in NPL as *dela* and *ala* is just as in PL, because, as in PL, the fully faithful forms do not incur any violation of SylCon.

Finally, the realization of /la/ as *ela* in this dialect is due to the dominance of *Pal » Dep.

Conclusions and Open Questions

In accounting for the preposition + article contractions attested in Medieval Leonese, this analysis shows a systematic relationship between morphology and phonology: The impetus from grammaticalization and markedness constraints to reduce the phonological form of short function words conflicts with the need for sufficient surface representation to ensure recoverability of meaning. This conflict is resolved by associating meaning not with individual segments but with individual features, a strategy that preserves sufficient phonological input to recover meaning despite the phonological shortening imposed by grammaticalization and markedness (figure 3.10).

If this solution resolved the tension between grammaticalization and preservation of meaning in Medieval Leonese, why did it not survive? Why didn't the contracted forms of the prepositions become productive morphemes, combining with other word classes, such as bare nouns? As Tuten (2003) notes, speakers of various dialects of Spanish (including Leonese) began to settle in Castile in the ninth century. The variety of dialects resulted in a koine in which no contraction occurred and which later became the standard. Although the constraint rankings particular to other Medieval Spanish dialects have yet to be analyzed, Tuten (2003, 115–17) lists dialects in which little or no contraction occurred and suggests that these analytical

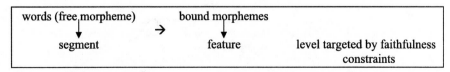

Figure 3.10 Model of Phonological Compensation for Morphological Reduction

and "transparent forms" were easiest for L1 speakers to acquire in this multidialectal setting. Due to the interference from competing dialects, it is impossible to tell how the Leonese morphological and phonological shortening would have progressed. Nonetheless, the data from the contraction of "small words" in Medieval Leonese provide insight into the relationship between the morpheme length and featural function.

NOTES

We owe thanks for comments and questions of substance, approach, and data to members of the audiences at GURT and at the 45th International Linguistic Association meeting (New York City, 2007), among them Loren Billings, Héctor Campos, Tom Cravens, Francisco Fernández Rubiera, Michael Ferreira, Gregory Guy, Regina Morin, Joel Rini, Donald Tuten, and José del Valle. The authors are responsible for any shortcomings of the present work.

1. Galician/Portuguese, Aragonese, and La Riojan show varying degrees of contraction. Leonese was selected for discussion because of its closer historical ties to Castilian, the national standard, being one of the strongest contributors to the medieval koine that emerged in Castile.

2. Interpretation of double *nn* and *ll* is somewhat problematic. Tuten is silent on what the double letter represents, and we interpret them as palatals. Menéndez-Pidal's *El dialecto leonés* (1962) seems to support this, though direct, clear statements are lacking—when mentioned directly, he refers to assimilation *(-n + l- > nn; -r, -s se asimilan a la l- del artículo, o se pierde)*. Statements about *ll* seem clearer. For instance, there are data cited from Lena such as *pagayos (pegarles), potcho (pollo < por lo)* (pp. 87–88; *potchas* also, as well as *cometcho < comello < comerlo*, p. 94, and *dache < da-le < darle*, p. 127; additional data cited throughout). The forms with palatal *y* or affricate *tch* plausibly and straightforwardly would result from the palatal lateral. For initial position, while palatalization of *l-* to *ll-* is abundantly attested, *n- > nn- > ñ* also occurs, *ño, ñunca*, and so on (Menéndez-Pidal 1962, p. 64, fn. 96; and Zamora Vicente 1967, 130–31).

3. We assume for all contractions the underlying form of *la*. Although it is reasonable to posit an underlying form of *lla*, given that this is the bare article form (table 3.1), such an analysis leaves unexplained its realization as *la* in contraction with *de* and *a*. We employ the feminine singular article as an exemplar throughout our analysis as all other article forms (with some minor exceptions for the masculine singular, ignored here) exhibit the same contraction patterns.

4. We assume that any identically valued feature in the input is sufficiently represented by a single occurrence in the output, perhaps as an instance of OCP-induced merger.

5. Bradley (2007) has pursued a similar line of argumentation in his gestural overlap account of Norwegian clusters, applying a Dispersion-Theoretic approach to coalescence of apicoalveolar /r/ with laminals /t, s, n, l/, which are realized as [ʈ, ʂ, ɳ, ɭ], where blending of adjacent tongue gestures obtains. In both this case and the case of coalescence-cum-palatalization in Leonese, recoverability is ensured, because, though distinct from underlying form, the surface form allows the listener to discern the features of the input segments; this is crucial for Leonese, as the input segments belong to different, and syntactic, morphemes.

6. We assume that *de la* and *a la* are phonologically contracted and orthographic variants of *dela* and *ala*, which are amply attested.

7. While a constraint prohibiting word-initial *l* may seem odd, especially when this constraint is satisfied by the marked process of palatalization, consider the structure of palatal [ʎ] versus nonpalatal [l] in figure 3.1. The fact that [ʎ] is characterized by two C-Places, while [l] is characterized by a C-Place and a V-Place, suggests that [l] is more sonorous and vowel-like than [ʎ], making [ʎ] a better choice for a syllable onset, as it yields a steeper sonority cline.

8. We again assume underlying form of *la*. Although it is reasonable to posit an underlying form of /ela/, given that this is the bare article form (table 3.2), such an analysis leaves unexplained the absence of forms such as **conela, *porela*, and so on.

9. We posit that the alternation between *ena* and *na* (table 3.2) is due to differing underlying forms of the preposition *en*, /en/ and /n/, the latter of which represents a more advanced stage of the grammaticalization of the preposition *en*, as it occurs only as a bound form in these contractions.

REFERENCES

Anttila, Arto. 2002. Variation and phonological theory. In *The handbook of language variation and change,* ed. J. K. Chambers, Peter Trudgill, and Natalie Schilling-Estes, 206–43. Malden, MA: Blackwell.

Baković, Eric J. 2001. Nasal place neutralization in Spanish. In *U Penn working papers in linguistics 7.1: Proceedings of the 24th annual Penn linguistics colloquium,* ed. Michelle Minnick Fox, Alexander Williams, and Elsi Kaiser, 1–13. Philadelphia: PWPL.

Bradley, Travis G. 2007. Morphological derived-environment effects in gestural coordination: A case study of Norwegian clusters. *Lingua* 117:950–85.

Casali, Roderick F. 1997. Vowel elision in hiatus contexts: Which vowel goes? *Language* 73:493–533.

Gouskova, Maria. 2001. Falling sonority onsets, loanwords, and syllable contact. In *CLS 37: Papers from the 37th annual regional meeting of the Chicago linguistic society.* Chicago: CLS.

Hooper, Joan Bybee. 1976. *An introduction to natural generative phonology.* New York: Academic Press.

Hopper, Paul J., and Elizabeth Closs Traugott. 1993. *Grammaticalization.* Cambridge: Cambridge University Press.

Lombardi, Linda. 2001. Why place and voice are different: Constraint interactions and feature faithfulness in optimality theory. In *Segmental phonology in optimality theory: Constraints and representations,* ed. Linda Lombardi, 13–45. Cambridge: Cambridge University Press.

McCarthy, John. 1995. Extensions of faithfulness: Rotuman revisited. Rutgers Optimality Archive.

Menéndez-Pidal, Ramón. 1962. *El dialecto leonés.* Oviedo: Instituto de Estudios Asturianos.

———. 1964. *Orígenes del español: Estado lingüístico de la Península Ibérica hasta el siglo XI.* 5th ed. Madrid: Espasa-Calpe.

Murray, Robert W., and Theo Vennemann. 1983. Sound change and syllable structure [: Problems] in Germanic phonology. *Language* 59:514–28.

Penny, Ralph. 1991. *A history of the Spanish language.* New York: Cambridge University Press.

Staaff, Erik. 1907. *Etude sur l'ancien dialecte léonais.* Uppsala. Almqvist and Wiksell.

Tuten, Donald. 2003. *Koineization in Medieval Spanish.* New York: Mouton de Gruyter.

Zamora Vicente, Alonso. 1967. *Dialectología española.* Madrid: Gredos.

Zubritskaya, Katya. 1997. Mechanism of sound change in optimality theory. *Language Variation and Change* 9:121–48.

II

Phonology

4

Distinguishing Function Words from Content Words in Children's Oral Reading

CAROL LORD, ROBERT BERDAN, AND MICHAEL FENDER
California State University, Long Beach

BY THE TIME they enter first grade, children acquiring language in a home where English is spoken typically show the English prosodic pattern in which content words receive stress but function words do not. However, when some of these children read text aloud, it is perceived as choppy, awkward, and word-by-word, without meaningful phrasal groupings and lacking appropriate expression, as if they are reading a word list (Weber 2006). A major factor contributing to the impression of word-by-word reading appears to be the lack of a stress distinction between content words and function words.

To investigate this interpretation, we performed acoustic analyses on recordings of samples of oral reading by nonfluent children, fluent children, and adults. We measured nuclear vowels in monosyllabic function words and content words for acoustic correlates of stress, including vowel length, intensity, pitch, and vowel quality. We found that the nonfluent children's function words tended to be relatively longer, louder, and higher in pitch, and their vowels were less likely to be reduced to schwa. Compared with the proficient readers, there was less distinction between their pronunciations of function words and content words.

Prosodic Features of Function Words

In many languages, possibly all, there is a distinction between lexical categories and functional categories. In English, lexical categories include nouns, verbs, and adjectives—that is, content words that carry the dominant semantic weight of utterances. Functional categories include prepositions, articles, auxiliaries, modals, complementizers, and conjunctions as well as other particles; these signal relationships among content words. Content words contain at least one stressed syllable. If a function word appears in a list, it receives the same stress as a content word; for example, *for* and *four* are pronounced the same, as are *him* and *hymn* and *to* and *two*. However, in discourse context the function words typically occur without stress; exceptions occur when the function word is focused or phrase-final (Bolinger 1975; Selkirk 1996; Sweet 1891).

Perception of stress in English appears to depend on a few major acoustic correlates: vowel duration, intensity, and pitch (Fry 1955, 1958; Hayes 1995; Tamburini and Caini 2005). Unstressed vowels in English typically are reduced to schwa, as in the first syllable of *about* and *connect,* and in the last syllable of *comet* and *medicine* (Shi et al. 2005). These are the acoustic correlates we examined and compared in function words and content words in this study.

Function Words and Fluent Reading

Once a reader is able to recognize individual words quickly and automatically, cognitive resources can be focused on text comprehension (LaBerge and Samuels 1974). In order to read a text aloud with appropriate stress patterns and intonation, the reader needs to group words into phonological phrases and to structure the syntactic and semantic elements to create a mental parse (Chafe 1988; Dowhower 1991; Kintsch 1998; Kuhn and Stahl 2003; Miller and Schwanenflugel 2006).

Prosodic patterns in oral speech provide information that helps the hearer construct a mental parse. In oral speech, function words are typically distinguished by lack of stress; however, English orthography provides the reader with no overt marking indicating presence or absence of stress. Function words constitute a significant portion of English discourse. Although there are only a few hundred function words in English, they make up at least 50 percent of the word tokens in everyday speech (Cutler 1993).

Evidence suggests that fluent readers may process function words differently from content words. In letter detection tasks conducted during reading, mature fluent readers are much better at noticing and marking a target letter (e.g., *t*) in content words than in function words. In contrast, younger novice readers do not show a distinction between content and function words on these tasks (Greenberg, Koriat, and Vellutino 1998; Saint-Aubin, Klein, and Landry 2005). Research with fluent readers using eye-tracking shows that function words are much more likely to be skipped than content words (Saint-Aubin, Klein, and Landry 2005). They are less likely to receive direct eye fixations, and they receive much shorter fixations (Rayner and Pollatsek 1989; factors such as word length and word frequency may account for some of these differences). Overall, studies suggest that fluent reading shows rapid lexical access for function words compared with content words (Segalowitz and Lane 2004).

In contrast, children learning to read may find function words difficult to master. One study found that children read function words less accurately than content words, whether in lists or in connected text (Blank 1985). Beginners as well as older delayed readers may read orally word-by-word, giving uniform stress to content and function words, due to difficulties in word identification or integration of meaning (Clay and Imlach 1971; Pinnell et al. 1995).

In reading research, reading fluency has been measured in terms of judgments of a reading sample, using a rubric with a four- to six-point scale (Kuhn and Stahl 2003; Pinnell et al. 1995; Rasinski 2003). Most recently, the Oral Reading Fluency Study of the National Assessment of Educational Progress (NAEP) used a four-level holistic rubric for rating fourth-grade oral reading fluency, focusing on three key elements: (a) grouping of words in phrases (manifested by intonation and pausing); (b) adherence to the author's syntax, indicating an awareness of the ideas expressed in the text; and (c) presence of expressive interpretation (Daane et al. 2005). With this rubric, a key element in student success is the use of appropriate stress patterns on function words.

Comparing Fluent and Nonfluent Readers

In this study, reading samples were collected from adults and children, and prosodic features of function words and content words were analyzed.

The children in our study were third graders in an urban public school in California. The school's average reading scores were at the thirty-eighth percentile on state reading assessments, and most of the children qualified for free or reduced-price school lunches, based on family income level. Six children were identified by their teachers as falling in the lower two quartiles in reading proficiency, with reading speed ranging from approximately seventy-five to one hundred correct words per minute. In addition, teachers identified six children with reading achievement scores at or above grade level. All children were classified as either native speakers of English or English proficient. The six adult readers were all college graduates. There was a mix of gender and ethnicity in all three groups.

The subjects were asked to read aloud two short narratives of about 250 words each; these were Dynamic Indicators of Basic Early Literacy Skills (DIBELS) passages at the second-grade reading level (Hintze, Ryan, and Stoner 2002). Digital recordings were made. In each narrative we identified thirty monosyllabic function words: the first ten prepositions, the first ten instances of infinitival *to,* and the first ten articles (*a, an, the*). We also identified thirty monosyllabic content words (nouns, verbs, and adjectives).

Using Praat software's acoustic display, we demarcated the beginning and end of the vowel nucleus of each target function word and content word (Boersma and Weenink 2007). Then, for each word, we made computational measures of vowel duration, intensity, pitch, and vowel quality. Vowel duration measures were in milliseconds. Intensity was measured in decibels at the midpoint of each vowel. To compensate for different recording levels across reading sessions, the mean intensity was calculated for each reading/recording session. This value was then subtracted from the midpoint vowel intensity of each token to produce the intensity values analyzed here. For each vowel, peak pitch was measured in hertz; these frequencies were subjected to a log transformation to linearize the scale and then standardized for each reader, giving a distribution of values for each reader with a mean of 0 and a standard deviation of 1. For vowel quality judgments, raters listened to all instances of the *to* infinitive and judged whether the vowel quality was a tense [u] or a reduced, centralized schwa vowel. Tense vowels were coded as 1 and all others as 0; each reader's score was the proportion of [u] pronunciations in his or her story. To obtain a comparable acoustic measure of extent of vowel reduction, we plotted formant 1 values against formant 2 values.

Results

Differences between adults and nonfluent children were found in comparisons of content and function word duration, intensity, pitch, and vowel quality.

Vowel Duration

For all three reader groups, the vowels of function words were shorter than the vowels of content words. However, the difference between content and function words was greatest for the adults. For these readers the duration of function word vowels was about 41 percent that of content words. For the fluent children the duration was

Table 4.1
Mean Vowel Duration by Word Class and Group

Group	Content	Function	Content + Function
Nonfluent (6)	201.4 ms (34.0 SD)	146.7 ms (33.6 SD)	174.0 ms
Fluent (6)	147.6 ms (30.0 SD)	87.9 ms (25.0 SD)	117.7 ms
Adults (6)	128.3 ms (37.1 SD)	52.2 ms (12.6 SD)	90.2 ms
All (18)	159.1 ms	95.6 ms	127.3 ms

about 60 percent, and for the nonfluent children it was about 72 percent. The mean duration values in milliseconds are shown in table 4.1.

Analysis of variance for group by word class by story ($3 \times 2 \times 2$) shows all main effects to be highly significant. The group effect ($f[2, 204] = 183.5, p < .0001$, $eta = .643$) shows significant difference in mean vowel length across the three groups of readers. Post hoc analysis (Scheffé) shows each group of readers to be significantly different from the other two groups: nonfluent readers with the longest mean vowel duration, adults with the shortest vowels, and fluent children in between. For all three groups, word class is also significant ($f[1, 204] = 304.4, p < .0001, eta = .599$): Vowels in the function words are shorter than vowels in the content words. The two-way interaction of word class and group is also significant: Adults shorten vowels of function words more than children do. Vowel length for function words is essentially unchanged across the two stories.

The relative duration of content word and function word vowels is shown in figure 4.1, where the slope of the lines shows that the greatest difference between content words and function words is for adults.

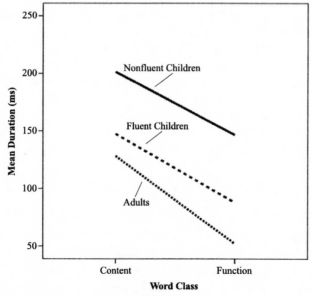

Figure 4.1 Vowel Duration by Group and Word Class

▓ Table 4.2
Mean Vowel Intensity by Word Class and Group

Group	Content	Function	Content + Function
Nonfluent (6)	2.85 db (1.84 SD)	1.41 db (3.07 SD)	2.13 db
Fluent (6)	3.02 db (1.48 SD)	0.77 db (2.51 SD)	1.90 db
Adults (6)	1.70 db (1.97 SD)	−1.83 db (2.21 SD)	−0.07 db
All (18)	2.53 db	0.12 db	1.32 db

Vowel Intensity

Measures of vowel intensity show that all readers produced louder vowels in content words than in function words (see table 4.2).

The difference among the reading groups in mean vowel intensity was significant ($f[2, 204] = 20.43, p < .0001, eta = .167$). Post hoc analysis (Scheffé) shows that this difference is between the adults and the two groups of children, with children showing greater vowel intensity, relative to the full reading session, than the adults. There is also a significant effect for word class ($f[1, 204] = 61.07, p < .0001, eta = .230$): Vowels in content words are spoken with greater intensity than vowels in function words. This differential is greater for adults than for either of the two groups of children. The story effect is not significant.

As figure 4.2 illustrates, the content words were louder than function words for all readers; however, the difference was greater for the adults.

Vowel Peak Pitch

A comparison of the peak pitch of content word and function word vowels showed that the function words were spoken at a lower pitch by the adults and the nonfluent

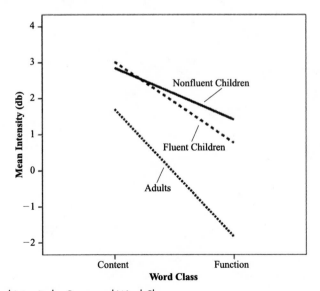

▓ Figure 4.2 Vowel Intensity by Group and Word Class

Table 4.3
Mean Standardized Peak Pitch by Word Class and Group

Group	Content	Function	Content + Function
Nonfluent (6)	.099 (.534 *SD*)	−.023 (.600 *SD*)	.038
Fluent (6)	−.122 (.401 *SD*)	.157 (.570 *SD*)	.017
Adults (6)	.159 (.480 *SD*)	−.029 (.326 *SD*)	.065
All (18)	.045	.034	.040

children; the difference between content and function words was smaller for the nonfluent children (see table 4.3).

Analysis of variance of the transformed pitch variable showed no significant effects for group of readers, for word class, or for story. In the interaction between reader group and word class ($f[2, 204] = 5.184$, $p = .006$, $eta = .048$), adults and nonfluent children showed quite similar behavior, each with lower mean pitch on function words than on content words. The fluent children, however, show exactly the opposite relationship, with higher mean pitch on function words than on content words.

As the difference in the slope of the lines in figure 4.3 illustrates, adults made greater pitch distinctions between content and function words than did the nonfluent children.

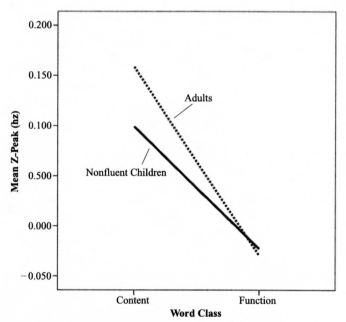

Figure 4.3 Peak Vowel Pitch by Group and Word Class

Table 4.4
Vowel Quality in Infinitival *to*, by Group

Group	Mean Proportion of [u]
Nonfluent (6)	.955 (.069 *SD*)
Fluent (6)	.487 (.231 *SD*)
Adults (6)	.073 (.071 *SD*)
All (18)	.505

Vowel Quality

Pronunciation of the [u] vowel in infinitival *to* differed strikingly across the three reader groups, as shown in table 4.4. Adults consistently reduced the vowel, and nonfluent children did not.

Analysis of variance shows large and significant differences in the mean proportion of [u] pronunciations across the three reading groups ($f[2, 204] = 104.948$, $p < .0001$, *eta* $= .875$). For the nonfluent readers, about 95 percent of the vowels were unreduced [u], and examination of individual readers shows that half of the children in this group used [u] categorically. The fluent children used [u] just under half of the time, and the adults used the unreduced form in only about 7 percent of the instances of infinitival *to*. Each group of readers is significantly different from the other two groups. Figure 4.4 illustrates the large differences between reader groups.

A representation of the extent of vowel reduction using Praat acoustic measures is shown in figure 4.5. Normalized values for formant 1 are on the vertical axis, with formant 2 on the horizontal axis. The resulting scatterplot approximates relative position on a vowel quadrilateral, with centralized/reduced instances appearing on the lower left. The circles represent adult pronunciations, and the squares represent non-

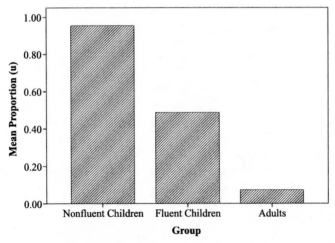

Figure 4.4 Mean Proportion of [u] by Group

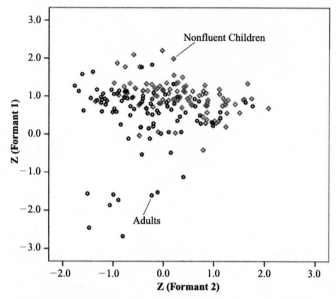

Figure 4.5 Vowel Quality of Infinitival *to*

fluent child pronunciations. As the figure shows, many of the adult vowels were significantly reduced, while the nonfluent children's were not. (For reasons of graphic clarity, we have not included the fluent children's pronunciations in this display; their formant values showed reduced, unreduced, and intermediate instances.)

Discussion

This study found that adults reading aloud consistently differentiated function words from content words with respect to measures that are considered to be acoustic correlates of stress: duration, intensity, and pitch. Function word vowel nuclei were shorter, not so loud, and lower in pitch than content word vowel nuclei. The results also showed that the differences between function and content words along these parameters were greater for adults than for children and that the differences were greater for the nonfluent children than for the fluent children. The difference between adults and children was strongest for vowel duration. For pitch, there was a small difference between adults and nonfluent children; however, the results for the proficient children are puzzling and bear further investigation, since they do not follow the trend of the other measures. The complex algorithm for pitch measures could have led to computational errors (Tamburini and Caini 2005).

The measures of vowel quality for infinitival *to* showed that adults typically reduced the vowel toward schwa, according to the pattern for unstressed syllables in English. In sharp contrast, nonfluent children rarely reduced the vowel, and fluent children showed a mixed pattern.

In identifying the nature and extent of differences in stress on function words, this study has served to clarify a key contributor to the perceived pattern of word-by-word prosody in the oral reading performance of nonfluent readers. These are the students who receive low ratings on our current national assessments of reading fluency.

How can we account for the word-by-word reading pattern? Function words in English are short, high-frequency lexical items, but they are more likely than content words to be spelled in ways that violate phonics generalizations (consider, e.g., function words *the, of, to*). Students are often drilled on these as "sight words," but, nevertheless, students who can read them readily in word lists often show the patterns we have described when reading them in connected text.

Some insight may be found from studying what these children are looking at while they are reading aloud. To read fluently with appropriate stress, a reader must be looking ahead in the text in order to construct appropriate phrasal word groups. In pilot studies using eye tracking, we have found consistent differences between fluent and nonfluent readers. In our limited sample, the eyes of fluent readers are generally two to four words ahead of the voice. However, for the nonfluent third graders that we have been observing, the eyes are often fixated on the word that follows the word being spoken. This may be an indication that cognitive resources are focused on next-word recognition and that there are too few words in the look-ahead queue to assign phrasal groupings.

A child takes approximately 400–600 ms to say a one-syllable content word. With a one-word look-ahead, if the reader spends 400–600 ms saying the word, this allows 400–600 ms to recognize the following word, which is apparently sufficient, for a child reading at a rate of 60–80 words per minute. A fluent adult takes only 75–150 ms to say a one-syllable function word. If the nonfluent child takes only 75–150 ms to say a word, the strategy of eyes-on-the-next-word is unlikely to provide adequate time for next-word recognition. Thus, by failing to de-stress function words, the child is able to maintain the spoken word stream and minimize between-word pauses in his or her oral performance.

The absence of a stress distinction between function words and content words by nonfluent readers deserves further study, particularly as these children gain in fluency, so that we can better understand the child's reading process. With clearer understanding, we may be able to assist reading professionals in developing more effective interventions.

NOTE

The authors acknowledge and appreciate the assistance of Nancy Caplow and Hide Okuno on this study.

REFERENCES

Blank, Marion. 1985. A word is a word—or is it? In *Biobehavioral measures of dyslexia,* ed. David B. Gray and James F. Kavanagh, 261–77. Parkton, MD: York Press.

Boersma, Paul, and David Weenink. 2007. Praat: Doing phonetics by computer (ver. 4.5.16) [Computer program]. www.praat.org/ (accessed March 1, 2007).

Bolinger, Dwight. 1975. *Aspects of language.* New York: Harcourt Brace Jovanovich.

Chafe, Wallace. 1988. Punctuation and the prosody of written language. *Written Communication* 5:396–426.

Clay, Marie M., and Robert H. Imlach. 1971. Juncture, pitch, and stress as reading behaviour variables. *Journal of Verbal Learning and Verbal Behavior* 10:133–39.

Cutler, Anne. 1993. Phonological cues to open- and closed-class words in the processing of spoken sentences. *Journal of Psycholinguistic Research* 32(2): 109–31.

Daane, Mary C., Jay R. Campbell, Wendy S. Grigg, Madeline J. Goodman, and Andreas Oranje. 2005. Fourth-grade students reading aloud: NAEP 2002 special study of oral reading (NCES 2006-469). U.S. Department of Education. Institute of Education Sciences, National Center for Education Statistics. Washington, DC: U.S. Government Printing Office.

Dowhower, Sarah L. 1991. Speaking of prosody: Fluency's unattended bedfellow. *Theory into Practice* 30:165–75.

Fry, D[ennis] B[utler]. 1955. Duration and intensity as physical correlates of linguistic stress. *Journal of the Acoustical Society of America* 27:765–68.

———. 1958. Experiments in the perception of stress. *Language and Speech* 1:126–52.

Greenberg, Seth N., Asher Koriat, and Frank R. Vellutino. 1998. Age changes in the missing-letter effect reflect the reader's growing ability to extract the structure from text. *Journal of Experimental Child Psychology* 69 (3): 175–98.

Hayes, Bruce. 1995. *Metrical stress theory: Principles and case studies.* Chicago: University of Chicago Press.

Hintze, John M., Amanda L. Ryan, and Gary Stoner. 2002. Concurrent validity and diagnostic accuracy of the dynamic indicators of basic early literacy skills and the comprehensive test of phonological processing. http://dibels.uoregon.edu/techreports/DIBELS_Validity_Hintze.pdf (accessed August 10, 2003).

Kintsch, Walter. 1998. *Comprehension: A paradigm for cognition.* New York: Cambridge University Press.

Kuhn, Melanie R., and Steven A. Stahl. 2003. Fluency: A review of developmental and remedial practices. *Journal of Educational Psychology* 95 (1): 3–21.

LaBerge, David, and S. Jay Samuels. 1974. Toward a theory of automatic information processing in reading. *Cognitive Psychology* 6:293–323.

Miller, Justin, and Paula J. Schwanenflugel. 2006. Prosody of syntactically complex sentences in the oral reading of young children. *Journal of Educational Psychology* 98 (4): 839–53.

Pinnell, Gay S., John J. Pikulski, Karen K. Wixson, Jay R. Campbell, Phillip B. Gough, and Alexandra S. Beatty. 1995. *Listening to children read aloud.* Report No. 23-FR-04. Washington, DC: National Center for Educational Statistics.

Rasinski, Timothy V. 2003. *The fluent reader: Oral reading strategies for building word recognition, fluency, and comprehension.* New York: Scholastic Professional.

Rayner, Keith, and Alexander Pollatsek. 1989. *The psychology of reading.* Englewood Cliffs, NJ: Prentice Hall.

Saint-Aubin, Jean, Raymond M. Klein, and Tina Landry. 2005. Age changes in the missing-letter effect revisited. *Experimental Child Psychology* 91:158–82.

Segalowitz, Sidney J., and Korri Lane. 2004. Perceptual fluency and lexical access for function versus content words. *Behavioral and Brain Sciences* 27 (2): 307–8.

Selkirk, Elisabeth. 1996. The prosodic structure of function words. In *Signal to syntax: Bootstrapping from speech to grammar in early acquisition,* ed. James L. Morgan and Katherine Demuth, 187–213. Mahwah, NJ: Lawrence Erlbaum Associates.

Shi, Rushen, Bryan Gick, Dara Kanwischer, and Ian Wilson. 2005. Frequency and category factors in the reduction and assimilation of function words: EPG and acoustic measures. *Journal of Psycholinguistic Research* 34 (4): 341–64.

Sweet, Henry. 1891. *A handbook of phonetics.* Oxford: Henry Frowde.

Tamburini, F., and C. Caini. 2005. An automatic system for detecting prosodic prominence in American English continuous speech. *International Journal of Speech Technology* 8:33–44.

Weber, Rose-Marie. 2006. Function words in the prosody of fluent reading. *Journal of Research in Reading* 29 (3): 258–69.

5

▓ Motivating Floating Quantifiers

LISA ROCHMAN
Ben Gurion University

▓ **THE RELATIONSHIP BETWEEN** information structure and prosody on the one hand, and the placement of "little words" on the other, is being explored in many languages in relationship to many different linguistic phenomena. In this chapter floating quantifiers (FQs) are shown to be a prime example of little words that are influenced by both prosody and information structure.[1] FQs in English are of particular interest because they are among a minority of elements that display some freedom in their placement in this fixed word-order language. This chapter investigates the relationship between FQs, information structure, and prosody and shows that FQs mark the focus and can be viewed as a type of focus marker whose placement is impacted by the prosody of the language.

Floating Quantifiers

There are three quantificational words in English that can appear in noncanonical positions, reportedly without a change in meaning: *all, both,* and *each* (Sportiche 1988).[2]

(1) All the children have greeted the teacher.

(2) The children (all) have (all) greeted the teacher.

In (1) the quantifier is in the canonical position for determiner quantifiers.[3] In contrast, the positions in (2) can only be occupied by FQ, as other quantifiers are ruled out, for example, (3).

(3) The children (*some/*many/*every) have (*some/*many/*every) greeted the teacher.

Although informants note no difference in sentences with an FQ as opposed to a nonfloating quantifier, there are consistent patterns of usage in natural speech. The existence of these patterns indicates that the choice between the nonfloating and floating word order is not haphazard or stylistic. This chapter addressed the following two questions regarding FQs:[4]

(4) a. What motivates the change in word order?

    b. What determines where the moved element occurs?

While a large body of work on FQ exists, its focus has been on syntactic accounts of how the FQ comes to occupy its noncanonical position.[5] The following section addresses question (4a), the motivation for the use of the floated word order. It is shown that information structure is the motivating factor in quantifier floating (q-float); FQs precede foci. The subsequent section then investigates question (4b), the positions where the FQ can occur, and concludes that this is determined by prosody.

Floating Quantifiers as Focus Markers
Focus Structure and Meaning of all

Before investigating what motivates q-float, this section presents the model of information structure used. Some of its concepts play a crucial role in the meaning that the FQ contributes to the sentence, and an informal approach to the semantics of *all*, based on Bobaljik (1995) and Dowty and Brodie (1984), is presented here. It is shown that *all* forces the predicate to be maximal in relationship to the subject, and this "maximalizing" interacts with focus structure in that it produces a contrastive focus that results in a sentence that has a reduced tolerance for alternatives.

Bobaljik (1995), based on Dowty and Brodie (1984), argues that the FQ *all* "causes the predicate to be maximal with respect to a group (or mass) argument" (Bobaljik 1995, 194).[6] Bobaljik views this as a type of strengthening—reducing the predicate's tolerance to weakening (1995, fn. 3, 201). Compare the following:

(5) The reporters harangued the candidate.

(6) The reporters all harangued the candidate.

(Bobaljik 1995, 198, citing Dowty 1986)

Sentence (5) is true if the majority of reporters harangued the candidate; the sentence is not falsified by a few reporters who did not participate in the haranguing. On the other hand, (6) is argued to be falsified by even one reporter not participating in the haranguing. I propose an addition to Bobaljik's claim: FQs also reduce the tolerance for alternatives.[7] This will be shown to produce the equivalent of a contrastive focus within which the alternative member(s) of the set have been eliminated as possible answers. It is the interaction of the FQ and the focus that contributes this contrastive interpretation. Some information structure basics are in order at this point.

This chapter adopts Erteschik-Shir's (1997) model of information structure termed *focus structure* (f-structure). Within this approach, every sentence contains both a main topic and a main focus and may contain subordinate (embedded) focus structure with further non–main topics and foci. *Topic* is defined as what the sentence is about, the pivot for assessment, while *focus* is what the speaker intends to direct the hearer's attention to, the answer to a *wh*-question. Crucial for us is Erteschik-Shir's restrictive and contrastive foci.

With contrastive foci, as in (7a), there is direct contrast between the members of the set, here *Janet* and *Ann* (underlining signals focus). And selection of one member results in the elimination of the other members (7b) of the set as a possible answer.

(7) Q: Who wants to marry John, Janet or Ann?

    A: <u>Janet</u> wants to marry John.

    B: #Janet wants to marry John. And I think Ann wants to also. (Erteschik-Shir 1997, 12)

Janet is selected from the set of {Janet, Ann}, and *Ann* is eliminated as a possible answer.

Restrictive foci require a specified contrast set to be available in the discourse, as in (8), but the contrast does not need to be direct, and the selection of a member of the set does not result in the elimination of other members as possible answers (8b).

(8) Q: Which one of John's friends wants to marry John?

    A: <u>Janet</u> wants to marry John.

    B: Janet wants to marry John. And I think Ann wants to also. (Erteschik-Shir 1997, 12)

Janet is selected from a set of possible (female) friends of John's, and the other members of the set remain as possible answers.

We turn now to see how f-structure influences q-float. The following examples show that FQs precede foci and the maximalizing function of *all* interacts with f-structure resulting in potential alternatives being eliminated.[8] In this way, *all* delineates the focus but also eliminates the possibility for alternatives.

Floating Quantifier Usage

The proliferation of FQ in sentences with pronouns, but not with full DPs, serves as an initial indicator that there may be an association between FQ and f-structure. Pronouns, when not used deictically, necessarily refer to something already in the discourse and therefore are obligatorily topics. Results obtained from analysis of a corpus showed that the frequency of FQs floated from pronouns make up over 96 percent of the cases, while FQs floated from full DP encompass less than 3 percent of the cases of FQs found in my investigation of a natural speech corpus.[9]

In the following examples we see the usage of floating and nonfloating quantifiers in conjunction with pronouns and full DPs. All examples are taken from natural speech corpora in order to ensure that the data obtained are representative of how speakers actually use FQ.

Example (9) is the quintessential example of an FQ and a pronoun; the quantifier floats from a pronoun and occurs before the predicate that is the focus.

(9) . . . and the brothers in that apartment, they were gonna go out and knock on all the doors, in their apartment, invite people to come to the worship service, cause no one could get out, they were *all* snowed in. (SBC file 20)

The focus of the sentence in (9) is *snowed in:* this implies "unable to leave." *All* strengthens the predicate and eliminates any other possible meanings such as "leaving," "leaving being difficult but possible," "leaving being delayed but possible," and so on. Although there is no overt contrast set here, *all* eliminates the possibility of any alternatives to the focus.

Example (10) is another case of an FQ and a pronoun.

(10) He—but was such a wimpy

Kim: physically . . . weak, uh person

Evelyn: and they *all* had asthma (SBC 022)

In the discourse prior to this excerpt several family members were introduced. In (10) Kim states that the people under discussion were physically weak. This introduces a restrictive set of reasons for physical weakness, perhaps something such as {ill health, asthma, emotional influences, etc.}. *Asthma* is selected from this restrictive set. The FQ facilitates the elimination of the other members of the set.

We turn to a case with a nonfloated quantifier and a full-DP subject.

(11) a. it was not a clean broadcast system

b. Like everything in the room,

c. *all* the metal objects would be receiving it constantly. (SBC 017)

In (11) *the metal objects* is being specified; what has been contextually established is that there are things in the room (11b), and then the speaker specifies which of these things are under discussion (11c) and eliminates the other things in the room. Therefore in this sentence the DP *the metal objects* functions as a contrastive focus, and we note that the quantifier does not float.

In the previous examples we saw FQ floated from pronouns but not from full DPs and a correspondence between the information structure and the use of the floated or nonfloated word order. Here we explore those cases that defy the pattern of FQ floating from pronouns but not full DPs and look for an explanation that holds across the nonstandard cases. The explanation is found in the f-structure status of the constituent following the FQ.

In example (12), the subject, *my family,* is the topic of the sentence, and the object, the location *Indiana,* is the contrastive focus of the sentence.

(12) Lajuna: I won't go to Indiana, see I don't have any family in Wisconsin

My family's *all* in Indiana. (SBC 044)

In this case we have a contrastive focus with the set encompassing {Wisconsin, Indiana}. Note the degraded status of the following continuation:

(13) I won't go to Indiana, see I don't have any family in Wisconsin

#My family's *all* in Indiana except for a few relatives in Wisconsin.

The continuation in (13) is degraded because *all* forces the second member of the set, *Wisconsin,* to be eliminated upon focusing the alternative member of the contrast set, *Indiana.* While FQs in natural speech usually float from pronouns, this example shows that when a speaker wants to emphasize the focus and create a contrastive focus they may opt to use an FQ. In this sentence the contrastive focus was direct, but what about cases where there is no overt contrast set specified before the focus? Such a case, taken from a natural speech corpus, is shown in (14).

(14) when you start pumping if your well has a large enough diameter,
    the water's all coming from the well, it's not coming from the aquifer.

The focus of this sentence is the place the water is coming from, *the well*. Because the speaker is contrasting water coming from the aquifer with water coming from the well, this is a case of contrastive focus. I would venture to say that *all* in this case alerts the listener that a contrastive focus follows and thus the contrast set occurring after the focus is not a problem.

In (15), like (14), we have a full DP and an FQ, and the restrictive set is specified after the selection of one member.

(15) . . . like the kids are *all* into pokemon right now
    and it uh they have these fads that go through   (Pitt et al. 2006, 1702b)

The speaker is selecting *Pokémon* from a set of possible fads. In this sense there is contrast between *Pokémon* and other fads, and it is a contrastive focus. Note that the following continuation does not follow well.

(16) # . . . but like the kids are *all* into pokemon right now and into Barney as well.

This continuation is odd because the sentence seems to be saying that the current fad is *Pokémon* and not something else. The same sentence as (16) without the FQ is perceived as better. The subject, *the kids,* is the topic. What we have here is a topical subject with an FQ occurring before a contrastive focus. These examples show that it is not the presence of a pronoun (or absence of a full DP) that dictates q-float but instead the f-structure roles of the elements involved.

The opposite case also occurs: a quantifier not floating from a pronoun. In the following sentence the subject is a contrastive focus and the object is the topic.

(17) a. LORI: Who was at Howard's End at the end?
    b. I thought it was Helen and the little boy.
    c. Linda: No, . . . *all of em* were at Howard's End. (SBC 023)

In (17c) the contrastive focus of the sentence is *all of them*. It is the quantifier itself, which is the contrastive element. In the discourse already are the members of a particular family, and these members form a restrictive set. The first speaker selects two members, and the second speaker contrasts these selected members with the entire group. In (17c) the focus of the sentence is the subject, and a nonfloated quantifier is employed. Because the focus is not in the predicate, there is no motivation for q-float.

The behavior of quantifiers and pronouns occurring sentence finally is an interesting test case for the idea proposed here. We have already discussed the tendency for FQ to float from pronouns. When we find pronouns and quantifiers occurring at the ends of sentences, we frequently find the nonfloated quantifier, although the floated order is perfectly acceptable.[10] In (18) we have a pronoun and a nonfloating quantifier occurring sentence finally.

(18) JOANNE: how can you remember all of them. (SBC 015)

This tendency for nonfloated quantifiers occurring sentence finally is a reflex of the fact that FQs occur floated before foci. Sentence finally, there is no motivation for floating. If we take the FQ to occur in order to mark the following constituent as the focus, sentence finally q-float is not motivated.

Last, we look at one more set of data that illustrates that informants perceive what follows the FQ to be the focus, and in particular a contrastive focus. In order to ensure that informants do perceive the FQ as marking what comes after it as focal, informants were given sentences and asked to choose the question that they corresponded to. In view of the fact that the foci can be identified by a *wh*-question (as mentioned earlier), these results show the determination of the focus based on the presence of the FQ. Informants were presented with sentences similar to (19).

(19) The children put the dogs *all* in cages.

The possible questions were as follows:

(20) Who put the dogs in cages? (subject focus)

(21) Did the kids put the dogs in boxes? (contrastive indirect object focus)

(22) What did the kids put in cages? (direct object focus)

(23) Where did the kids put the dogs? (indirect object focus)

(24) What did the children do? (VP focus)

(21) and (23) were most frequently selected as the most likely possible questions corresponding to the answer in (19). In order to ensure that it is the FQ that creates this interpretation, informants were asked to correlate (25), without the FQ, to one of the previously mentioned questions.

(25) The children put the dogs in cages.

The majority of informants opted for (24), which asks for a VP focus. Evidently, the presence of the FQ ensures that the focus is on the indirect object (IO), while in the absence of the FQ there is no favoring toward IO focus (see Göbbel 2005).

Examples (9) through (18) are representative of the use of floating/nonfloating quantifiers in natural speech. The predominance of FQ with pronouns and corresponding lack of FQ with full DPs indicate minimally that there is a correlation between pronouns and quantifier floating and full DPs and nonfloating. Bošković (2004, 706) proposes that DP objects overtly shift in English and that pronouns undergo further movement (cliticisation) to a higher position.[11] Q-float occurs when the pronoun raises higher, and this accounts for the lack of q-float with full-DPs. A puzzling issue here is that in natural speech we find weak pronouns and no q-float (*all'v'em*), particularly sentence finally. The weak pronoun is expected to raise. We also find q-float from nonweak pronouns, again unexpected in an approach of this type. An f-structure approach predicts that FQ will be found more frequently with subject pronouns because, if the subject is the topic, most likely the focus will occur in the predicate, and FQs occur before foci. Examples (19) and (25) ensure that it is indeed f-structure that determines the use of the FQ. What we have seen is that there is a strong correlation between the f-structure of a sentence and the presence and absence of an FQ.

The FQ *all* in a sentence leads to the results in which the following constituent is interpreted as a contrastive focus. As such, the FQ can be viewed as a focus marker. F-structure, though, plays no role in determining the exact position of the FQ within the linear string. In the next section I explore the positions that FQs occur in and show that that is determined by the prosody.

The Phonology of Quantifier Float

In this section I turn to the second question posed at the outset of this paper: What determines where the FQ can occur? In the previous section I showed that the determination to use the floated or nonfloated order was based on the information structure of the sentence. The determination to use the floated order still leaves open the exact linear position in which the FQ occurs. I take the syntactically allowed positions as a starting point and show that the position of the FQ in the linear string is determined by the prosody of the language. For reasons of space, I limit the discussion to sentences with full-DP subjects and auxiliary verbs. The idea that prosody plays a determining role when the syntax allows more than one word order is not new (see Guasti and Nespor 1999, among others). Moreover, I show that the patterns of FQ placement in natural speech are a result of prosodic constraints in the language, and this in turn can explain the absence of certain word orders in natural speech.

The prosodic structure of English is crucial to understanding FQ placement, so first I present a very brief overview of it. Syntax-prosody mapping is often couched in Optimality Theoretic constraints, and here I briefly present a few mapping constraints: Align-XP/R and Wrap-XP (Selkirk 2000; Truckenbrodt 1995, 1999). The former states that for every XP there is a phonological phrase such that the right edge of the XP corresponds to the right edge of the phonological phrase. Wrap-XP states that every XP is contained in one phonological phrase.[12] In addition to these constraints, there is the Align-Focus, R, a constraint requiring the alignment of the right edge of a focus constituent with the right edge of a prosodic phrase. Within each phonological phrase there must be, minimally, one accented syllable (Selkirk 2000, among many others). In English the default position for the phrase level accent is rightmost.

An additional constraint, outside the optimality theory (OT) framework, on English prosody is discussed by Speyer (2005), who notes a rule of English intonation that he termed the *Trochaic Requirement* (TR). This rule requires a weak element between two accents:

(26) (o) Ó o Ó o . . .   (Speyer 2005, 7)

Following Speyer, this weak element can be either a phonologically weak word or a pause.

Summarizing the effect of these constraints on English, thus far we know that we commonly find the following:

(27) a. The subject is in its own phonological phrase while the object can phrase with the verb

   b. There is a prosodic boundary to the right of the focus

   c. Every phrase must have an accent

   d. There cannot be two adjacent accents (TR)

What does this predict for sentences with an FQ? First, I note that the syntax allows the FQ to occur in several positions.[13]

(28) The children (all) might (all) have (all) greeted the teacher.

Because none of these positions result in an ill-formed sentence, we expected to find instances of all these word orders in natural speech. But that is not the case. FQs only occur in the last position in natural speech. I explore the absence of FQ in the two nonutilized positions in turn.

   Example (29) illustrates the first possible position that the FQ can occur in; the FQ occurs to the right of the DP.

(29) The children all have greeted the teacher.

We could logically conceive of two possible ways that this could be phrased, with the DP separate from the FQ (30) or with the DP phrased with the FQ (31).

(30) (The children) (all . . .)

(31) (The children all)

Brisson (1998), among others, has shown that the pronoun + FQ unit does not form a constituent. The same can be shown of DP + FQ—it does not form a constituent. Therefore there is no reason to assume that the DP + FQ must phrase together. The prosodic strength of FQ has been noted repeatedly (McCloskey 2000, among others). FQs are consistently pitch accented. Because FQs are not prosodically weak, they cannot be phrased with the DP, which is usually pitch accented, without violating TR. Welby (2003, citing Nakatani 1997) notes that the literature shows that even nonfocused DP subjects are frequently pitch accented and occur in their own phonological phrase (PPh). Thus, not surprisingly, we find informants use (30) and not (31).

   This predicts that if there is an auxiliary verb the FQ will phrase with the weak auxiliary verb, as in (32), and thereby avoid any prosodic violations.

(32) (The children) (all have seen the movie).

Natural speech confirms that when there is an FQ and a full DP the quantifier occurs phrased with the auxiliary verb and not the full DP. But the word order we get is not the one in (32). Instead, the FQ occurs to the right of the auxiliary verb.[14]

(33) (The children) (have all . . .)

(34) (The children've)(all . . .)

If there are several weak function words, the FQ occurs to the right of the final one, as in (35).[15]

(35) (The children) (might have all . . .)

This could stem from a preference to place heavier elements at edges (Selkirk 1995). For example, Guasti and Nespor (1999) discuss the preference in coordinated structures to place the heavier element second (to the right). Because informants find no meaning difference or grammatical problem with the FQ in any position in regards to the auxiliaries, the syntax and semantics must be neutral to the placement of the FQ, and it is the prosodic/phonological component determining the placement. The FQ occurs to the right of the auxiliaries because it is the heavier constituent of this group and heavy constituents are preferred rightmost—as close to the edge as possible.[16] Because we frequently get a prosodic boundary following the FQ, this placement provides an added bonus that may not be haphazard—a boundary between the topic and focus is formed.

Conclusion

The relationship between FQ and information structure has been overlooked in the literature on quantifier float. This chapter has explored the motivation for q-float and showed that it is f-structure that provides this motivation. Quantifiers that occur in floated positions do so in order to mark a focus that follows them. The final placement of FQ has been shown to be determined by the prosody of the language. FQs are dependent on information structure for determining if their presence is warranted, syntax for determining their possible positions, and prosody for determining their final position. This forces us to assume that their position is fixed at the phonetic form (PF) interface.

NOTES

I would like to thank Nomi Erteschik-Shir for her help and support during this research. This work also benefited from the comments and feedback of the participants of GURT 2007.

   1. I persist with the tradition of using the term "floating quantifiers" to identify *all, both,* or *each* located in non–determiner phrase (non-DP) initial position. I use the term *nonfloating* quantifiers to identify those that occur DP initially but could occur in a noninitial position.
   2. It is argued that there are scope differences. See Bošković (2004) for a syntactic account of this and Rochman (unpublished manuscript) for an information structure account of the scope differences.
   3. The status of *all* (determiner, quantifier, etc.) will not be dealt with here.
   4. This chapter confines itself to *all,* for reasons of space.
   5. For a survey of the work on FQs, see Bobaljik (2001). The questions of motivation and placement have been addressed for Korean, where it was shown that the hierarchical focal status of the quantifier in reference to other constituents determines its location (Han 1999). McCloskey (2000) discusses the role of prosody in q-float in West Ulster English. In exploring the semantics of *all,* floated and none, some researchers have dealt with meaning differences that could be interpreted as motivation for using an FQ.
   6. See Brisson's (1998) arguments that it is the sentence without *all* that can be subject to pragmatic weakening while the sentence with *all* is not vulnerable to this. (See also Bobaljik 1995, 199 fn 2.)
   7. This in some ways is similar to the claim made for *any* by Kadmon and Landman (1993). But they propose that *any* differs from *all* in that only the former has the widening effect that causes the reduced tolerance for exceptions.

8. The interaction is presented informally; the formal semantics of this interaction need to be fleshed out.
9. This is based on a count in the Santa Barbara Corpus (Du Bois et al. 2000; Du Bois et al. 2003; Du Bois and Englebretson 2004). Some utterances were not included in the statistics. Due to space constraints, I refer the reader to Rochman (unpublished manuscript) for a full explanation of the criteria.
10. See Rochman (unpublished manuscript) for a breakdown of the behavior of sentence final pronouns/FQ in natural speech.
11. Lasnik (1999) uses height test to show that object pronouns are higher than full DPs (Bošković 2004).
12. In English, Wrap-XP and Align-XP, R, are argued to be equally ranked (Selkirk 2000).
13. FQs that occur in positions that result in syntactic violations are completely ill formed and judged as impossible by informants (see McCloskey 2000).
14. Note that phrasing could be as in (a) as the addition of the weak auxiliary prevents any violations of TR. See Rochman (unpublished manuscript) for a discussion of this.

  (a) (The children've all) (seen the movie).

15. With the exception of *been*.
16. For an account of how the FQ comes to occupy this position, see Rochman (unpublished manuscript).

REFERENCES

Bobaljik, Jonathan D. 1995. Morphosyntax: The syntax of verbal inflection. PhD diss., Massachusetts Institute of Technology.

———. 2001. Floating quantifiers: Handle with care. In *The second Glot international state-of-the-article book,* ed. Lisa Cheng and Rint Sybesma, 107–48. New York: Mouton de Gruyter.

Bošković, Zeljko. 2004. Be careful where you float your quantifiers. *Natural Language and Linguistic Theory* 22:681–742.

Brisson, Christine. 1998. Distributivity, maximality, and floating quantifiers. PhD diss., Rutgers University.

Dowty, David. 1986. A note on collective predicates, distributive predicates and "all." In *Proceedings of the third Eastern State Conference on Linguistics,* ed. Fred Marshall, Ann Miller, and Zhengsheng Zhang, 97–115. Columbus: Ohio State University.

Dowty, David, and Belinda Brodie. 1984. A semantic analysis of "floated" quantifiers in a transformation-less grammar. In *Proceedings of the Third West Coast Conference on Formal Linguistics,* ed. Mark Cobler, Susan MacKaye, and Micheal Wescoat, 75–90. Stanford, CA: CSLI.

Du Bois, John W., Wallace L Chafe, Charles Meyer, and Sandra A. Thompson. 2000. Santa Barbara corpus of spoken American English, Part 1. Philadelphia: Linguistic Data Consortium.

Du Bois, John W., Wallace L. Chafe, Charles Meyer, Sandra A. Thompson, and Nii Martey. 2003. Santa Barbara corpus of spoken American English, Part 2. Philadelphia: Linguistic Data Consortium.

Du Bois, John W., and Robert Englebretson. 2004. Santa Barbara corpus of spoken American English, Part 3. Philadelphia: Linguistic Data Consortium.

Erteschik-Shir, Nomi. 1997. *The dynamics of focus structure.* New York: Cambridge University Press.

Göbbel, Edward. 2005. Focus in double object constructions. *Linguistics* 43:237–74.

Guasti, Maria Teresa, and Marina Nespor. 1999. Is syntax phonology-free? In *Phrasal phonology,* ed. René Kager and Wim Zonneveld, 73–98. The Netherlands: Nijmegen University Press.

Han, Jeonghan. 1999. Grammatical codings of information structure in Korean: A role and reference grammar account. PhD diss., University of Buffalo.

Kadmon, Nirit, and Fred Landman. 1993. Any. *Linguistics and Philosophy* 16:353–422.

Lasnik, Howard. 1999. Chains of arguments. In *Working minimalism,* ed. Samuel David Epstein and Norbert Hornstein, 189–215. Cambridge, MA: MIT Press.

McCloskey, James. 2000. The prosody of quantifier stranding under *wh*-movement in West Ulster English. Unpublished ms.

Nakatani, Christine. 1997. The computational processing of intonational prominence: A functional prosody account. Unpublished PhD diss., Harvard University.

Pitt, Mark A., Laura Dilley, Kyle Johnson, Scott Kiesling, William Raymond, Elizabeth Hume, and Eric Fosler-Lussier. 2006. *Buckeye corpus of conversational speech.* Columbus: Department of Psychology, Ohio State University.

Rochman, Lisa. The role of f-structure and intonation in quantifier floating. PhD diss., Ben Gurion University of the Negev.

Selkirk, Elisabeth O. 1995. Sentence prosody: Intonation, stress, and phrasing. In *The handbook of phonological theory,* ed. John A. Goldsmith, 550–69. Cambridge: Blackwell.

———. 2000. The interaction of constraints on prosodic phrasing. In *Prosody: Theory and experiment,* ed. Merle Horne, 231–61. Dordrecht: Kluwer.

Sportiche, Dominique. 1988. A theory of floating quantifiers and its corollaries for constituent structure. *Linguistic Inquiry* 19:425–49.

Speyer, Augustin. 2005. Topicalization and the trochaic requirement. *Penn Working Papers in Linguistics* 10 (2): 243–56.

Truckenbrodt, Hubert. 1995. Phonological phrases: Their relation to syntax, focus, and prominence. PhD diss., Massachusetts Institute of Technology.

———. 1999. On the relation between syntactic phrases and phonological phrases. *Linguistic Inquiry* 30:219–55.

Welby, Pauline. 2003. Effects of pitch accent type and status on focus projection. *Language and Speech* 46 (1): 53–81.

Syntax

6

Applicative Phrases Hosting Accusative Clitics

LUIS SÁEZ
Universidad Complutense de Madrid

IN THIS CHAPTER I offer an explanation for the puzzling behavior exhibited in certain environments by a particular class of standard Spanish "little words": accusative pronominal clitics. Those environments derive from the presence of a special sort of Spanish verbs that I will call "*ayudar*-verbs"; they are illustrated in (1):

(1) Ana *ayudó / perjudicó / molestó* a la   chica.
    "Ana helped / harmed / bothered   the girl."

Ayudar-verbs resemble standard dyadic monotransitives in the sense that they manifest a single internal object bearing accusative case. Accusative case assignment is evidenced in (2), where the object of (1) is substituted for by the accusative pronominal clitic *la*.[1]

(2) Ana *la*   ayudó.
    Ana 3.sg.fem.AccCL helped.3.sg.
    "Ana helped her."

Therefore, at first glance, any standard configuration for monotransitives might also be considered to be adequate for *ayudar*-verbs. In spite of this, in this chapter I will offer several pieces of evidence showing that a double object construction (DOC) underlies these verbs. This proposal will eventually explain the puzzling behavior exhibited by accusative pronominal clitics in these environments.

Puzzling Behavior of Accusative Clitics in *Ayudar*-Verb Environments

The problem I will focus on here has to do with the so-called *me-lui* constraint (Perlmutter 1971). As is well known, this constraint dictates that a dative pronominal clitic cannot co-occur with a first-/second-person accusative clitic, as illustrated in (3) for Spanish:

(3) Tú   *se*   *la/*me/*te*   enviaste a Juan.
    you 3.sg.DatCL 3/1/2.sg.AccCL sent.2.sg. to Juan
    "You sent it/her/me/you to Juan."

Romero (1997) and Ormazábal and Romero (1998a, 1998b) offer an account of this phenomenon centered around the [+animate] feature. First, they assume Demonte's (1995) proposal showing that Spanish sentences containing a triadic verb with a dative clitic are the correlates of English DOCs, where, as is well known, the dative (a goal) tends to be animacy related. The parallelism with English DOCs can be checked by comparing the grammatical English glosses in (4a) ("you sent a book to Ana/you sent a book to Madrid") with the ungrammatical English gloss ("*you sent Madrid a book") appearing in (4b):

(4) a. Tú enviaste un libro a Ana /Madrid.
     you sent.2.sg. a   book to Ana/Madrid
     "You sent a book to Ana/Madrid."
   b. Tú le   enviaste un libro a Ana / *Madrid.
     you 3.sg.DatCL sent.2.sg. a   book to Ana/Madrid
     "You sent Ana/*Madrid a book."

Further facts lead Ormazábal and Romero to proposing an exhaustive featural characterization of pronominal elements centered around the [+animate] feature: As previously observed, dative clitics are [+animate]; however, direct-object strong pronouns in verb-related argumental positions are [+animate] too. First-/second-person accusative clitics are also marked for [+animate], as they refer to the human protagonists of discourse (speaker and hearer). By contrast, third-person accusative clitics are [-animate]. Once provided with this featural characterization, Ormazábal and Romero explain the ungrammaticality in (3) as the result of two pronouns (the dative *se* and the first/second accusative *me/te*) competing for checking their [+animate] feature with one single animacy-related functional head.

A relevant feature of this approach concerns the fact that ungrammaticality arises when the competing [+animate] pronouns are co-arguments. For instance, let us consider the analytical causative constructions in (5), where two [+animate] pronouns co-occur: a dative clitic *me*, "me," referring to the first-person causee subject, and an accusative strong pronoun, *ella*, "her," interpreted as the patient role of the causee verb *conocer*, "to know." In such a situation, ungrammaticality results only when restructuring has taken place, that is, when a monoclausal configuration has been obtained. Such restructuring is not necessary in (5a), where the accusative clitic *la*, "her," doubling the strong pronoun undergoes enclisis to the causee verb; however, restructuring is necessary in (5b), where the accusative clitic has undergone clitic climbing. As shown in (5c), the grammaticality is restored if the strong pronoun is removed; as previously stated, direct object strong pronouns are characterized by Ormazábal and Romero as [+animate], thus differing from third-person accusative clitics in this respect:

(5) a. Tú   me   hiciste   conocer*la*   a ella. (biclausal)
     you 1.sg.AccCl made.2.sg. know.INFIN-3.sg.fem.AccCL to her
     "You made me know her."
   b. *Tú me   *la* hiciste conocer   a ella.
                                                      (restructuring)
   c. Tú me *la* hiciste conocer. (restructuring)

I propose that it is in these particular constructions, analytical causatives, that *ayudar*-verbs reveal significant peculiarities that distinguish them from other transitive verbs. Let us consider the examples in (6) and compare them to the ones in (5).

(6) a. Tú   me   hiciste ayudar*la*   a ella.   (biclausal)
       you 1.sg .AccCl made help.INFIN-3.sg.fem.AccCL to her
       "You made me help her"

    b. * Tú me   *la* hiciste ayudar   a ella.
                                                             (restructuring)

    c. * Tú me   *la* hiciste ayudar.   (restructuring)

(6a) is predictably grammatical, because, although there are two [+animate] pronouns, they belong to different clauses, hence competition between them does not take place. (6b) is predictably ungrammatical, because both pronouns belong to the same clause and, as a consequence, compete for checking. Surprisingly, (6c) shows that, unlike (5c), the grammaticality of the monoclausal configuration cannot be restored by simply omitting the offending strong pronoun. This is a very striking fact that, as far as I know, has been totally bypassed in the theoretical literature concerning DOCs.[2] Of course, such ungrammaticality means that a second offending [+animate] element still remains after omitting the strong pronoun. The only conceivable candidate for carrying this offending feature must be another pronominal element, obviously the third-person accusative clitic itself (*la*). However, recall that (5c) clearly showed that third-person accusative clitics cannot be inherently marked as [+animate]. As a way out of this puzzle, I propose that the third-person accusative clitic of *ayudar*-verbs inherits that feature from the particular configuration displayed by these verbs.

The Configuration Displayed by *Ayudar*-Verbs
I propose that *ayudar*-verbs display the DOC configuration represented in (7):

(7)

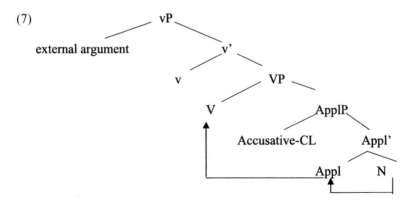

According to such a configuration, in *ayudar*-verbs a V° is selecting an ApplP, and *ayudar*-verbs are the result of "conflating" a nominal head (a kind of cognate theme), the null applicative head and V°. "Conflation" is a process that has figured prominently in Hale and Keyser's work on argument structure (see Hale and Keyser

2002, chap. 3, for details). They define it as a "fusion of syntactic nuclei," that is, a process according to which the phonological matrix of the head of a complement, say *n*, ends up located in the head *X* governing such a complement. The process may involve more than two heads: Given a sequence of heads $<X, \ldots, n - 1, n>$, each one governing the complement headed by the next, the phonological content of the most embedded one (say *n*) may end up under the highest one (*X*) provided that $<X \ldots n - 1>$ lack phonological content. In (5), X = V° governs the complement headed by n − 1 = Appl°, and n − 1 = Appl° governs the complement headed by n = N°. As a consequence, the phonological matrix of the cognate theme N°, for instance *ayuda*, "help," ends up in V°, giving rise to the verb *ayudar*, "to help."

As for the location of the ApplP in (7), proper justification can be provided. Pylkkänen (2002) distinguishes two sorts of ApplPs: high ApplPs and low ApplPs. Low ApplPs are selected by V° [as in (7)]; high ApplPs are higher than VP, as in the configuration represented in (8):

(8)

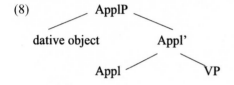

In high ApplPs, Appl° selects a VP, that is, an event; therefore they are compatible with both transitive and intransitive verbs and may host a dative pronoun referring to the benefactive of the event. This is illustrated in (9) for Albanian.

(9) I   vrapova.
    3.sg.Dat.CL run.1.sg.
    "I ran for him."

High ApplPs do not exist in Spanish, as shown by (10), the Spanish correlate of (9).

(10) *le*   corrí   yo.
     3.sg.Dat.CL ran.1.sg. I

In low ApplPs, Appl° obligatorily selects a theme object; therefore they are only compatible with transitive verbs. Spanish only has low ApplPs (although see Cuervo 2003 for a different view), as shown by the fact that once the verb *correr*, "run," in (10) is transitivized by adding *los cien metros*, "the hundred meters," the dative *le* is possible.

(11) *Le*   corrí   yo los cien   metros.
    3.sg.Dat.CL ran.1.sg. I   the hundred meters
    "I ran the hundred meters for him."

However, the benefactive interpretation of *le* in (11), coupled with my claim that Spanish only has low ApplPs, might seem to conflict with Pylkkänen's typology for ApplPs, because she relates the benefactive interpretation to high ApplPs and a source (possessive)/recipient interpretation to low ApplPs. I claim, though, that there is no actual conflict, as the benefactive interpretation of (11) is a mere inference obtained from a more basic source/possessive interpretation. According to this interpretation, the hundred meters are initially "related to" (or "belong to") a person as a task, and the task ends up transferred to a different person [in (11), the speaker]. This new way of looking at the interpretation of sentences like (11) explains that, as shown in (12), the direct object of (11) must be definite, that is, conceived as a distance previously assumed to "belong to" somebody else (the referent of the pronominal clitic *le*) as a task to be performed:

(12) *Le   corrí   yo cien   metros.
     3.sg.Dat.CL ran.1.sg. I   hundred meters
     "I ran hundred meters for him."

Moreover, the task to be transferred might be of a static nature, which makes the prediction, borne out by (13a), that Spanish low ApplPs could also be compatible with static predicates. This fact apparently escapes Pylkkänen's second test distinguishing high and low ApplPs. According to this test, low ApplPs are incompatible with static predicates, as in (13b), as they convey a transfer-of-possession interpretation incompatible with static predicates. I propose instead that (13b) is ungrammatical because, as has been commonly observed, English lacks source ApplPs.

(13) a. Le   sostuve yo la bolsa.
        him.Dat.CL.3.sg. held   I   the bag
        "I held the bag for him."
     b. *I held him the bag.   (Pylkkänen 2002, 24)

I conclude, then, that Spanish ApplPs in *ayudar*-verb environments are also selected by V°, that is, they are low ApplPs too. As shown in (7), the accusative clitic of *ayudar*-verbs is generated in the specifier of the low ApplP. In this position it obtains the goal interpretation in the conceptual-intentional interface, according to a configurational interpretation of theta-roles à la Hale and Keyser (1993). Therefore, in order to derive the ungrammaticality of (6c) by relying on Ormazábal and Romero's (1998a, 1998b) approach, it may be proposed that the feature [+animate] is part of the bundle of features forming the applicative head and that, as a consequence, the pronominal clitic located in the specifier of the ApplP must inherit such a feature in some way, thus giving rise to animacy competition in monoclausal causative environments.

Further Arguments in Support of the Configuration in (7)

One piece of evidence supporting the idea that the object of *ayudar*-verbs is actually the goal argument of a masked DOC is the fact that they never co-occur with a dative element. (14) shows their incompatibility with a possessor dative (*al equipo,* "to the team"):

(14) Juan (*le)   ayudó   a los miembros del   / *al   equipo.
     Juan 3.sg.DatCl helped.3.sg. to the members of the/ to the team
     "Juan helped the team members."

The fact that *ayudar*-verbs are never possible with a dative constituent can be derived from my proposal that the internal object of these verbs is a DOC goal, because, as is well known, indirect objects can never coexist with further datives. For instance, (15) shows the incompatibility of the indirect object *al niño,* "to the child," with a possessor dative like *a Ana:*

(15) *Juan *le*   dio   un beso al   niño *a Ana.*
     Juan 3.sg.DatCl gave.3.sg. a   kiss to the child to Ana
     "Juan kissed Ana's child."

A new argument in support of the configuration in (6) relies on research by Bosque and Masullo (1997) focusing on a particular interpretation of quantificational adverbs such as *mucho,* "very much." With intransitive verbs, adverbs like *mucho* may have three main interpretations: the eventive one, the durative one, and the inherent one. I illustrate these three interpretations with the example in (16):

(16) Llueve   mucho.
     "It is raining very much."

In this example, the eventive interpretation of *mucho* conveys the existence of many events of raining; that is, the sentence would mean that it rains very often. According to the durative interpretation, there is an event of raining, and that event is lasting for a very long time. The inherent interpretation conveys an evaluation of the amount of fallen rain (there is a lot of water). Bosque and Masullo (1997) propose that this interpretation results from a structure similar to (17).

(17)

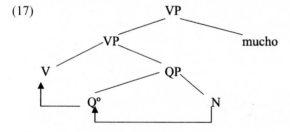

In this structure, the unergative verb *llover,* "rain," is the result of conflating a nominal head meaning "rain" and a light verb. This process also involves a quantificational head providing a variable for the VP modifier *mucho,* thus enabling the inherent reading.

Leaving aside the technical details, the interesting point for this chapter of Bosque and Masullo's proposal is that the inherent reading of *mucho* reveals the existence of a nominal element in the syntax performing as the complement of a light verb. This proposal correctly predicts that transitive verbs should prevent the inherent interpretation for adverbs like *mucho,* as these verbs already have an overt object, and as a consequence, there is no room for the quantified nominal complement. This incompatibility is illustrated in (18).

(18) Autorizaron   (*mucho)   una manifestación
     authorized.3.pl very much a   demonstration
     "They authorized a demonstration (*very much)."

However, Bosque and Masullo point out that certain transitive verbs, such as *ayudar*, "to help," do admit the inherent interpretation of *mucho;* this compatibility is illustrated in (19).

(19) Ana ayudó   a la   chica mucho.
     "Ana helped   the girl   very much."

Bosque and Masullo relate the exceptional behavior of verbs like *ayudar* to the fact that they alternate with light verb constructions; for instance, *ayudar* alternates with the equivalent expression *dar ayuda,* "provide help." As represented in (20), my proposal for *ayudar*-verbs provides room for both the overt accusative object (the goal) and the abstract correlate of the light verb constructions pointed out by Bosque and Masullo, that is, an abstract noun meaning "help." This abstract noun may now be selected by a quantifier head, which explains the exceptional availability of the inherent reading of *mucho* with these transitive verbs.

(20)

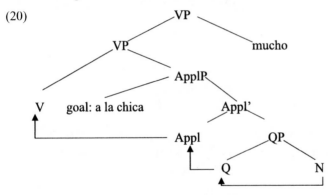

A third argument in support of the configuration in (7) has to do with depictives. Pylkkänen (2002) points out that depictive secondary predicates are incompatible with indirect objects in English. For instance, (21), where the depictive *hungry* tries to attribute a property to Mary, is completely ungrammatical:

(21) *I gave Mary the meat *hungry.*

Pylkkänen derives this impossibility from the incompatibility between the semantic type of depictives and the semantic type of the low ApplP hosting indirect objects (see Pylkkänen 2002 for details). Therefore the ungrammatical result triggered by the presence of a depictive constitutes a test for the presence of low ApplPs.

Ayudar-verbs are incompatible with depictives, as illustrated in (22):

(22) *Juan ayudó   a María *enfadada.*
     "Juan helped   Mary angry."

As a consequence, it is reasonable to conclude that the transitivity of these verbs hides a low ApplP hosting the accusative constituent in its specifier.

Case Assignment

I have proposed that *ayudar*-verbs display a DOC configuration with a low ApplP. As represented in (7), this explains that their complement must be taken into consideration for animacy competition in analytical causative environments, as ApplPs convey a [+animate] feature. However, this hypothesis must deal with a case-related problem that immediately arises. Demonte (1995) and Romero (1997) show that sentences such as (23a), where the clitic *le* is doubling the goal *a María,* "to María," are the Spanish correlates of English DOCs. However, such a clitic exhibits dative case, and, moreover, the goal cannot become a subject under passivization, as illustrated in (23b):

(23) a. Juan le   dio   a María el libro.

Juan 3.sg.DatCL gave.3.sg to María the book

"J. gave M. the book."

   b. *María fue dada un libro.

"María was given a   book."

Consequently it must be concluded that, in Spanish DOCs, goals exhibit dative case. However, recall that the goal of constructions with *ayudar*-verbs exhibits accusative case, as it may be replaced by an accusative clitic, as illustrated in (2). Moreover, it may become a subject under passivization, as illustrated in (24):

(24) Ella fue ayudada.

"She was helped."

It seems, then, that the goals of *ayudar*-verbs are the faithful counterpart of English DOC goals as far as case properties are concerned; indeed, the grammaticality of the English gloss of (23b) shows that English DOCs may passivize with no problem and that, as a consequence, their goal is invariably marked with accusative case.

Of course, the two phenomena observed with regard to *ayudar*-verb environments—the existence of theme conflation and the availability of accusative case and raising-to-subject for goals—cannot be two independent facts unrelated to each other. Informally speaking, it seems as if, when theme conflation takes place, the accusative case usually assigned to the theme can now be "transferred" to the goal argument.

I will derive the apparently exceptional behavior of these goals from the principle in (25), a version of the one proposed by Alsina (1997) in relation to Romance causatives:

(25) Dative case can only be assigned to the (thematically) more prominent of two internal arguments.

According to (25), structural dative case cannot be assigned if there is only one internal argument in the predicate. I will assume that (25) is a severe case restriction holding for case assignment in Spanish. As an effect of (25), a constituent in the specifier of an ApplP must regularly receive dative case, because it normally co-occurs with a theme argument. However, in certain instances where the theme does not structurally manifest itself, as in the conflation cases analyzed here, the goal must receive accusative case.

One piece of evidence supporting (25) concerns, of course, the case behavior of causee subjects in causative constructions; recall that it is in connection to causative constructions that Alsina puts forth a principle similar to (25).

Under restructuring, the clitic corresponding to the causee subject in Spanish causative constructions exhibits dative case if the causee verb selects an object represented by an accusative clitic undergoing clitic climbing; by contrast, if no accusative clitic is selected by the causee verb, the clitic corresponding to the subject of the causee verb manifests itself as accusative. I illustrate these contrasting facts with the examples in (26)/(27). We have obtained (26b) from (26a) through substitution for the low argumental phrases of (26a) by a clitic, plus a restructuring process (notice that clitic climbing has taken place). As a result, we observe that the causee subject in (26a) must be replaced by a dative pronominal clitic *se,* because it co-occurs with a predicate-mate accusative clitic replacing the theme object *la canción,* "the song." By contrast, the causee subject in (27a) may only be replaced by an accusative clitic *la* in (27b), as the causee verb is intransitive.

(26) a. Juan hizo   cantar la canción a María.
       Juan made.3.sg to.sing the song   to María
     b. Juan *se*   la   hizo   cantar.
       Juan 3.sg.DatCL. 3.sg. AccCL made.3.sg to.sing
       "Juan made Mary/her sing the song/it."

(27) a. Juan hizo   cantar a María.
       Juan made.3.sg to.sing to María
     b. Juan *la*   hizo   cantar
       Juan 3.sg.AccCL. made.3.sg to.sing
       "Juan made Mary/her sing."

In these examples it is possible to see that the same restriction holding for the specifier of an ApplP also holds for subjects of causee verbs when they become internal arguments of the causer verb, provided that a theme predicate-mate is present. Therefore we can say that (25) is a general principle holding for case assignment to internal arguments.

A further piece of evidence supporting (25) concerns the behavior of Spanish verbs like *pagar,* "pay"/*servir,* "serve." These verbs must assign dative case to their goals if the theme object is present, as shown in (28a); by contrast, when the theme is absent, as in (28b), the goal must obtain accusative case.

(28) a. *le/*la*   serví   a ella el café.
       3.sg.DatCL/3.sg.fem.AccCL served.1.sg. to her the coffee
       "I served her a coffee."

b. *La* serví.

"I served her."

Therefore, it seems reasonable to conclude that a principle like (25) is constraining structural case assignment in Spanish.

Inanimate Objects

The presence of an animacy-feature in the ApplP selected by *ayudar*-verbs seems to be seriously compromised by the fact that those verbs are sometimes able to appear with nonanimate complements, as illustrated in (29).

(29) Esas   cosas   perjudican la   salud.

      "Those things harm   the health."

Consequently a modification of my original hypothesis relying on a concept different from "animacy" but preserving the fundamental role of ApplP would be highly desirable. Luckily, this new perspective is provided by Ormazábal and Romero (2007) in their updated account for the *me-lui* constraint. Ormazábal and Romero (2007) notice that ApplPs are not inherently related to animacy; they illustrate this fact with the example in (30):

(30) Le   pongo   la   pata a   la   mesa.

      3.sg.DatCL put.1.sg. the leg   to the table

      "I will assemble the leg on the table."

Importantly, even though the clitic *le* in environments like (30) is not related to animacy, it triggers *me-lui* constraint effects, as illustrated in (31b) [which contrasts with (31a)]:

(31) CONTEXT: I'm fed up; if you mention that the table is missing a leg once again and do nothing to fix it . . .

     a. . . . te   pongo   a ti (de pata) en la   mesa.

        . . . 2.sg.AccCL put.1.sg   you as leg   in the table

     b. *. . . te   le   pongo   a ti (de pata) a   la   mesa.

        . . . 2.sg.AccCL 3.sg.DatCL put.1.sg   you as leg   to the table

        "I assemble you as a leg in the table."   (Ormazábal and Romero 2007)

This means that an account of the *me-lui* constraint based on animacy competition cannot be true. Instead, Ormazábal and Romero propose the constraint in (32), coupled with the empirically (and cross-linguistically) well-supported claim that animacy always triggers object agreement and the reasonable assumption that indirect object clitics are a manifestation of applicative object agreement (2007; see their work for details):

(32) *Object Agreement Constraint (OAC):* If the verbal complex encodes object agreement, no other argument can be licensed through verbal agreement.

The reason why Spanish third-person accusative clitics do not trigger *me-lui* constraint effects [recall example (3)] is that they are instances of determiner cliticization, which explains that they cannot be doubled [see (33)]; instead, Spanish dative (and first-/second-person accusative) clitics necessarily trigger such effects, because, as evidenced by their availability to undergo doubling [see (34)], they are instances of agreement:

(33) *La   vimos   la   casa.
     3.fem.AccCL saw.1.sg the house
     "We saw the house."   (Ormazábal and Romero 2007)

(34) Les   compré   un libro a los primos.
     3.pl.DatCL bought.1.sg. a   book to the cousins
     "I bought my cousins a book."   (Ormazábal and Romero 2007)

Clearly, the accusative clitic located in the specifier of *ayudar*-verbs is not a manifestation of applicative object agreement, as no doubling is possible in these cases:

(35) *La   ayudé a una chica.
     3.sg.fem.AccCL helped to a girl
     "I helped a girl."

As a consequence, accusative clitics hosted by ApplPs are determiners undergoing cliticization. However, I also claim that this process simultaneously triggers obligatory abstract applicative object agreement. The abstract nature of this agreement is quite natural, given that the accusative clitic is cliticizing to the verbal head, thus preventing the overt manifestation of applicative agreement most probably due to morphological reasons.

It is the combination of abstract applicative agreement and animacy-related object agreement that explains the ungrammaticality of (6c) as a violation of the principle in (32).

The situation just described concerning accusative clitics with *ayudar*-verbs significantly resembles the behavior of goal clitics in Spanish "laísta" dialects. In these dialects, accusative clitics may be interpreted as goals, as illustrated in (36), where the feminine accusative clitic *la* is referring to the recipient of the book:

(36) Juan la   dio un libro.
     Juan 3.sg.AccCL gave a book
     "Juan gave her a book."

Romero (2001) offers several pieces of evidence supporting the proposal that sentences like (36) are the Spanish equivalent of English DOCs, where the goal exhibits accusative case too. If this is true, we could say that the accusative clitic in examples like (36) occupy the specifier of an ApplP in the same way that *ayudar*-verb goals do. Importantly, although it is located in the ApplP, the clitic cannot be doubled, a fact also pointed out by Romero.

(37) *Juan *la*   dio un libro *a una chica.*

Juan 3.sg.AccCL gave a book to a   girl

"Juan gave a girl a book."

Moreover, no agreement clitic may show up co-occurring with the accusative clitic either:

(38) *Juan *la*   *le*   dio un libro.

Juan 3.sg.AccCL 3.sg.DatCL gave a   book

"Juan gave her a book."

As a consequence, it is reasonable to conclude that both "laísta" goal clitics and standard Spanish *ayudar*-verb goal clitics are instances of the same phenomenon: Determiner cliticization takes place in an ApplP environment, and, as a result, the applicative agreement morpheme heading the ApplP must remain silent, presumably due to morphological reasons.

NOTES

I thank the audience of GURT 2007, as well as Ignacio Bosque and Juan Romero. Of course, all errors are my own. This work has been financed by the Servicio de Investigación of the Universidad Complutense de Madrid as a result of the author's taking part of the research group "Relations between Lexicon and Syntax in Spanish" (Departamento de Lengua Española y Teoría de la Literatura y Literatura Comparada, Facultad de Filología).

1. Spanish has a series of four third-person nonreflexive accusative clitics (neu./masc. sg. *lo,* fem.sg. *la,* masc.pl. *los,* fem.pl. *las*) and a series of two third-person nonreflexive dative clitics (sg. *le,* pl. *les*), plus one special third-person nonreflexive dative clitic, the "spurious" *se,* unmarked for gender/number and restricted to co-occurring with other clitics.

2. As for the descriptive literature, the contrast between cases like (4b) and (5b) has also been almost totally ignored. One exception is Cano (1987, 353), who points out the difference between his pair of examples in (1) [with innocuous restructuring in (1b)] and the pair in (2) [with restructuring triggering ungrammaticality in (2b)]:

   (1) a. Lo   vi   manejar*lo.*

       3.sg.masc.AccCL saw.1.sg drive.INFIN-3.sg.masc.AccCL

       b. Se   *lo*   vi   manejar.

       3.DatCL 3.sg.masc.AccCL saw.1.sg drive.INFIN

       "I saw him drive it."

   (2) a. Lo   vi   castigar*lo.*

       3.sg.masc.AccCL saw.1.sg punish.INFIN-3.sg.masc.AccCL

       b. *Se *lo*   vi   castigar.

       3.DatCL 3.sg.masc.AccCL saw.1.sg punish.INFIN

       "I saw him punish him."

REFERENCES

Alsina, Alex. 1997. Causatives in Bantu and Romance. In *Complex predicates,* ed. Alex Alsina, Joan Bresnan, and Peter Sells, 203–46. Stanford, CA: CSLI Publications.

Bosque, Ignacio, and Pascual J. Masullo. 1997. On verbal quantification in Spanish. In *Studies on the syntax of Central Romance languages,* ed. Olga Fullana and Francesc Roca, 9–64. Girona: Universitat de Girona.

Cano, Rafael. 1987. *Estructuras sintácticas transitivas en el español actual.* Madrid: Gredos.

Cuervo, María Cristina. 2003. Datives at large. PhD diss., Massachusetts Institute of Technology.

Demonte, Violeta. 1995. Dative alternation in Spanish. *Probus* 7:5–30.

Hale, Kenneth, and Samuel Jay Keyser. 1993. On argument structure and the lexical expression of syntactic relations. In *The view from building 20,* ed. Kenneth Hale and Samuel Jay Keyser, 53–109. Cambridge, MA: MIT Press.

———. 2002. *Prolegomenon to a theory of argument structure.* Cambridge, MA: MIT Press.

Ormazábal, Javier, and Juan Romero. 1998a. Attract-F. A case against case. Paper presented at the 21st GLOW Colloquium, Tilburg, April 16.

———. 1998b. On the syntactic nature of the me-lui and the person-case constraint. *Anuario del Seminario de Filología Vasca Julio de Urquijo* 32:415–34.

———. 2007. The object agreement constraint. *Natural Language and Linguistic Theory* 25:315–47.

Perlmutter, David. 1971. *Deep and surface structure constraints in syntax.* New York: Holt, Rinehart and Winston.

Pylkkänen, Lina. 2002. *Introducing arguments.* PhD diss., Massachusetts Institute of Technology.

Romero, Juan. 1997. *Construcciones de doble objeto y gramática universal.* PhD diss., Universidad Autónoma de Madrid.

———. 2001. A note on case (mis)match in Spanish. *Cuadernos de Lingüística VIII:* 97–104.

7

The Little *DE* of Degree Constructions

REMUS GERGEL
Universität Tübingen

THIS CHAPTER ANALYZES one function of the Romanian "little word" *de*. I claim that it serves as a morphosyntactic exponent in degree constructions. The first two sections illustrate problematic outcomes for a standard (universal) representation of degree constructions employing diagnostics used, for example, in Beck, Oda, and Sugisaki (2004). The next two sections discuss the pertinent morphosyntactic properties of Romanian and the paradox arising from a positive setting for degrees as far as the basic morphological and syntactic facts of the language are concerned together with some apparent negative outcomes, for example, in questions and subcomparatives. The paradox is resolved in the penultimate section. I propose an analysis for the role of the morpheme *de* as an exponent inserted in the relevant degree constructions under a functional degree-sensitive head, implemented here as Deg°. The final section analyzes an independent domain involving the adjectival *de*.

Degree Analysis(/es)—Essentials

This section introduces the minimal tenets of the standard representation of comparatives (and degree constructions more generally) that will be relevant in the discussion later. As there is a good deal of work supporting the view of degree representations in syntax-semantics for languages like English (cf. Kennedy 1999; Klein 1991; von Stechow 1984), we will not go into the details of the analysis of those languages. As we are concerned here with syntactic facts, we simply introduce one common analysis in this respect (following, e.g., Kennedy 1999, in main outline). A gradable adjective bears a relationship to a *degree*. The minimal assumption is that a degree element is a sister to a gradable adjective phrase (AP). In Kennedy's (1999) terms the adjective has an extended projection, a familiar pattern syntactically. One possibility, then, is (1).

(1)   DegP analysis, simplified structure

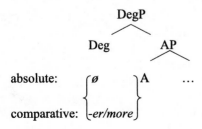

The decisive question for my purposes will be whether and where specifically degree representations originate in the syntax and how their dependencies become visible morphosyntactically. Where degree elements structurally end up is well known: Following Chomsky (1977), previous investigations of comparatives argued that they have representations akin to *wh*-clauses. A basic dependency is (2).

(2) a. $[_{CP}$ [wh-Op]   ...... [t_{wh} ...]...

    b. $[_{CP}$ [deg-Op]   ...... [t_{deg} ...]...

Problems with the Standard Analysis: The Case of Japanese

A series of recent studies point to particular types of cross-linguistic variation within comparative constructions (cf. Beck, Oda, and Sugisaki 2004; Reglero 2007; Snyder 1995; Snyder, Wexler, and Das 1995, among others). For example, Beck, Oda, and Sugisaki (2004) point out that the traditional degree-based analysis cannot explain crucial Japanese data pertaining to comparative structures. Among them, one finds subcomparatives and degree questions, cornerstones of the standard degree-based views [cf. (3) and (4)].

(3) *Kono tana-wa [ano doa-ga hiroi yori (mo)] (motto) takai.
    this shelf-Top [that door-Nom wide YORI (mo)] (more) tall
    This shelf is taller than that door is wide.   (Beck, Oda, and Sugisaki 2004)

(4) a. How smart is John?
    b. John-wa   dore-kurai   kasikoi no?
       John-Top which degree smart   Q
       To which degree is John smart?   (Beck, Oda, and Sugisaki 2004)

The subcomparative is ruled out in Japanese, and the degree question is a paraphrase. A language *L* may then have (English-style) deg-variables—or, for example, use non-compositional, pragmatic strategies instead. Beck, Oda, and Sugisaki propose the parameter in (5).

(5) Degree abstraction parameter   (DAP; Beck, Oda, and Sugisaki 2004)
    A language {does/does not} have binding of degree variables in the syntax.

Starting from the essential variationist observation, there are two main issues that require further exploration from a morphosyntactic perspective. First, how is (5) realized in a given *L*? Second, how can it be realized? More specifically, what shows, for example (to a learner of *L*), that there is a possible degree-based representation in a syntactic derivation of *L*? The following section focuses on these questions for Romanian and argues that a morphosyntactically overt function word is involved. Thus while Romanian does not seem to show any unusual type of comparison strategy (i.e., from the wider typological perspective; see Stassen 1985), it can nonetheless be instructive for how a particular surfacing realization ties in with the diagnostics of variationist research on degrees. Next it provides a test of the representation of degree constructions at various levels and argues that—despite some conflicting appearances—it is positive (with a number of crucial cases represented through an overt exponent).

Essentials of Low- and High-Degree Morphosyntax

This section gives the basic facts relating to the syntactic locus from which a Deg-head could project (namely, adjectival morphology) and the level where it could end up (clausal *wh*-syntax) to test for potential sources of a different parameter setting.

Adjectival Morphology

Romanian has the pattern sketched in (6) for the absolute and the comparative.

(6) a. Ion e inteligent.   b. Maria e mai inteligentă   (decât Ion).

    Ion is intelligent   Maria is more intelligent.FEM (than Ion)

There is, of course, nothing a priori unusual about such patterns. The language has (analytic only) comparative morphology. Beyond that, in the adjectival domain one finds a series of otherwise usual morphological facts obtaining in Romance (also beyond comparative morphology; e.g., including adjectival agreement patterns).[1] A first conjecture would be that *mai,* "more," is a good candidate for a comparative Deg-head. A second conjecture would be that a silent absolute Deg° is available in the other (*mai*-less) cases [cf. (6a), as usually assumed, e.g., for English (Kennedy 1999)].

Wh-clauses

At the clausal level, the morphosyntactic facts of the language do not give rise to suspicion either. Although there is multiple *wh*-movement, *wh*-phrases essentially move to the left edge of the clause in Romanian [with superiority in conjunction with the D-linking-based "violations" applying; Comorovski 1996; cf. (7) and (8)].

(7) Cine ce (crezi că) a văzut?

    who what (think.2sg. that) has seen

    Who (do you think) saw what?

(8) *Ce (pe) cine (crezi că) a văzut?

    what PE who (think.2sg. that) has seen

    Who (do you think) saw what?

Moreover, certain pied-piping effects obtain (cf. Grosu 1994 and references therein).

Comparative "Complementizer(s)"

Romanian has two main ways to introduce comparatives. One is *decât,* "than," which is felicitous with clausal and phrasal comparatives. More colloquial is the *ca* version of "than," felicitous with phrasal comparatives. This is, again, a not uncommon situation cross-linguistically (namely, with essentially two types of comparative introducers; Hankamer 1973).[2] In particular, I will focus on the clausal type of comparatives in the language to test crucial data that become visible at the sentential level. To sum up: From the evidence at the structurally lowest and highest syntactic levels, that is, word-level and clausal syntax, we would expect a syntactic degree parameter to be set positively.

Puzzles in the Middle

If a language has a Deg-head, and given the previously detailed essentials, one expects such phenomena as the following: (a) Deg-questions, (b) subcomparative structures, and (c) comparatives behaving uniformly in the language. This section makes the observation that despite the regular comparative morphology and the available (movement-based) *wh*-syntax, degree constructions in Romanian seem to share some of the unwelcome consequences (for a standard analysis) evidenced by Japanese.

Main Puzzle 1: Degree Questions

The first problem encountered, if we tried to follow the previously mentioned reasoning, is that Romanian does not have simplex degree questions.[3] Merging an appropriate *wh*-word to a licit declarative structure fails, as in (9a). Moreover, controlling for potentially interfering movement does not yield grammatical structures either [cf. (9b) through (9f)].

(9) a. *Cât Ion e inteligent?   d. *Cât Ion inteligent e?
    b. *Cât inteligent e Ion ?   e. *Cât inteligent Ion e?
    c. *Cât e inteligent Ion?   f. *Cât e Ion inteligent?
        WH Ion is intelligent (and permutations for constituents X_i, $2 \leq I \leq 4$ above)
        How intelligent is Ion?

The position of the *wh*-word is constant at the left edge in the examples in (9).

Main Puzzle 2: Subcomparatives

The same is true of subcomparatives, that is, a simple Merge strategy of the usual lexical items does not yield the results usually expected. Merging two degree-based clauses does not yield a well-formed subcomparative. Sentence (10) illustrates this fact.

(10) *Raftul e(ste) mai lung decât camera e lată.
     shelf.the is more long than room.the is wide
     The shelf is longer than the room is wide.

Trying to allow for more flexibility in word order (e.g., focus movement; see Reglero 2007 for persuasive argumentation for some Spanish cases)[4] is not applicable as such in Romanian either. In particular, structures like (11) are ungrammatical.[5]

(11) *Raftul e(ste) mai lung decât lată e (ste) camera.
     shelf.the is more long than wide is room.the
     The shelf is longer than the room is wide

Two predictions of the standard analysis do not seem to be borne out. One might conjecture the opposite from the previous section, for example, that Romanian lacks syntactic degree representations. However, there is evidence to the contrary, which the following section explores.

"DE-Support"

This section argues that despite the apparent deficient outcomes observed earlier, there is, crucially, a morphosyntactically well-motivated strategy used in the language (i.e., Merge of a little word), which salvages the problematic derivations. More specifically, the overt morphological form *de* is merged to the gradable adjective and saves the relevant derivations, that is, degree questions and subcomparatives in particular. The descriptive claim is stated as follows. We suggest that the overt morpheme *de* is last-resort merged to the Deg position and marks it as such [cf. (12)].

(12)

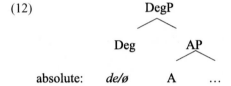

absolute: *de*/ø   A   …

Repair in Degree Questions

With the exponent *de* merged, degree questions are grammatical, as in (13a). The same repair effect obtains in the pied-piping variants, as shown in (13b).

(13) a. Cât e de inteligent Ion?   b. Cât de inteligent e Ion?
      how is DE intelligent Ion   how DE intelligent is Ion
      How intelligent is Ion?   How intelligent is Ion?

In differential degree questions (*cu cât*, "by how much"), where *mai* is necessarily present, a first indication for the complementary distribution of *mai* and *de* is observed. Thus the (predicted) incompatibility between *de* and *mai* obtains [cf. (14)].

(14) Cu cât e mai (*de) inteligentă Maria?
     with how much is more (DE) intelligent.FEM Maria
     By how much is Maria more intelligent?

The same holds on the multiplicative scale [*de cîte ori,* "how many times"; cf. (15)].

(15) De   câte   ori   e mai   (*de) scump un iaz decît un om?(web-based)
     DE$_{(NUM)}$ how-many times is more DE expensive a   lake than a   man

Moreover, *de/mai* competition is also evidenced beyond degree questions (see next section).

While the particular phenomena in Romanian are language specific, last-resort mechanisms are more general and well known in other domains and languages.[6] In this connection, it is worth considering *do*-support briefly, which is not found in the English form in the Germanic cognates. Nonetheless subset effects of it are detectable elsewhere (cf., e.g., Houser et al. 2006, among many others). An interesting counterpart to the asymmetric Germanic situation can be found in some areas in Romance, for example, if we compare Romanian with Spanish. Spanish does not have *de*-support (in the Romanian pattern); it shows it, however, in a subset of the environments, for example, in some degree questions [cf. (16) through (17) with data from (Chilean) Spanish provided by Héctor Campos (p.c.)].[7]

(16) Cómo es Juan *de* inteligente?   (17) Cómo *de* inteligente es Juan?
    how   is Juan of intelligent   how of intelligent is Juan

Repair in Subcomparatives

Recall that simple subcomparatives are not licensed. There are, however, repair strategies that improve their acceptability. While the issues posed by subcomparatives in general overload the scope of this chapter, I focus here on one ingredient in their structure, namely, Merge of degree *de*. The existence of subcomparatives, as of degree questions, has previously been noted in the literature. However, this has happened without analyzing the role played by *de* as a degree head in the relevant contexts [which was also not the focus of the previous contributions concerned with the issues; cf. (18)].

(18) Maria e cu mult mai deşteaptă decât e Zamfira de frumoasă.

    Maria is with much more clever.F than is Zamfira DE beautiful.FEM

    Maria is far cleverer than Zamfira is beautiful.   (adapted from Grosu 1994)

While there is a series of factors involved in such examples, they are syntactically of a relevant sort, and the reported examples involve the morpheme *de*.[8]

The Relationship to the Comparative Morpheme

The supportive *de* and the grammaticalized comparative *mai,* "more," do not co-occur. Certain co-occurrence restrictions thus extend beyond Deg-questions [cf. (19)].[9]

(19) a. *Radu e mai de inteligent.   b. *Radu e de mai inteligent
    Radu is more DE intelligent.   Radu is more DE intelligent.

On the Status of the Absolute

Having seen the basic distribution in conjunction with *mai,* "more," note that degree-based *de* is in complementary distribution with the silent absolute [cf. (20)].

(20) * Ion e de inteligent.

    I. is DE intelligent.

This is corroborating evidence for a hypothesis in favor of an exponent of a degree-based functional little word—*de* merged to grammaticalized degree morphemes makes the derivations crash.[10] But how do we then account for the complementary set of *de*-examples seen, that is, those the acceptability of which increases with *de* merged? The first idea that comes to mind is that an overt head is needed. However, this is neither empirically sufficient in general [e.g., (20) does not show this necessity] nor theoretically satisfactory. As Corver (1997, 130) points out, a step that would try to motivate last resort this way would be but a sheer stipulation.[11] A somewhat more developed hypothesis would be that *de*-Merge is last resort. Applied to our case, the morpheme *de* would then not be possible in a simple (predicative) position, but it would come to rescue derivations when special conditions call for it. Considering the nature of the contexts in which the morpheme appears, a more specific venue recommends itself even more strongly, namely, one inspired by *Distributed Morphology* (DM; cf. Embick and Noyer 2001, on *do*-support and references therein). While classical theories of *do*-support involve failure of affix lowering, in some cases it seems that broader generalizations may be gained via DM. For current purposes, let us recall, for instance, that Romanian comparatives are not affixal and that A′-properties are involved in degree constructions in general. The point we capitalize on is that abstract morphemes are largely determined by syntactico-semantic configurations. This offers a theoretically motivated venue for phrasing the findings. The exponent *de* marks degree dependencies of adjectives in the contexts discussed earlier (and in at least one additional case to be discussed later). Merging *de* can then be envisaged as late insertion of the same abstract morpheme over the relevant contexts.

Independent Evidence and *de*-"Repair"

In questions or subcomparatives, the structurally low member of the dependency is marked via *de*-insertion. Under the copy theory of movement, one can ask whether there are configurations in which a structurally high copy is marked similarly.

Predicate doubling (PD) is a well-known cousin of topicalization. Arguably, PD leaves (parts of) both the foot and the head of a chain spelled out at the level of phonological form (PF). PD is well known, for example, from verb doubling in Romance (but also, e.g., from Germanic/African/Semitic and indeed other varieties). Some varieties of Spanish have the construction in (21) (cf. Vicente 2007 on detailed recent discussion).

(21) Comprar, Juan ha comprado un libro.   (Vicente 2007)

    buy.INF J has bought a book but later not CL has read

    As for buying, Juan has bought a book, although he didn't read it later.

To illustrate the current connection, we first raise the question of whether PD appears with adjectival predicates. Call this type PDA. Although not a necessary condition in general, in Romanian PDA there is a connection to degree constructions through the exponent used. PDA is licit only with the *de*-exponent merged. Further, the relevant *de* involved is degree sensitive: gradable adjectives (absolute and relative ones) are licit [cf. (22) through (23)], while nongradable ones are in general disallowed [cf. (24)].

(22) *(De) înaltă/bogată nu e înaltă/bogată.

    DE tall/rich.FEM NEG is tall/rich. FEM

    She is not tall/rich.   (Tall/rich she is not.)

(23) *(De) strîmbă nu e strîmbă.

DE bent NEG is bent

It is not bent.

(24) *(*De) american/mort nu-i american/mort.

DE American/dead not is American/dead

He is not American/dead.

The two asterisks in (24) indicate that besides the ungrammatical *de*-less variant, with nongradable predicates, as the ones given in (24), *de* cannot attach and the construction is not felicitous. Though the two classes of phenomena have certain distinctive features (e.g., notably in Spell-out), in Romanian they also have a clear connection. This fact offers the opportunity to analyze the little-word exponent of present concern in a somewhat different environment.

The three key factors involved in PDA are gradability, topicalization, and double Spell-out, with *de* attaching to the structurally higher adjective. While the class of the (gradable) adjective may speak for itself, notice also that it is not the case that topicalization per se clashes with adjectives like *mort,* "dead" [cf. (25)].

(25) Moartă nu-i.

dead.FEM NEG-is

She is not dead.

It is also not the case that *doubling* per se is ruled out with predicates with such meanings. The following, using a verbal predicate (plus a different, that is, supine, *de*), is just as acceptable (cf. also other languages/varieties with verbal doubling via the infinitive).

(26) De murit n-a murit.

die.SUP has not died

As for dying, (s)he has not died.

Let us next consider the phrase-structural status of the fronted adjectives. Complements do not participate in PDA [cf., e.g., (27) through (28)].

(27) *Mîndru de fică-sa nu-i mîndru de fică-sa.

proud of daughter-his NEG-is proud of daughter-his

He's not proud of his daughter.

(28) *Dependenți de petrol nu sunt dependenți de petrol.

dependent.PL on gas NEG are dependent.PL on gas

They do not depend on gas.

Similarly, specifiers do not move along with the adjective. Only heads then move. We may hypothesize that A moves to Deg. But how does the complex A + Deg head then move on? Recalling that A´-properties are involved in questions and subcomparatives, the issue is: Does the same hold for the less orthodox PDA? On closer inspection, the global properties of PDA reveal themselves as being also in line with A´-movement. We can show this through the following examples, illustrating that PDA is not clause bounded and that it obeys all the major island constraints on movement.

(29) De bogat nu cred că-i bogat.
     DE rich NEG believe that-is rich
     I don't believe that he's rich.

(30) *De bogat n-am auzit poveștile că-i bogat.
     DE rich NEG have heard stories.the that-is rich
     I didn't hear the stories that he's rich.

(31) ?*De bogat am cunoscut un fotbalist care-i bogat.
     DE rich I have known a soccer player who-is rich
     I have known a soccer player who is rich.

(32) *De bogat și-a cumpărat o vilă dupa ce a aflat că e bogat.
     DE rich SE-has bought a villa after that has learnt that is rich
     He acquired a villa after he learnt that he was rich.

(33) ?*De bogat nu e nici bogat nici sărac.
     DE rich NEG is neither rich nor poor
     He's neither rich nor poor.

The combined results we have obtained so far amount to the structure given in (34).

(34)

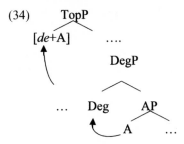

Let's note at this point that while under traditional syntactic assumptions the structure may raise syntactic-ontological questions, namely regarding the status of heads and phrases, it is not clear that these questions are well motivated (cf. Chomsky [1995] and Vicente [2007]). The present findings may well support the latter views.

The crucial part from the discussion of PDA for present purposes is that the adjectival process only occurs when a *de*-exponent marks the adjectival dependency.

In sum, despite regular morphology, the Romanian adjective does not seem to invariably "project up" by itself (cf. the status of simplex degree question and subcomparatives); *de*-Merger salvages such structures. Descriptively this happens through last resort, possibly for the consistent setting of a parameter of degree-based representations. The realization of the parameter is tied to the presence of the relevant functional head and its appropriate exponent in accordance with the syntactico-semantic environment.

NOTES

I am indebted to the colleagues who offered their valuable feedback in Chicago (University of Illinois at Chicago), Georgetown (GURT 2007), Philadelphia (University of Pennsylvania), and Tübingen (Comparative Constructions project 2006, 2007), and in particular S. Beck, J. Bobaljik, H. Campos, M. den Dikken, D. Embick, E. Göbbel, K. González-Vilbazo, J. Kabatek, L. López, M. Romero, as well as my consultants. All errors are fully mine.

1. But cf. the distinct determiner system; see Campos (2005) for a thorough discussion.
2. See Price's (1990) tensed verb constraint for Spanish, but cf. subcomparatives as (a):

   (i) *María leyó más libros que revistas leyó Juan.*
       Maria read more books than journals read Juan.   (Reglero 2007)

3. By *simplex,* we mean exactly what happens in languages like English: (Re)Merge the appropriate *wh*-word at the left edge of the clause to form a degree question.
4. Reglero's discussion (2007) focuses on number-based subcomparatives. It would be interesting to ascertain whether the movement strategies may be transported to degree subcomparatives; some speakers report structures as (a) as (only) marked as "literary." Notice that even if the focus strategy does not turn out to transfer to degree adjectives, this is not a limitation of Reglero's approach, which is not concerned with them.

   (a) ?Juan es más alto que gorda es Maria.
       Juan is more tall than fat   is Maria

   Turning back to Romanian, fronting the adjective does not improve subcomparatives.
5. Using verb movement and a low subject (cf. Cornilescu 2000), we obtain a distinct inversion structure, which we apply later with the overt morphosyntactic support.
6. For last resort in another domain in Romanian, cf. the discussion in Campos (2005).
7. To be sure, not every *wh*-word has the same distribution: e.g., *cuánto* (literally "how much") does not allow both variants, as evidenced by (Modern) Spanish (i).

   (i) a. Cuánto es Juan de inteligente?
          how   is Juan of intelligent
       b. *Cuánto de inteligente es Juan?   Héctor Campos (p.c.)

   Due to limited space, I must abandon discussion of different uses of *de* and its cognates. Though there may be a cognitive connection to Deg-constructions (plus the historical one), the distributions are, based on my preliminary investigation, distinct. A particularly striking example is the number-based *de* of French (cf. Snyder 1995).
8. One of the factors is that the two properties are not compared on the same scale or dimension. The pragmatic effect of this alteration is considerable (cf. Kennedy 1999). However, many attested subcomparatives are of this type [cf. also English (a)].

   (a) This practice stems from the fact that it is almost impossible to write questions that are more difficult than the questioner is smart (*Journal of Educational and Behavioral Statistics,* vol. 22, 1997).

   I suggest with Klein (1991) a (structure-preserving) homomorphism from the relevant degree scales to real numbers, in which case comparisons will be sanctioned. This does not mean equaling degree scales with real numbers. While they may have similar structures (e.g., density in some cases), they are not identical in general. Thus number-based and adjective-based degree constructions may behave distinctly, as they do. There are additional factors that I must leave out because of space considerations. Turning back to Romanian, while there are additional syntactic and semantic points in such examples, conservative and liberal speakers (with regard to subcomparatives) that were confronted with relative judgments confirmed an improvement on structures involving *de* in pragmatically less elaborate structures, if more subtly, too [cf. (b)].

   (b) ?Raftul e mai lung decît e camera de lată.
       shelf.D is more long than room.D is DE wide
       The shelf is longer than the room is wide.

A further remark is that since alternative nominalizations of the adjectives may be invoked, one might wonder whether a generalized blocking (descriptively) obtains.

9. Equatives, unlike genuine comparatives, co-occur with the morpheme *de* [cf. (a)].

(a) Radu e la fel de inteligent.
    R. is at sort DE intelligent
    Radu is (just) as intelligent.

Some of the specific differences may indeed have to do with grammaticalization. Note that (the relevant) *mai*, "more," is an overt morpheme relatively clearly associated in the language with a morpheme of superiority. It is plausible to assume that no need to mark a degree-sensitive morpheme can be invoked (including the crucial perspective of a learner). The circumlocution construction *la fel*, on the other hand, has some distinct properties: for example, it can be used with other related meanings; conversely, and perhaps more importantly, it has competitors as an equative; finally, it is transparent (cf. glosses). While these points involve additional issues, discussion of which would lead the present study too far afield, overall there is no clear one-to-one identification of a degree-sensitive exponent. Thereby no "competition" of two exponents arises, and the exponent *de* would be required for a licit degree construction. An alternative is that *de* is incorporated.

10. Cf. also **foarte de* + A. *Foarte*, "very," is bleached of other meanings in Romanian.

11. I use Corver's general observation without transferring his solution. A theta-theoretic postulation is, in particular, irrelevant for the processes at hand.

REFERENCES

Beck, Sigrid, Toshiko Oda, and Koji Sugisaki. 2004. Parametric variation in the semantics of comparison: Japanese vs. English. *Journal of East Asian Linguistics* 13:289–344.

Campos, Héctor. 2005. Noun modification and last resort operations in Arvantovlaxika and in Romanian. *Lingua* 115:311–47.

Chomsky, Noam. 1977. On *wh*-movement. In *Formal syntax,* ed. Peter Culicover, Thomas Wasow, and Adrian Akmajian, 71–132. New York: Academic Press.

———. 1995. *The minimalist program.* Cambridge, MA: MIT Press.

Comorovski, Ileana. 1996. *Interrogative phrases and the syntax-semantics interface.* Dordrecht: Kluwer.

Cornilescu, Alexandra. 2000. The double subject construction in Romanian. In *Comparative studies in Romanian syntax,* ed. Gabriela Alboiu and Virginia Motapanyane, 83–133. Amsterdam: Elsevier.

Corver, Norbert. 1997. *Much*-support as last resort. *Linguistic Inquiry* 28:119–64.

Embick, David, and Rolf Noyer. 2001. Movement operations after syntax. *Linguistic Inquiry* 32:555–95.

Grosu, Alexander. 1994. *Three studies in locality and case.* London: Routledge.

Hankamer, Jorge. 1973. Why there are two "than"s in English. Proceedings of the 9th annual meeting of the Chicago Linguistics Society. Chicago, IL, 179–91.

Houser, Michael, Line Mikkelsen, Ange Strom-Weber, and Maziar Toosarvandani. 2006. Gøre-support in Danish. Paper presented at the 21st CGSW, University of California, Santa Cruz, April 1.

Kennedy, Christopher. 1999. *Projecting the adjective: The syntax and semantics of gradability and comparison.* New York: Garland.

Klein, Ewan. 1991. Comparatives. In *Semantics. An international handbook of contemporary research,* ed. Arnim von Stechow and Dieter Wunderlich, 673–91. Berlin: de Gruyter.

Price, Susan. 1990. *Comparative constructions in Spanish and French syntax.* London: Routledge.

Reglero, Lara. 2007. On Spanish comparative subdeletion constructions. *Studia Linguistica* 61:130–69.

Snyder, William. 1995. Language acquisition and language variation: The role of morphology. PhD diss., Massachusetts Institute of Technology.

Snyder, William, Kenneth Wexler, and Dolon Das. 1995. The syntactic representation of degree and quantity: Perspectives from Japanese and child English. In *Proceedings of the West Coast Conference on Formal Linguistics XIII,* ed. Raul Aranovich, William Byrne, Susanne Preuss, and Martha Senturia, 581–96. Stanford, CA: CSLI.

Stassen, Leon. 1985. *Comparison and universal grammar.* Oxford: Blackwell.

Stechow, Arnim von. 1984. Comparing semantic theories of comparison. *Journal of Semantics* 3:1–77.

Vicente, Luis. 2007. The syntax of heads and phrases. PhD diss., Leiden.

8

The Complementizer *The*

HEATHER LEE TAYLOR
University of Maryland, College Park

THIS CHAPTER CONCERNS comparative correlatives [in (1) and (2)] and the "little word" *the* that obligatorily begins both phrases/clauses. The syntactic structure of such expressions is far from apparent.

(1) *The* more a student studies, *the* better grades she will receive

(2) *The* longer the storm lasts, *the* worse the damage is

A comparative correlative looks like two nominals, obligatorily headed by the determiner *the,* with no clear indication of what the relationship between these two "nominals" is. English comparative correlatives consist of two phrases, no more and no less, as seen in (3) through (5). This characteristic is not limited to comparative correlatives in English; to the extent that comparative correlatives have been documented cross-linguistically, all languages require that exactly two phrases/clauses be present.[1]

(3) *The more a student studies

(4) *The better grades she will receive

(5) *? The more a student studies, the better grades she will receive, the better job she'll land

Because we do not have evidence at this point to make a distinction between the two parts of the comparative correlative or to determine their syntactic status in terms of a category, I will temporarily refer to them as phrases, and individually to the "first phrase" and the "second phrase" as it corresponds to their linear order, as in (6). This terminological issue will be resolved below.

(6) <u>The more a student studies</u>, <u>the better grades she will receive</u>
      first phrase   second phrase

In English, both the first phrase and the second phrase obligatorily begin with the little word *the*. The unacceptability of (7a) is due to the absence of *the* in the first clause, in (7b) in the second clause, and last, in (7c), the absence of *the* in both clauses unsurprisingly also results in unacceptability.

(7) a. * More a student studies, the better grades she will receive

    b. * The more a student studies, better grades she will receive

    c. * More a student studies, better grades she will receive

Another characteristic of comparative correlatives (CCs) is that A′-movement of a constituent within either the first or the second phrase can occur (Culicover and Jackendoff 1999). To see this clearly, consider (8) through (10) [Culicover and Jackendoff's examples (68) through (70)]. Both the first and the second phrase in the CC in (8) have an object of a verb, *this problem* and *the folks up at corporate headquarters,* respectively, and these objects can be targeted for A′-movement out of its phrase. In (9) we see movement of each for the purpose of forming a relative clause, and in (10) each object can be topicalized. Culicover and Jackendoff argue that movement of a *wh*-phrase in order to form a question is not possible, but in (11), when a CC is embedded under a certain class of predicates (*think, believe, say*), each object can be replaced with an appropriate *wh*-phrase and A'- moved to form a question.[2]

base sentence

(8) The sooner you solve this problem, the more easily you'll satisfy the folks up at corporate headquarters.

relative clause

(9) a. ✓ This is the sort of problem which$_1$ the sooner you solve t$_1$, the more easily you'll satisfy the folks up at corporate headquarters.

    b. ✓ The folks up at corporate headquarters are the sort of people who$_1$ the sooner you solve this problem, the more easily you'll satisfy t$_1$.

topicalization

(10) a. ✓ This problem$_1$, the sooner you solve t$_1$, the more easily you'll satisfy the folks up at corporate headquarters.

    b. ✓ The folks up at corporate headquarters$_1$, the sooner you solve this problem, the more easily you'll satisfy t$_1$.

wh-question formation

(11) a. ✓ Which problem$_1$ do you think that the sooner Bill solves t$_1$, the more easily he'll satisfy the folks up at corporate headquarters

    b. ? Who$_1$ do you think that the sooner that Bill solves this problem, the more easily he'll satisfy t$_1$?

These collective characteristics of CCs provide some clues to what the syntactic structure of the expressions is and what the nature of the word *the* turns out to be. What I suggest here is that the word *the* that obligatorily appears at the start of both the first and the second phrase of the English CC is a complementizer. The CC consists of two CPs, the first adjoined to the second. The complementizer selects for a FocusP (FocP), something we would expect of a complementizer phrase (C^0) and not of a determiner.

This chapter is broken into five sections. The first considers a treatment of CCs as a type of equative and explores the lack of empirical support for that analysis. The next section is a presentation of other analyses of the English CC's *the*. The following section contains the analysis that the *the* in English CCs is in fact a complementizer. The next section expands this proposal by providing evidence from Nominal Extraposition expressions in English and cross-linguistic evidence from CCs in Basque. The final section presents my conclusions.

Comparative Correlatives as Equatives

Cross-linguistically, CCs consist of exactly two phrases. In English, both of these phrases obligatorily begin with the word *the*. These two characteristics hold for equatives as well, as exemplified in (12). An equative consists of two and only two arguments of a copular verb, and those arguments are nominals that can begin with the determiner *the*. The structure of an equative, using the lexical items in (12) to demonstrate, is that in (13).

(12) The president of AT&T is (also) the president of Cingular

(13)

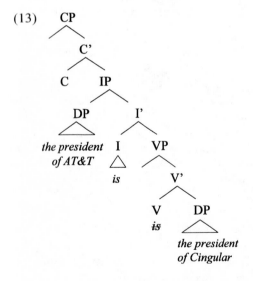

If CCs are a type of equative, this suggests that its structure consists of a main verb, a null copula, which takes two arguments, the first and second phrases. Thus the structure of the CC in (14) would look much like the structure of the equative in (12). This is illustrated in comparing (13) and (15).

(14) The more a student studies, the better grades she will receive

---

(left column, partially cut off at binding)

lish as a degree head (Deg^0), and the mor- complement of this degree head.

clause

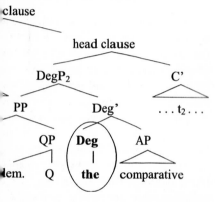

e key components. First, the word *the* is wo analyses differ in a number of ways, ance of the definite determiner. Second, nething other than a degree head. Last, in uses is filled, allowing no possibility for essive cyclically. The proposal put forth components. As in these analyses, *the* is e determiner. In contrast to these analy- degree head (following Kennedy 1997), osition in both the main and subordinate nt out of the clauses is permitted.

orily begin with the word *the*. I propose oth clauses of the CC are CPs. The first the main clause. In both the main and e takes a FocP complement.[3] The mor- modifies occupy Spec,FocP. FocP imme- s given immediately following as it is

(15)

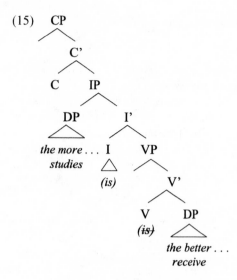

Evidence for This Analysis

One unusual characteristic of equatives is that movement out of both the subject a_ object is permitted, as in (16) and (17). This mirrors extraction behaviors observ_ for CCs in (8) through (11). This appears to offer support for a similar analysis both types of expression.

(16) [Which company]$_1$ is the president of t_1 also the president of Cingular?

(17) [Which company]$_2$ is the president of AT&T also the president of t_2?

Treating CCs as a type of equative would explain the observations made at tł beginning of the chapter. CCs have two, but not one or three or more phrases, b_ cause a copular verb takes only two arguments. Movement out of the phrases of a C would be permitted the same way that it is in equatives. Last, and most important_ the investigation here, the word *the* that appears at the start of each phrase could l_ classified as a determiner, the D^0 that heads the DP.

Strong Evidence against the Equative Analysis

As it turns out, this analysis has been considered, and rejected, in the literature. Cul_ cover and Jackendoff (1999) present two strong pieces of evidence maintaining th_ this analysis cannot be correct. First, when a CC hosts a tag question, it is the se_ ond phrase that obligatorily hosts this tag, as in (18), (19), and (20).

(18)   The earlier Bill arrives home, the more time the kids spend with him

(19) * The earlier Bill arrives home, the more time the kids spend with him, doesn't he?

(20) ✓ The earlier Bill arrives home, the more time the kids spend with him, don't they?

---

(23)

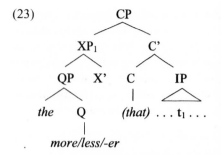

Den Dikken (2005) instead treats *the* in E_ pheme *more/less/-er* is part of an AdjP, tł

(24)   he_

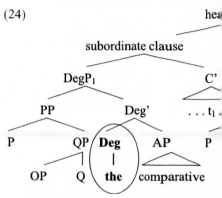

These prior detailed analyses have tł given a label other than determiner. Thes_ yet both conclude that *the* cannot be an i_ the morpheme *more/less/-er* is treated as s_ both of these analyses, Spec,CP of both _ A′-movement out of a clause to proceed s_ in the next section will address each of th_ analyzed as something other than the def_ ses, though, the morpheme *more/less/-er* i_ and the structure has an available Spec,C_ clauses so that successive cyclic A′-move_

The Is a Complementizer
Proposal for the Structure of CCs

Both of the clauses of the English CC obl_ that this *the* is a complementizer and tha_ clause, the subordinate clause, is adjoine_ subordinate clauses, the complementizer pheme *more/less/-er* and the constituent _ diately dominates IP. The entire structu_ sists of two CPs, the first adjoined to the second. The complementizer selects for a FocusP (FocP), something we would expect of a complementizer phrase (C[0]) and not of a determiner.

This chapter is broken into five sections. The first considers a treatment of CCs as a type of equative and explores the lack of empirical support for that analysis. The next section is a presentation of other analyses of the English CC's *the*. The following section contains the analysis that the *the* in English CCs is in fact a complementizer. The next section expands this proposal by providing evidence from Nominal Extraposition expressions in English and cross-linguistic evidence from CCs in Basque. The final section presents my conclusions.

Comparative Correlatives as Equatives

Cross-linguistically, CCs consist of exactly two phrases. In English, both of these phrases obligatorily begin with the word *the*. These two characteristics hold for equatives as well, as exemplified in (12). An equative consists of two and only two arguments of a copular verb, and those arguments are nominals that can begin with the determiner *the*. The structure of an equative, using the lexical items in (12) to demonstrate, is that in (13).

(12) The president of AT&T is (also) the president of Cingular

(13)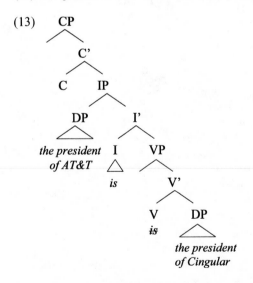

If CCs are a type of equative, this suggests that its structure consists of a main verb, a null copula, which takes two arguments, the first and second phrases. Thus the structure of the CC in (14) would look much like the structure of the equative in (12). This is illustrated in comparing (13) and (15).

(14) The more a student studies, the better grades she will receive

(15)

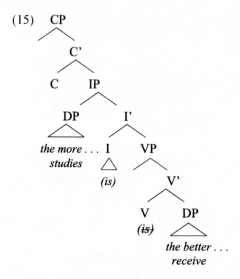

Evidence for This Analysis

One unusual characteristic of equatives is that movement out of both the subject and object is permitted, as in (16) and (17). This mirrors extraction behaviors observed for CCs in (8) through (11). This appears to offer support for a similar analysis of both types of expression.

(16) [Which company]$_1$ is the president of t_1 also the president of Cingular?

(17) [Which company]$_2$ is the president of AT&T also the president of t_2?

Treating CCs as a type of equative would explain the observations made at the beginning of the chapter. CCs have two, but not one or three or more phrases, because a copular verb takes only two arguments. Movement out of the phrases of a CC would be permitted the same way that it is in equatives. Last, and most important to the investigation here, the word *the* that appears at the start of each phrase could be classified as a determiner, the D^0 that heads the DP.

Strong Evidence against the Equative Analysis

As it turns out, this analysis has been considered, and rejected, in the literature. Culicover and Jackendoff (1999) present two strong pieces of evidence maintaining that this analysis cannot be correct. First, when a CC hosts a tag question, it is the second phrase that obligatorily hosts this tag, as in (18), (19), and (20).

(18)   The earlier Bill arrives home, the more time the kids spend with him

(19) * The earlier Bill arrives home, the more time the kids spend with him, doesn't he?

(20) ✔ The earlier Bill arrives home, the more time the kids spend with him, don't they?

Second, when the CC is embedded under a predicate that triggers subjunctive mood, that mood is hosted on the verb in the second phrase, not the first. Culicover and Jackendoff (1999) provide evidence from English, reproduced here in (21) and (22). Though morphological evidence of subjunctive mood in English is weakly used by most speakers, the judgments for (21) and (22) are robust. Furthermore, cross-linguistically, languages that contrast indicative and subjunctive mood by use of morphological marking also display this use of subjunctive mood on the second clause.

(21) a. ✓ I demand that the more John eats, the more he pay(s)

    b. * I demand that the more John eat, the more he pay(s)

(22) a. ✓ It is imperative that the more John eats, the more he pay(s)

    b. * It is imperative that the more John eat, the more he pay(s)

Given this evidence, it is clear that the two phrases of the CC are not on equal standing. The second phrase displays all the characteristics of a main clause, and the first phrase does not. If CCs had a structure like equatives, these characteristics of a main clause would be seen in different constituents: tag questions would form on the null copula and the subject, and subjunctive mood would be hosted on the null copula (or rather not heard at all because the verb would be null). Further, even if an analysis of CCs as a type of equatives did not suffer the previously stated problems, this analysis still does not provide an explanation for why the arguments in the CC require the determiner *the*. This is not a general property of equatives; the internal structure of the two arguments in equatives can have a wide array of structures, with or without the definite determiner (see Adger and Ramchand [2003] for extensive discussion of this point). Thus if CCs are a type of equative and the word *the* is a determiner, the treatment of the word *the* would still require some special explanation.

It appears that treating CCs as a type of equative is the wrong way to proceed. The evidence we have just seen forces us to conclude that CCs consist of a main clause (the second) and a subordinate clause (the first). Yet now the word *the* seems very curious. A word normally classified as a determiner is obligatorily appearing at the start of something that is not a nominal (the entire first or second clause).

Previous Analyses of CCs' *the*

Perhaps it is the case that *the* in CCs is not a determiner at all but a lexical item of some other category. If this were the case, it would provide a way to label the main clause (the second) and the subordinate clause (the first) something other than DP. Two separate proposals for English CCs are reviewed here, Culicover and Jackendoff (1999) and den Dikken (2005).

Culicover and Jackendoff (1999) treat the comparative as a quantifier and the word *the* as a determiner of that quantifier (following Bresnan 1973), sitting in Spec,QP. This quantifier phrase (QP) is in the specifier of an XP, which in turn is in the specifier of a complementizer phrase (Spec,CP). The XP is coindexed with a trace in inflection phrase (IP), where this constituent is logically understood. The structure is illustrated in (23).

(23)

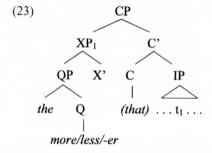

Den Dikken (2005) instead treats *the* in English as a degree head (Deg[0]), and the morpheme *more/less/-er* is part of an AdjP, the complement of this degree head.

(24)

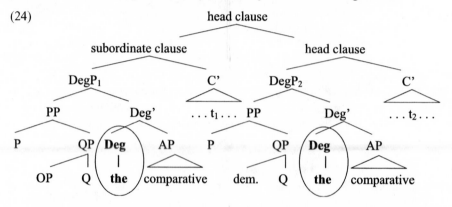

These prior detailed analyses have three key components. First, the word *the* is given a label other than determiner. These two analyses differ in a number of ways, yet both conclude that *the* cannot be an instance of the definite determiner. Second, the morpheme *more/less/-er* is treated as something other than a degree head. Last, in both of these analyses, Spec,CP of both clauses is filled, allowing no possibility for A′-movement out of a clause to proceed successive cyclically. The proposal put forth in the next section will address each of these components. As in these analyses, *the* is analyzed as something other than the definite determiner. In contrast to these analyses, though, the morpheme *more/less/-er* is a degree head (following Kennedy 1997), and the structure has an available Spec,CP position in both the main and subordinate clauses so that successive cyclic A′-movement out of the clauses is permitted.

The Is a Complementizer
Proposal for the Structure of CCs
Both of the clauses of the English CC obligatorily begin with the word *the*. I propose that this *the* is a complementizer and that both clauses of the CC are CPs. The first clause, the subordinate clause, is adjoined to the main clause. In both the main and subordinate clauses, the complementizer *the* takes a FocP complement.[3] The morpheme *more/less/-er* and the constituent it modifies occupy Spec,FocP. FocP immediately dominates IP. The entire structure is given immediately following as it is

abstractly construed for any CC in English [in (25)], and then specifically [in (26)] as it applies to the CC in (1).

(25)

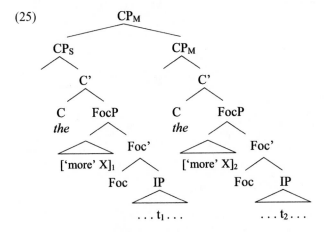

(26)

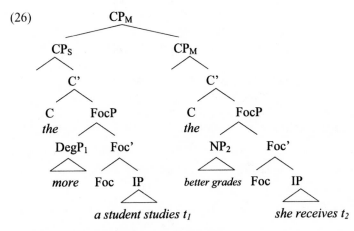

The structure of degree phrase (DegP) that I adopt here is Kennedy's (1997), in (27). If the modified constituent is adjective phrase (AdjP), adverb phrase (AdvP), or IP, it is this DegP that occupies Spec,FocP. In the case of IP modification, Deg^0 has no complement. In the case of noun phrase (NP) modification, DegP is adjoined to NP (following Kennedy and Merchant's [2000] proposal for attributive comparative deletion), and as with IP modification, Deg^0 has no complement. In the case of NP modification, then, it is the NP to which the DegP is adjoined that holds the position of Spec,FocP.

(27)

```
        DegP
        /\
      XP   Deg'
      /\   /\
 measure  Deg  (AP)
 phrase
```

Why not classify *the* as a definite determiner so that it is part of the comparative constituent in Spec,FocP? I follow Taylor's (2006) proposal that the comparative constituent in Spec,FocP has been base-generated in its canonical position and A′-moved to this higher position. Further evidence for this is the existence of almost synonymous expressions to CCs, like that in (28). These have been referred to as CC′ (Culicover and Jackendoff 1999) and ICC (Inverted Comparative Correlative; Culicover and Jackendoff 2005, 505). In ICCs, the main clause appears first linearly, and the subordinate clause follows. Also in ICCs, the word order of the main clause is different from the word order of the main clause in the CC. In (28) and (29), the main clause contains the compared constituent *worse* (suppletive form of "bad" + "more"). In (28), this compared constituent has raised to Spec,FocP and is preceded linearly by *the*. But in (29), where the compared constituent appears in its base-generated position, the word *the* is missing. If it is assumed that CCs and ICCs are derivationally related, the absence of the word *the* in the ICC suggests that it is not a part of the comparative constituent.

(28) The damage is worse, the longer the storm lasts

(29) The longer the storm lasts, the worse the damage is

The *Induces* that-*trace Effect*
As proposed, the complementizer *the* is phonologically overt, therefore it should have the same effect as an overt complementizer . . . and it does—it induces *that*-trace effect. (30d) and (30e) are unacceptable. If we hypothesize that this unacceptability is also due to a *that*-trace effect induced by the C⁰ *the*, then the presence of a heavy AdvP between the comparative string and the *wh*-trace should improve the expression. Indeed, this is exactly what happens, as can be seen in (30f) and (30g).

(30) a.   I said that *the* more Bill eats vegetables, the less Mary wants sweets

    b. ✓ What$_1$ did I say that *the* more Bill eats t_1, the less Mary wants sweets

    c. ✓ What$_1$ did I say that the more Bill eats sweets *the* less Mary wants t_1?

    d. * Who$_1$ did I say that *the* more t_1 eats vegetables, the less Mary wants sweets?

    e. * Who$_1$ did I say that the more Bill eats vegetables, *the* less t_1 wants sweets?

    f. ✓ Who$_1$ did I say that *the* more for all intents and purposes t_1 eats vegetables, the less Mary wants sweets?

    g. ?? Who$_1$ did I say that the more Bill eats vegetables, *the* less for all intents and purposes t_1 wants sweets?

More Evidence for the Proposal
If the word *the* in CCs is a complementizer, a bolster for this claim could be found in two kinds of empirical observations. First, thus far the complementizer *the* is unique to CCs. We would be fortunate if this complementizer could be found in other types of expressions in English. Second, no other language for which CCs have so far been documented begins both clauses with what looks like a definite determiner

(but see Beck [1997] for a proposal that German *je* and *umso/desto* can be glossed as "the," and Roehrs, Sprouse, and Wermter [2002] for a more lengthy discussion of the contrast between these two lexical items in comparative correlatives). However, if another language used a lexical item that was unique to CCs, this would suggest that the relatively unique lexical item *the* of English CCs is not so ad hoc. As it turns out, both of these bolsters exist.

The Complementizer the *in Other Expressions in English*

The examples in (31) are named nominal extraposition (NE) by Michaelis and Lambrecht (1996), who examined the data in detail. The sentences appear to consist of a saturated expression (*It's amazing/perfect/sickening*), followed by head noun and a relative clause, as evidenced by the data in (32). But if the apparent relative clauses in (31) are indeed relative clauses, this constitutes a problem for the selectional properties of the predicates that precede them. Normally, the predicates *amazing, perfect,* and *sickening* subcategorize for a CP, as in (33). If the predicate is followed by a nominal other than the apparent relative clauses in (31), the result is unacceptable, as in (34).

(31) a. It's amazing the people you see here these days

    b. It's perfect the way the sun sets in the winter

    c. It was sickening the amount of waste there was

(32) a. [The people you see here these days] are weird

    b. [The way the sun sets in the winter] is beautiful

    c. Please give me a report of [the amount of waste there was]

(33) a. It's amazing [$_{CP}$that [we survived]]

    b. It's perfect [$_{CP}$that [the weather cooperated]]

    c. It was sickening [$_{CP}$that [the waste was so excessive]]

(34) a. * It's amazing the people/that person/those people/a person/some people

    b. * It's perfect the way/that way/those ways/a way/some ways

    c. * It was sickening the amount/that amount/those amounts/an amount/some amount

If we treat the *the* at the start of these apparent nominals as a complementizer, then these clauses are CP complements of the predicates. It is not that the predicates *amazing, perfect,* and *sickening* in NEs have taken a complement other than CP, or that a relative clause has been right dislocated; rather, the predicates in NEs have taken a CP complement just as they do in expressions like (32). Further evidence that the word strings beginning with *the* in (31a) through (31c) are CPs comes from NEs that take other kinds of CPs, such as (35), and Michaelis and Lambrecht's (1996) virtually synonymous examples (32a) and (32b), reproduced here as (36a) and (36b).[4]

(35) It was sickening [how much waste there was]

(36) a. It's amazing [what things children say]

    b. It's amazing [the things children say]

Cross-linguistically, we see many languages (Dutch, Spanish, Brazilian Portuguese, and Latin, as reported by den Dikken [2005], for example) use a morpheme meaning "how much/how more" to introduce the adjunct clause of a CC. Russian and Turkish introduce the first clause with a similar type of string—a *wh*-item corresponding to *what* + much is used [see (41) and (42)].

(37)   Dutch

Hoe meer je   leest, **hoe meer** je   begrijpt
How more you read how more you understand
"The more you read, the more you understand"

(38)   Spanish

Cuantos   Más problemas resolvió Joan, mejor puntuación recibió
How-much more problems solved Joan better score   she-received
"The more problems Joan solved, the better score she received"

(39)   Br. Portuguese

Quanto   mais problemas a   Joana resolve, melhores notas ela recebe
How-much more problems the Joana solves better   scores she receives
"The more problems Joan solved the better score she received"

(40)   Latin[5]

Quanto   in pectore hanc rem   meo magis voluto, tanto   mi
How-much-ABL in heart   this   matter my   more   ponder that-much-ABL me
aegritudo auctior est in animo
grief   greater is in spirit
"The more I turn this matter over in my mind, the greater grief is in my soul"

(41)   Russian

Chem   bol'she vina,   tem   veseleye
What-INST more   wine-GEN that-INST merrier
"The more wine, the merrier"

(42)   Turkish

Ne   kadar rahatla-r-   sa-   k, o kadar vakit kaybed- er-   iz
what much relax   aorist COND. 1P it much time lose-   aorist 1P
"The more we relax, the more we waste time"

Unique Lexical Items in Languages Other Than English

In Basque CCs, two lexical items, *gero* and *eta,* appear together and introduce both clauses of the CCs, as in (43). *Gero eta* is unique to CCs. Elsewhere in Basque, *gero* and *eta* appear independent of one another—*gero* is an adverb meaning "after," and *eta* is a conjunction meaning "and." Within CCs the two words must both be present, and they must be adjacent; to restate, nothing can intervene between the two in a CC, and neither *gero* nor *eta* can occur alone in the CC. Yet there is nothing compositional about the lexical items that would render a meaning in the CC equivalent to that of "the more" in English. This suggests that Basque speakers treat the *gero eta* in CCs as a single lexical item and one that exists only in CCs.

(43)   Basque

Gero eta Jonek   sagar gehiago bildu, **gero eta** pastel gehiago egiten

CC   John-ERG apples more   pick, CC   pies   more   did

zituen   bere amak

AUX-TRNS-PAST his   mom-ERG

"The more apples John picked, the more pies his mother baked"

Conclusion

This chapter has largely looked at the microsyntax of one specific word, *the,* in English comparative correlatives. But from this investigation of one small lexical item, the syntactic structure of this type of expression can be understood as very similar to other expressions in the grammar. Further, another unusual type of expression, nominal extrapositions, can also be analyzed without proposing anything special within the grammar. From this analysis, the question arises as to what it means for a single lexical item to have two different category types. Semantic analyses of the definite determiner have encoded features such as maximality and uniqueness, and perhaps these features are part of the compositional semantics of comparative correlatives. Work on this question as it relates to these data and elsewhere in the grammar remains to be investigated.

NOTES

1. The languages thus far are Maltese (Beck 1997), Standard Arabic (Taylor 2006), Berber (den Dikken 2005), Hebrew (Beck 1997), Turkish (Taylor 2006), Khalkha Mongolian (den Dikken 2005), Basque (Taylor 2006), Malayalam (Taylor 2006), Spanish (Taylor 2006; Abeillé, Borsley, and Espinal 2006), Italian (Taylor 2006), Portuguese (Brazilian and European) (Taylor 2006), French (den Dikken 2005; Beck 1997; Abeillé, Borsley, and Espinal 2006), Latin (Michaelis 1994; den Dikken 2005), German (McCawley 1988; Beck 1997; Roehrs, Sprouse, and Wermter 2002; den Dikken 2005), Dutch (Beck 1997; den Dikken 2005), Danish (Beck 1997), Swedish (Culicover and Jackendoff 1999), Russian (Beck 1997; den Dikken 2005), Polish (Borsley 2003; den Dikken 2005), Bulgarian (Beck 1997), Greek (Taylor 2006), Hindi (den Dikken 2005; Taylor 2006), Japanese (den Dikken 2005; Taylor 2006), Korean (Beck 1997), Mandarin Chinese (McCawley 1988), and Hungarian (Beck 1997; den Dikken 2005).

2. For more extensive discussion of this point, see Taylor (2006) and Taylor (unpublished manuscript).

3. This FocP was simply "FP" in prior writings by this author, meaning "functional projection." However, there is evidence from Greek that this functional projection is indeed a Focus projection (Kapetangianni and Taylor 2007). I follow the analysis in that paper and assume that this functional projection in English in FocP, just as it is in Greek.

4. Michaelis and Lambrecht (1996) provide these examples to contrast NEs with Right Dislocation, such as (i-a) and (i-b).

   (i) a. ✓ They're amazing, the things children say.
       b. * They're amazing, what things children say.

   Despite the presence of the examples in (9a) and (9b) in their paper, they do not consider the possibility that *the* is a complementizer rather than a determiner.

5. This example is originally given by Michaelis (1994) and is repeated as example (10) by den Dikken (2005).

REFERENCES

Abeillé, Anne, Robert Borsley, and Maria-Teresa Espinal. 2006. The syntax of comparative correlatives in French and Spanish. In *Proceedings of the HPSG06 conference,* ed. Stefan Müller, 6–26. Bulgarian Academy of Sciences, Varna, Bulgaria: CSLI Publications.

Adger, David, and Gillian Ramchand. 2003. Predication and equation. *Linguistic Inquiry* 34:325–59.

Beck, Sigrid. 1997. On the semantics of comparative conditionals. *Linguistics and Philosophy* 20:229–71.

Borsley, Robert. 2003. On the Polish periphery: Comparative correlatives in Polish. In *GLiP-5: Proceedings of fifth Generative Linguistics in Poland conference,* ed. Piotr Banski and Adam Przepiórkowski, 15–28. Warsaw: Polish Academy of Science.

Bresnan, Joan. 1973. Syntax of the comparative clause construction in English. *Linguistic Inquiry* 4:275–343.

Culicover, Peter, and Ray Jackendoff. 1999. The view from the periphery: The English comparative correlative. *Linguistic Inquiry* 30:543–71.

———. 2005. *Simpler syntax.* Oxford: Oxford University Press.

Dikken, Marcel den. 2005. Comparative correlatives comparatively. *Linguistic Inquiry* 36:497–532.

Kapentangianni, Konstantia, and Heather Lee Taylor. 2007. Comparative correlatives in Greek: The syntax of *oso.* Presented at Workshop on Greek Syntax and Semantics, at Massachusetts Institute of Technology, May 20–22. http://the-source.dlp.mit.edu:16080/greeksynsym/papers/Kapetangianni_Taylor.pdf (accessed August 23, 2008).

Kennedy, Christopher. 1997. *Projecting the adjective: The syntax and semantics of gradability and comparison.* PhD diss., University of California, Santa Cruz.

Kennedy, Christopher, and Jason Merchant. 2000. Attributive comparative deletion. *Natural Language and Linguistic Theory* 18:89–146.

McCawley, James. 1988. The comparative conditional constructions in English, German and Chinese. In *Proceedings of the fourteenth annual meeting of the Berkeley Linguistics Society,* ed. Shelly Axmaker, Annie Jaiser, and Helen Singmaster, 176–87. Berkeley: University of California, Berkeley,

Michaelis, Laura. 1994. A case of constructional polysemy in Latin. *Studies in Language* 18 (1): 45–70.

Michaelis, Laura, and Knud Lambrecht. 1996. Toward a construction-based theory of language function: The case of nominal extraposition. *Language* 72:215–47.

Roehrs, Dorian, Rex Sprouse, and Joachim Wermter. 2002. The difference between desto and umso: Some mysteries of the German comparative correlative. *Interdisciplinary Journal for Germanic Linguistics and Semiotic Analysis* 7:15–25.

Taylor, Heather Lee. 2006. Out on good syntactic behavior. Generals paper, University of Maryland, College Park. http://www.ling.umd.edu/~htaylor/Taylor_895.pdf (accessed June 2006).

———. Unpublished manuscript. Moving out of adjuncts. University of Maryland at College Park.

9

What Is There When Little Words Are Not There?

Possible Implications for Evolutionary Studies

LJILJANA PROGOVAC
Wayne State University

▓ **THE GOAL OF THIS CHAPTER** is to provide a theoretical argument, using the tools of the syntactic framework of minimalism (e.g., Chomsky 1995), that certain small clauses (syntactic objects with no or few "little words"), which can be found in root contexts as well as in other unexpected uses, may represent "living fossils" from a root small-clause stage in language evolution (see Jackendoff 2002 for the idea of syntactic fossils). In addition to the root small-clause stage, the clausal development may also have gone through a protocoordination stage, on its way to developing specific functional categories. These claims are consistent with (a) a syntactic analysis of what counts as an increase in complexity, (b) well-known grammaticalization processes, (c) "living fossil" evidence, and (d) stages in language acquisition. Not only does this approach help situate syntax in an evolutionary framework, but it also sheds light on some crucial aspects of syntax itself, as will be shown.

Grammar without Little Words: Root Small Clauses

Consider the following utterances with no (or almost no) little words [(1), (3), and (5)], rarely discussed in the syntactic literature, and compare them with full finite counterparts [(2), (4), and (6)]. (In this chapter I only consider small clauses with one argument, in order to abstract away from the factor of transitivity, which involves an additional layer of morphosyntactic structure.)

Mad Magazine/incredulity clauses   (Akmajian 1984)

(1)   a) *Him retire!?*   b) *John worry?!*   c) *Her happy?!*
Cf. (2) a) *He is going to retire.*   b) *John worries.*   c) *She is happy.*
        "Irrealis" clauses expressing wishes/commands

(3)   *Me first!/Family first!/Everybody out!*
Cf. (4) *I am first./Family should be first./Everybody must go out.*
        Clauses anchored in a context (e.g., here-and-now, photograph, etc.)

(5)   *Class in session./Problem solved./Case closed./Me in Rome.*

Cf. (6) *The class is in session./The problem is solved./The case is closed./I am in Rome.*

In contrast to the corresponding finite sentences, the clauses in (1), (3), and (5) show no evidence of tense or nominative case checking: The verb is either entirely absent or surfaces in a nonfinite form, while the pronouns exhibit default (accusative) case in English (Akmajian 1984; see also Roeper 1999 and Schütze 2001 for default grammars/default case). In the spirit of the widely accepted analysis of embedded small clauses proposed by Stowell (1983), adopted in Chomsky (1995), and in the spirit of Barton's (1990) approach to nonsententials in general, Progovac (2006) analyzes (1), (3), and (5) as tenseless *root* small clauses (RootSCs), where the semantic consequence of no tense is argued to be the prevalence of nonindicative/irrealis interpretations among such clauses [(1), (3)].[1]

This approach explains why RootSC subjects in (5) occur without articles, which are obligatory in full sentential counterparts (6): The absence of articles in this case signals the absence of a determiner phrase (DP), reinforcing the idea that RootSCs do not check structural case. In current syntactic theory DP is required for structural case checking (e.g., Longobardi 1994). In other words, the realizations of RootSC syntax illustrated earlier are shorter by at least two categories of little words, in comparison to their full sentential counterparts: tense bearers (including copulas and finite auxiliary verbs) and articles.

Moreover, small clauses with default case subjects cannot embed (are not recursive), providing a challenge for the hypothesis put forth in, for example, Chomsky (2005) and Hauser, Chomsky, and Fitch (2002) that Merge alone can account for all the recursive power of language (see Pinker and Jackendoff 2005 for a reply).

(7) a) **Him worry [me first]?!/b) *I consider [case closed]./c)*I want [problem solved].*

Notice that the embedded clauses in (7b) and (7c) would become grammatical if an article were used, suggesting that they check structural case, the so-called exceptional case marking (ECM). Appropriate functional categories/projections/relations need to be available in order to license embedding of any kind, whether an ECM mechanism for small clauses, or complementizer phrase (CP) for finite subordination (see Progovac 2007b for elaboration; also Deutscher 2000 and references cited there; Progovac et al. 2006). I return to this issue later in the chapter.

In sum, small clauses are found both as embedded ECM complements, with structurally case-marked subjects, and as RootSCs, whose subjects carry default case (no case). The next section speculates on the reasons for the existence of small clauses in general, and of RootSCs in particular.

Evolutionary Perspective

It is often assumed that syntax is all or nothing, the stand summarized in the following quote from Berwick (1998, 338–39; see also Bickerton 1998): "In this sense, there is no possibility of an 'intermediate' syntax between a non-combinatorial one and full natural language—one either has Merge in all its generative glory, or one has no combinatorial syntax at all." However, if my analysis of RootSCs is correct, then a coherent grammar with much less syntactic complexity than full sentential grammar is not only possible but also is still in relatively productive use (see Progovac 2007a on how syntactic complexity can be measured and how it can evolve). Indeed, the existence of RootSCs opens up a possibility to consider the evolution of syntax in a gradualist fashion, in the spirit of Pinker and Bloom (1990).

In this perspective, one can see RootSCs as "living fossils" from an evolutionary stage of syntax dominated by RootSCs (see Jackendoff 2002 for the idea of a syntactic fossil). Ridley (1993, 525) defines "living fossils" as species that have changed little from their fossil ancestors in the distant past, such as lungfish, and that have continued to coexist with more complex species. What I consider here to be preserved is the RootSC syntax, and our ability to tap into it, rather than particular details of modern-day realizations of such syntax. For example, while the absence of structural case is the defining property of this grammar, the particular realizations of non-case-marked subjects will vary across languages.

Initial plausibility for a RootSC evolutionary stage comes exactly from the existence of these living fossils found in modern-day languages (more realizations of such fossilized syntax will be discussed in the following sections). Further corroborating evidence comes from language acquisition. The so-called two-word stage in first language (L1) acquisition abounds in subject–predicate utterances that can be analyzed as RootSCs, as well as by probable absence of Move(ment) (see, e.g., Lebeaux 1989; Ouhalla 1993; Platzak 1990; Potts and Roeper 2006; Radford 1990).[2] Lock and Peters (1996) conclude that recent views on the relationship between ontogeny and phylogeny permit using ontogeny to corroborate evolutionary inferences.

Furthermore, the emergence of tense/tense phrase (TP) in children parallels the historical development (grammaticalization) of tense/indicative from injunctive in pre–Indo-European (Progovac 2006). According to Kiparsky (1968), the unmarked tense/mood form, injunctive, was initially able to express both indicative and nonindicative meanings, but once tense and indicative emerged in pre-IE, injunctive specialized only for nonindicative/irrealis readings. This indicates not only that it is possible to proceed from a pre-TP stage to a TP stage but also that this developmental scenario can lead to the division of labor in mood expression that is attested today in adult speech between RootSCs and their finite counterparts.

Suppose now that functional projections (e.g., aspect, light verb phrase (vP) shell for transitivity, tense) started to be added over the layer of the small-clause core, perhaps in order to make precise the hierarchy of thematic roles through case relations, as well as to render the expression of time and truth automatic and precise. In this sense, the layers of more recently emerged functional projections were superimposed over the layers of more ancient structures, letting the latter survive but in marginalized roles. Similar stratification accounts have been proposed for brain development, as well as for the development of complexity in general, where newly emerged patterns become dominant and "rework" older patterns into conformity with them (see Rolfe's [1996] "recency dominance"; also Vygotsky 1981). This idea of evolutionary layering of syntax is explored further in Progovac (2007a). The next two sections extend the evolutionary perspective to shed light on the existence of small clauses elsewhere.

Why Every Sentence Begins as a Small Clause

It is a remarkable discovery on the part of linguists, and a recent one, too, that every sentence in its underlying representation is in fact a small clause, which gets transformed into a sentence only upon subsequent merger of tense and/or other comparable functional projections (see, e.g., Burzio 1981; Chomsky 1995; Kitagawa 1986; Koopman and Sportiche 1991; Stowell 1981). For example, the sentence with a copular verb such as "John is tall" derives from the underlying small clause "John tall," where the subject "John" moves from the subject position of the small clause to the specifier position of the sentence (TP):

(8) $[_{TP}$ *is* $[_{SC}$ *John tall*$]]. \rightarrow [_{TP}$ *John* $[_{T'}$ *is* $[_{SC}$ t *tall*$]]]$

Similarly, as illustrated in (9), the sentence/TP "He will worry" starts out as a small clause "He worry," which gets transformed into a full sentence (TP) only upon the merger of Tense ("will") and upon the subsequent Move of "he" into the specifier of TP to check nominative case:

(9) $[_{TP}$ *will* $[_{SC}$ *he worry*$]]. \rightarrow [_{TP}$ *he* $[_{T'}$ *will* $[_{SC}$ t *worry*$]]]$

Notice that the verb *worry* is selected without any tense or case features here.

Parker (2006, 285) raises the question of why one should have Move in the syntactic theory, in addition to Merge, given that even in the minimalist framework Move is considered to be more costly than Merge. This question can be related to that of why every sentence should begin as a small clause in the first place. But if the small clause core of the sentence can be seen as a vestige of the evolutionary tinkering with building sentential structure, then Move can be seen as a force that connects different layers of sentential derivation, as determined by such evolutionary tinkering. In other words, the building of the sentence bottom up, from small clause to TP, may be seen, metaphorically, as retracing the steps of the evolutionary development of the sentence. Neither bottom-up sentence building, nor small-clausal beginnings of the sentence, nor Move would then need to be considered as conceptual necessities.

Why There Are Bare Small Clauses in Parataxis/Adjunction and Coordination

In addition to the root contexts, bare small clauses (i.e., small clauses whose subjects are not structurally case marked, in contrast to ECM small clauses) are also found with parataxis/adjunction and with coordination, exhibiting similar morphosyntactic properties as RootSCs, including the lack of tense and the lack of structural case on subjects.

Even though, as pointed out in the first section, bare small clauses do not embed within each other, they can participate in loose, typically binary paratactic combinations, usually found in proverbs or wisdoms:

(10) *Nothing ventured, nothing gained./Easy come, easy go.*

When two small clauses combine paratactically in this fashion, they appear to be on an "equal footing" with respect to each other, and their relationship is then interpreted as one of temporal ordering and/or causation, expressed iconically by the relative ordering of the two clauses. On the other hand, when a bare small clause attaches paratactically to a finite sentence/TP, such a small clause is perceived as an adverbial/adjunct, which again usually receives temporal/causal interpretation, as in (11) and (12) (these are discussed in Jackendoff [2002] to suggest a possible pre-TP stage in the evolution of human language):

(11) *[Us having left], he reverted to his old ways.*

(12) [Him having gone to Rome], I can now focus on my work.

However, the interpretation in this case is no longer determined by the relative ordering of the two clauses but is at least partly determined by their grammatical status: The finite clause is the main clause regardless of the order.

Bare small clauses also occur coordinated with full finite clauses, again in positions in which their subjects have no way of receiving structural case (example from Jespersen 1954):

(13) *I am not going to have any woman rummaging about my house, and [me in bed].*

Examples such as these would be characterized as involving "unlike coordination," violating the coordination of likes constraint (CLC), the principle that allows only phrases/clauses of the same type to coordinate (see, e.g., Chomsky 1957). It may well be that this unexpected coordination possibility is yet another example of vestigial treatment of small clauses as root clausal objects. The following section discusses possible stages in the evolutionary development of clauses, which include not only paratactic RootSC stage but also a protocoordination stage.

Possible Stages in the Evolution of Clauses: Multiple Breakthroughs

The grammaticalization of finite subordination typically takes parataxis as a starting point and proceeds through a(n intermediate) coordination stage (see, e.g., Deutscher 2000; Traugott and Heine 1991, and references cited there). Here I tentatively suggest that predication/clause may also have gone through a similar sequence of stages in its evolutionary development: RootSC stage, protocoordination stage, and then a specific functional category stage, as illustrated below. This sequence constitutes a progression from least syntactically integrated (parataxis), to more integrated (coordination), to most integrated (specialized functional categories/projections).

Parataxis with Intonation/Prosody: Suprasegmental Glue

If the presyntax stage of language (protolanguage, in the sense of Bickerton [1998]) utilized only single-word utterances, then the first syntactic stage may have combined two such utterances into a meaningful two-word utterance (see, e.g., Deutscher 2005; Jackendoff 2002). Such initial combinations may not have 5 distinguished from a sequence of one-word utterances by much more than prosody. Nonetheless this ability to Merge would have marked a great breakthrough in the evolution of language—it would have made possible a more precise expression of relationships between words/concepts.

(14) Presyntax: *John. Happy./Me. First.* Syntax: *John happy./Me first*!

According to Burling (2005, 170), intonation/prosody likely served as the first type of glue to hold two words together in a single utterance. Interrogatives in English can still be expressed either solely by prosody [rising intonation (15a)] or by both rising intonation and "rising syntax" [the raising to C, in (15b)], resulting in substantial redundancy:[3]

(15) a. *Mary is already at home?*   b. *Is Mary already at home?*

There are reasons to believe that intonation and prosody were available before syntax. Piattelli-Palmarini and Uriagereka (2004, 354) mention that intonation, prosody, and emphasis, which are modulated analogically rather than discretely, have nonnegligible analogs in other species (see also Burling 2005; Deacon 1997; Pulver-müller 2002, and references cited there). Moreover, while lesions in certain left-hemispheric areas of the brain cause severe language impairments, right-hemispheric lesions usually lead to more subtle language-related difficulties affecting prosodic and pragmatic processing (Joanette, Goulet, and Hannequin 1990, 40).

Deacon (1997, 234) points out that vocal communication has inherited many features of a partly automatic, partly controllable motor system, so that most speech sounds involve both muscle systems: automatic and controlled. Most tonal variation plays a paralinguistic role in speech prosody, and most of this occurs subconsciously and automatically with the corresponding shifts in affect. "It is as though we haven't so much shifted control from visceral to voluntary means but *superimposed* one upon the other" (Deacon 1997, 244, emphasis added). This situation in phonology is reminiscent of the idea of the layering of grammar, where the layer of TP gets superimposed upon a layer of small clause, a more primary structure.

Note in this respect that irrealis small clauses in (1) and (3) are characterized by exaggerated intonation.

Coordination: All-Purpose Segmental Glue
Here, I tentatively explore the possibility that, just as seems to be the case with finite subordination, predication may have gone through a coordination stage, that is, a stage in which the subject and the predicate were connected with more than just suprasegmental glue (prosody). Suppose that Merge was so advantageous to language users that it was beneficial to signal it redundantly and robustly, not only by relatively transient prosodic cues but also by a segment dedicated solely to that purpose, a proto-coordinator. It could have been only much later that this all-purpose glue got differentiated into specific functional categories and projections, such as tense, aspect, and so on (see next section).

In fact, in some languages one still finds vestiges ("living fossils") of coordinators in predicative functions. For example, the incredulity clauses in German can optionally feature a conjunction (Potts and Roeper 2006; see also Progovac et al. 2006):

(16) *Ich (und) Angst haben*?!

    I   and   fear   have-INF

    "Me afraid?!"

Next, Deutscher (2000, 33–34) argued that Akkadian (Semitic language spoken between c. 2500 to 500 BC) used the coordinative particle *ma* in predicative functions (17). There was no verbal copula in Akkadian, which may imply the use of root small clauses.

(17) *Napištsti māt-im   eql-um-**ma***

    soul.of   land-GEN   field-NOM-MA

    "The soul of the land is the field."

Thus both German and Akkadian can use a coordinator to connect the subject with the predicate.

Moreover, Bowers (1993) analyzes English *as* as a realization of the head of Pr(edication) P(hrase), which is used in embedded small clauses (18):

(18) *She regards [Mary <u>as</u> a fool]./She regards [Mary <u>as</u> crazy].*

English *as* (as well as Akkadian *ma*) can serve not only to cement predication (interclausally) (18) but also as coordinator connecting clauses (19):

(19) *Peter will come to the party, as will John./As she was approaching, the door opened.*

The emergence of this kind of protocoordinator would have provided another crucial breakthrough in the development of the clause: a little word without much meaning of its own but that would have performed an important function in solidifying the advantages of the first major syntactic breakthrough—Merge.

Some corroborating evidence for a protocoordination stage may come from language acquisition, but much further research is needed to substantiate the plausibility of this idea. It is frequently reported in acquisition literature that some children use "fillers" in places where one would expect functional categories. While researchers sometimes attribute the presence of these fillers to the presence of specific functional categories, a more conservative approach may be that these are just all-purpose connectors (protocoordinators), serving to connect words into utterances (see, e.g., Peters and Menn 1993; Veneziano and Sinclair 2000, and references cited there). According to these researchers, the fillers are vocalizations that do not correspond to particular words/morphemes and that initially seem to range over various kinds of functional categories/positions. It is only later that they differentiate and specialize, starting to occur in specific positions. Such fillers are often a syllabic nasal [m] or an ə, as the following example illustrates (Peters and Menn 1993):

(20) *[m] pick [ə] flowers.* (English learning boy, age 1;6)

Specific Functional Category Stage

Finally, such protocoordinators (such as *ma* or *as*) could have then differentiated/grammaticalized into specific functional categories, such as predication head, tense head, aspect head, and so on. This would have constituted another syntactic breakthrough and the beginning of modern syntax, which can now not only use little words as all-purpose glue to connect words/clauses but also use them to build specialized functional projections, introducing a variety of specialized grammatical meanings.

According to Chomsky (2005) and Hauser et al. (2002), the principle of Merge was the only important evolutionary breakthrough for syntax: Once Merge was introduced, it was able to apply recursively and to account for all recursion, including subordination. My proposal here is that additional breakthroughs (and intermediate stages) were necessary to lead to modern syntax, including possibly the one that provided all-purpose segmental glue (protocoordination) and the one that provided specialized functional glue with which to build specialized functional projections. One such specialized functional breakthrough would have been the development of finite subordination, the emergence of the CP layer, yet another layer of structure over the TP domain.

There are (at least) two reasons to consider such gradual emergence of syntax in evolution: well-defined stages in language acquisition and living fossils, as discussed in this chapter, which in fact are not subject to syntactic subordination (see Progovac 2007a, 2007b for additional reasons).

Concluding Remarks

This evolutionary approach, which sees small clauses as vestiges/"living fossils" of the evolutionary development of syntax, not only makes it possible to situate syntax in a gradualist evolutionary framework (in the spirit of Pinker and Bloom 1990) but also begins to shed light on the very nature of syntax. First of all, it can explain why bare small clauses (small clauses with default case subjects) are found in root contexts, as well as with coordination and parataxis/adjunction. This approach also provides some rationale for the otherwise unexpected finding in theoretical syntax that every sentence is built upon a layer of small clause. Decomposing/unpacking syntax into simpler (evolutionary) stages/layers may also derive some subjacency effects, as I argue elsewhere (Progovac 2007b).

In this approach, it was the little words, or more precisely their gradual grammaticalization, that enabled humans to avail themselves of complex syntax, rather than the other way around.

NOTES

Thanks to the Wayne State University Humanities Center for the travel grant to pursue this project. For many good comments and discussions regarding various ideas in this paper, I am very grateful to Martha Ratliff, Relja Vulanović, Eugenia Casielles, Ellen Barton, Kate Paesani, Pat Siple, David Gil, Dan Seeley, Natasha Kondrashova. My thanks also to the audiences at 2007 GURT; 2007 ILA, New York; 2007 Max Planck Workshop on Complexity, Leipzig; 2007 ISU Conference on Recursion; and 2007 FASL, Stony Brook, especially Rafaella Zanuttini, Richard Kayne, Eric Reuland, John Locke, Tecumseh Fitch, Stephanie Harves, and Ken Safir. All errors are mine.

1. But see Cardinaletti and Guasti (1995) for alternative views of small clauses.

2. For references and discussion of alternative views, see, e.g., Guasti (2002).

3. Also, focus and topic/comment in English are rarely signaled by syntactic movement but typically solely by prosody.

REFERENCES

Akmajian, Adrian. 1984. Sentence types and the form-function fit. *Natural Language and Linguistic Theory* 2:1–23.

Barton, Ellen. 1990. *Nonsentential constituents: A theory of grammatical structure and pragmatic interpretation.* Amsterdam: Benjamins.

Berwick, Robert C. 1998. Language evolution and the minimalist program: The origins of syntax. In *Approaches to the evolution of language: Social and cognitive bases,* ed. James R. Hurford, Michael Studdert-Kennedy, and Chris Knight, 320–40. Cambridge: Cambridge University Press.

Bickerton, Derek. 1998. Catastrophic evolution: The case for a single step from protolanguage to full human language. In *Approaches to the evolution of language: Social and cognitive bases,* ed. James R. Hurford, Michael Studdert-Kennedy, and Chris Knight, 341–58. Cambridge: Cambridge University Press.

Bowers, John. 1993. The syntax of predication. *Linguistic Inquiry* 24:591–656.

Burling, Robbins. 2005. *The talking ape: How language evolved.* Oxford: Oxford University Press.

Burzio, Luigi. 1981. *Intransitive verbs and Italian auxiliaries.* PhD diss., Massachusetts Institute of Technology.

Cardinaletti, Anna, and Maria Teresa Guasti, eds. 1995. *Syntax and semantics 28: Small clauses.* San Diego, CA: Academic Press.

Chomsky, Noam. 1957. *Syntactic structures.* The Hague: Mouton.

———. 1995. *The minimalist program.* Cambridge, MA: MIT Press.

———. 2005. Three factors in language design. *Linguistic Inquiry* 36:1–22.

Deacon, Terrence W. 1997. *The symbolic species: The co-evolution of language and the brain.* New York: W. W. Norton.

Deutscher, Guy. 2000. *Syntactic change in Akkadian: The evolution of sentential complementation.* Oxford: Oxford University Press.

———. 2005. *The unfolding of language: An evolutionary tour of mankind's greatest invention.* New York: Henry Holt.

Guasti, Maria Teresa. 2002. *Language acquisition: The growth of grammar.* Cambridge, MA: MIT Press.

Hauser, Marc, Noam Chomsky, and W. Tecumseh Fitch. 2002. The language faculty: What is it, who has it, and how did it evolve? *Science* 298:1569–79.

Jackendoff, Ray. 2002. *Foundations of language: Brain, meaning, grammar, evolution.* Oxford: Oxford University Press.

Jespersen, Otto. 1954. *A modern English grammar.* Part III, *Syntax.* London: Allen and Unwin.

Joanette, Yves, Pierre Goulet, and Didier Hannequin. 1990. *Right hemisphere and verbal communication.* New York: Springer-Verlag.

Kiparsky, Paul. 1968. Tense and mood in Indo-European syntax. *Foundations of Language* 4:30–57.

Kitagawa, Yoshihisa. 1986. *Subjects in English and Japanese.* PhD diss., University of Massachusetts, Amherst.

Koopman, Hilda, and Dominique Sportiche. 1991. The position of subjects. *Lingua* 85:211–58.

Lebeaux, David. 1989. Language acquisition and the form of the grammar. PhD diss., University of Massachusetts, Amherst.

Lock, Andrew, and Charles R. Peters, eds. 1996. *Handbook of human symbolic evolution.* Oxford: Clarendon Press.

Longobardi, Giuseppe. 1994. Reference and proper names: A theory of N-Movement in syntax and logical form. *Linguistic Inquiry* 25:609–65.

Ouhalla, Jamal. 1993. Functional categories, agrammatism and language acquisition. *Linguistische Berichte* 143:3–36.

Parker, Anna R. 2006. Evolution as a constraint on theories of syntax: The case against minimalism. PhD diss., University of Edinburgh.

Peters, Ann M., and Lise Menn. 1993. False starts and filler syllables: Ways to learn grammatical morphemes. *Language* 69:742–77.

Piattelli-Palmarini, Massimo, and Juan Uriagereka. 2004. Immune syntax: The evolution of the language virus. In *Variation and universals in biolinguistics,* ed. Lyle Jenkins, 341–77. Oxford: Elsevier.

Pinker, Steven, and Paul Bloom. 1990. Natural language and natural selection. *Behavioral and Brain Sciences* 13:707–84.

Pinker, Steven, and Ray Jackendoff. 2005. The faculty of language: What's special about it? *Cognition* 95:201–36.

Platzak, Christer. 1990. A grammar without functional categories: A syntactic study of early child language. *Nordic Journal of Linguistics* 13:107–26.

Potts, Christopher, and Tom Roeper. 2006. The narrowing acquisition path: From expressive small clauses to declaratives. In *The syntax of nonsententials: Multidisciplinary perspectives,* ed. Ljiljana Progovac, Kate Paesani, Eugenia Casielles, and Ellen Barton, 183–201. Amsterdam: Benjamins.

Progovac, Ljiljana. 2006. The syntax of nonsententials: Small clauses and phrases at the root. In *The syntax of nonsententials: Multidisciplinary perspectives,* ed. Ljiljana Progovac, Kate Paesani, Eugenia Casielles, and Ellen Barton, 33–71. Amsterdam: Benjamins.

———. 2007a. Layering of grammar: Vestiges of evolutionary development of syntax in modern-day languages. Presented at the Workshop on Language Complexity as an Evolving Variable, Max Planck, Leipzig, April 2007.

———. 2007b. When clauses refuse to be recursive: An evolutionary perspective. Presented at the ISU Conference on Recursion in Human Languages, Normal, IL, April.

Progovac, Ljiljana, Kate Paesani, Eugenia Casielles, and Ellen Barton, eds. 2006. *The syntax of nonsententials: Multidisciplinary perspectives.* Amsterdam: Benjamins.

Pulvermüller, Friedemann. 2002. *The neuroscience of language: On brain circuits of words and serial order.* Cambridge: Cambridge University Press.

Radford, Andrew. 1990. *Syntactic theory and the acquisition of English syntax.* Oxford: Blackwell.

Ridley, Mark. 1993. *Evolution.* Oxford: Blackwell Scientific.

Roeper, Thomas 1999. Universal bilingualism. *Bilingualism: Language and Cognition* 2 (3): 169–86.

Rolfe, Leonard. 1996. Theoretical stages in the prehistory of grammar. In *Handbook of human symbolic evolution,* ed. Andrew Lock and Charles R. Peters, 776–92. Oxford: Clarendon Press.

Schütze, T. Carson. 2001. On the nature of default case. *Syntax* 4 (3): 205–38.

Stowell, Timothy. 1981. *Origins of phrase structure.* PhD diss., Massachusetts Institute of Technology.

———. 1983. Subjects across categories. *Linguistic Review* 2–3:285–312.

Traugott, Elizabeth C., and Bernd Heine. 1991. *Approaches to grammaticalization.* Vol. 2, *Typological studies in language* 19. Amsterdam: Benjamins.

Veneziano, Edy, and Hermine Sinclair. 2000. The changing status of "filler syllables" on the way to grammatical morphemes. *Journal of Child Language* 27:461–500.

Vygotsky, Lev S. 1981. The genesis of higher mental functions. In *The concept of activity in Soviet psychology,* ed. James V. Wertsch, 144–88. New York: M. E. Sharpe.

10

Spanish Personal *a* and the Antidative

OMAR VELÁZQUEZ-MENDOZA AND RAÚL ARANOVICH
University of California, Davis

SPANISH IS OFTEN CONSIDERED to have flexible word order. This flexibility extends to the relative placement of verbal complements in ditransitive clauses. A theme may precede a goal, appearing immediately to the right of the verb, as in (1a), or it may follow the goal, as in (1b). There is, however, an intriguing restriction on word order among complements. When the theme is a pronoun, the goal cannot be placed between the theme and the verb, as seen in (2).

(1) a. *Miguel le entregó sus hijos a la niñera.*　　　　　　　　　　V-DO-IO
　　　Miguel 3.sg.dat give.past his children to the nanny
　　　"Miguel gave his children to the nanny."

　　b. *Miguel le entregó a la niñera sus hijos.*　　　　　　　　　　V-IO-DO
　　　Miguel 3.sg.dat give.past to the nanny his children
　　　"Miguel gave the nanny his children."

(2) a. *Miguel se los entregó a ellos a la niñera.*　　　　　　　　　$\text{V-DO}_{pro}\text{-IO}$
　　　Miguel 3.sg.dat 3.pl.masc.acc give.past anim them.masc to the nanny
　　　"Miguel gave them to the nanny."

　　b. **Miguel se los entregó a la niñera a ellos.*　　　　　　　　*V-IO-DO_{pro}
　　　*Miguel 3.sg.dat 3.pl.masc.acc give.past to the nanny anim them.masc
　　　"Miguel gave them to the nanny."

In recent years, the theoretical status of dative arguments in Spanish has generated intense debate (Cuervo 2003; Demonte 1995). Some studies suggest that Spanish has a rule of dative shift (i.e., an applicative rule) similar to the one responsible for the double object construction in English. While it may be tempting to attribute the contrast between (2a) and (2b) to a restriction on the application of the applicative rule, we argue instead that variations in word order among verbal complements in Spanish ditransitives are the result of an antidative rule, following Dryer (1986). According to this analysis, Spanish objects are sensitive to a distinction between primary object (PO) and secondary object (SO). The complement that is immediately adjacent to the verb in ditransitives is a PO. The PO/SO distinction is also relevant for the distribution of personal *a,* the syntactic particle that marks animate direct objects in Spanish. Personal *a,* we argue, cannot occur on SOs, and this is why pronominal themes (which must bear the accusative marker *a*) are not allowed to appear after the goal.

In this chapter, first we introduce the applicative analysis of the English double object construction and contrast such analysis with Dryer's alternative approach. We define the notions of PO and SO and then explain the antidative rule. Second, we show how the antidative analysis accounts for word order variation in Spanish ditransitives and how the notion of an SO is relevant for the distribution of personal *a.* Third, we show that as a consequence of antidative pronominal themes cannot occur in the position that follows the goal in a ditransitive, thus accounting for the ungrammaticality of (2b). The section that follows offers independent evidence in support of our analysis, coming from a restriction on relativization in ditransitives. Fifth, we focus on the analysis of alternations in Spanish ditransitives proposed in Cuervo (2003) and highlight the differences between her approach and ours. This section is followed by some concluding remarks.

Applicatives and Antidatives

In English there are pairs of sentences, such as those in (3a) and (3b), in which the two arguments of a verb like *give* (theme and goal) occur in different configurations.

(3) a. John gave the book to Mary.

   b. John gave Mary the book.

According to one analysis of these sentences (Larson 1988; Perlmutter and Postal 1983), the theme in (3a) is realized as a direct object (DO) and the goal as an indirect object (IO) (marked by the preposition *to*). This is often referred to as the "ditransitive" construction. (3b) is derived by a rule that promotes the IO to DO, placing it right next to the verb (without the preposition *to*). The theme in (3b) is a "second object" often analyzed as an adjunct. We will refer to this construction as the "double object" construction.

In this chapter, however, we revisit a different approach to dative alternations, which is proposed by Dryer (1986).[1] In Dryer's analysis, the double object construction has an IO (the goal) and a DO (the theme). English, being a primary object language, characterizes its IO in a double object construction with the same morphosyntactic feature as the DO in a monotransitive: immediate adjacency to the verb. The DO in a double object construction is, then, an SO:

(4) John gave Mary the book.
   S   IO   DO
            PO   SO

A question remains, however, about the correspondence between (3a) and (3b). Dryer suggests that there is still a correspondence between (3a) and (3b) but that the rule relating the two is different: (3a) is the product of a rule (the antidative rule) that promotes the SO to PO.

For the SO to become a PO, a ditransitive clause has to turn into a monotransitive. To achieve this, the goal has to be realized as an oblique in (3a). This is an important way in which Dryer's analysis departs from the traditional views about English ditransitives: the goal, introduced by the preposition *to* in (3a), is not a surface IO, and the theme does not change its grammatical function in (3a) and (3b), remaining as the DO in both cases. This is the essence of Dryer's Antidative Hypothesis.

It is important for our purposes to highlight the pragmatic value of the PO/SO contrast. Typically the IO is more topical than the DO, as it tends to be human or one of the "local" persons (first or second). In a ditransitive clause, then, an IO is less topical than the canonical subject but more topical than the DO. Thus it follows that the PO function is a grammaticalization of the "secondary topic" notion.

"Antidative" in Spanish

The relative word order of Spanish DOs and IOs is mostly free. Like English, Spanish word order in ditransitives allows for either the theme or the goal to immediately follow the verb, as shown in (5).

(5) a. *Miguel le entregó sus hijos a la niñera.*

Miguel 3sg.dat give.past his children to the nanny

"Miguel gave his children to the nanny."

b. *Miguel le entregó a la niñera sus hijos.*

Miguel 3sg.dat give.past to the nanny his children

"Miguel gave the nanny his children."

Extending Dryer's antidative analysis to Spanish, in this chapter we treat sentence (5b) as basic and sentence (5a) as derived. The structure in (6) shows the relational network of (5).

(6) a. P   S   SO   PO
    ----
    entregar Miguel hijos niñera (= 5b)

b. P   S   SO   PO
    P   S   PO   Obl
    ----
    entregar Miguel hijos niñera (= 5a)

Our interpretation of the antidative analysis, now applied to Spanish ditransitives, is that sentence (5a) is derived from (5b) by the antidative rule that places the original PO in *chômage,* allowing for the promotion of the original SO in the initial stratum as a PO in the final stratum. As a consequence of that, the initial PO (*a la niñera*) is demoted to oblique.[2]

Based on the representation of sentences (5a) and (5b) given in (6a) through (6b), we claim that the antidative rule is responsible for the relative word order of the theme and the goal. As noted earlier, we analyze the complement *sus hijos* in (5a) as a PO but as an SO in (5b), and the argument *a la niñera* as a PO in (5b) and as an oblique in (5a). In other words, we propose that the "basic" word order of Spanish ditransitives is

V-IO-DO and that the V-DO-IO order is derived. While the alternation has no effect on grammatical relations, it changes the PO/SO status of the arguments: The complement that directly follows the verb in ditransitive constructions is always a PO, but in derived sentences (i.e., sentences of the V-DO-IO type), the goal is a demoted PO. Worth noting is that antidative in English assigns a change in the grammatical functions of the dative goal in derived sentences, whereas antidative in Spanish does not. This is why the preposition *to* is included in obliques in English in derived sentences of the type *John gave the book to Mary,* in which the goal is an oblique, and excluded in the basic order *John gave Mary the book,* in which the goal is a PO. Yet it seems appropriate at this point to clarify the relationship between POs/SOs and DOs/IOs.

When Dryer introduces the notions of PO and SO, he initially defines them in terms of the grammatical relations DO and IO—the PO is the DO in a monotransitive clause and the IO in a ditransitive clause. But when he reevaluates the theoretical status of the PO and SO functions, he takes a different approach, stating that "it may be better to view PO and SO as primitive notions on a pair with DO and IO, and thus to use a principle relating the various primitive notions DO, IO, PO and SO to each other" (Dryer 1986, 835). In English, the principle relating these notions to each other states that IOs in ditransitives must be POs. The status of this principle as a language universal, however, is not entirely clear. It is possible that languages differ from each other in the way that the primitive notions are related to each other. What we are proposing, then, is that Spanish IOs need not be POs, but can also be the equivalent of a PO that has been put *en chômage* by the advancement of the SO to PO.

Unlike English, Spanish is unable to mark the object primacy of the dative PO in double object constructions through the exclusion of the preposition *a,* the dative marker, because the grammatical functions of Spanish dative arguments do not change in either of the two word orders. A PO [e.g., *a la niñera* in (5b)] that is demoted to oblique and placed after the theme [e.g., *a la niñera* in (5a)] is still an IO. As shown in (7a) through (7b), this is why a PO in basic sentences and a demoted PO in derived sentences can be doubled by a dative clitic, regardless of the relative position of the dative argument within the sentence (refer to section on the applicative accounts of Spanish ditransitives for the notion of clitic reduplication).

(7) a. *Le di el libro a María.*

   3.sg.dat give.past the book to Mary

   "I gave the book to Mary."

   b. *Le di a María el libro.*

   3.sg.dat give.past to Mary the book

   "I gave Mary the book."

Conversely, while no change in the grammatical functions of Spanish IOs takes place regarding their status as POs or SOs, the morphosyntactic properties of the Spanish themes do reflect a syntactically grammaticalized difference between an accusative SO in basic sentences and an accusative PO in derived ones. In Spanish, when the theme follows the verb, if it is animate it may have personal *a* both in monotransitives [as shown in (8a)] and in ditransitives [as in (8b)].[3]

(8) a. *Veo a un vampiro.*

    1.see anim a vampire

    "I see a vampire."

  b. *El secretario le contó (a) los obreros al ingeniero.*

    The secretary 3sg.dat count.past (anim) the laborers to the engineer

    "The secretary counted the laborers for the engineer."

But personal *a* does not occur in every animate accusative argument. Its presence is ungrammatical, for instance, in the accusative nominal of the V-IO-DO basic sentence structure, as (9b) exemplifies. For purposes of illustration, we repeat the examples in (1) and relabel them as (9).

(9) a. *Miguel le entregó (a) sus hijos a la niñera*   V-DO-IO

    Miguel 3.sg.dat give.past (anim) his children to the nanny

    "Miguel gave his children to the nanny."

  b. *Miguel le entregó a la niñera (*a) sus hijos.*   V-IO-DO

    Miguel 3.sg.dat give.past to the nanny (*anim) his children

    "Miguel gave the nanny his children."

Thus, by analyzing the theme as a PO when it immediately follows the verb in a ditransitive such as (9a), we can offer a general statement of the conditions that determine the distribution of personal *a:*

(10) **PO *a*-marking hypothesis:** personal *a* may or may not occur on POs, but it cannot occur on SOs.

Therefore a theme that follows a goal [e.g., *sus hijos* in (9b)] cannot have personal *a,* not even if animate. The inability of the accusative theme *sus hijos* to take personal *a* in (9b), we propose, is an indication of this constituent's status as an SO. The nominal *sus hijos* in (9a), conversely, may take personal *a* due to its PO status.[4] If this is the case, it follows that Spanish grammaticalizes the notion of POs/SOs through the PO *a*-marking hypothesis, in which personal *a* introduces highly topical complements (human noun phrases [NPs], pronouns, definite complements, etc.) and thus distinguishes them from less topical object arguments.

But one of the problems that were pointed out in the introduction was that the flexible word order that Spanish verbal complements display [which was presented in (1)] becomes rigid when the themes are NPs headed by pronouns, as shown in (2). For purposes of exemplification, (2) will be relabeled as (11).

(11) a. *Miguel se los entregó a ellos a la niñera.*   V-DO$_{pro}$-IO

    Miguel 3.sg.dat 3.pl.masc.acc give.past anim them.masc to the nanny

    "Miguel gave them to the nanny."

  b. **Miguel se los entregó a la niñera a ellos.*   *V-IO-DO$_{pro}$

    Miguel 3.sg.dat 3.pl.masc.acc give.past to the nanny anim them.masc

    "Miguel gave them to the nanny."

Unlike NPs headed by common nouns, pronominal themes must always be preceded by personal *a*. When this requirement is added to the PO *a*-marking hypothesis, only the V-DO$_{pro}$-IO order is grammatical. In other words, when a pronominal theme follows the verb [as (11a) illustrates], the theme is a PO and may therefore take personal *a*. This coincidence aligns with the fact that the accusative pronoun that heads the theme [in (11a), for example] needs the personal *a* because every accusative pronoun needs personal *a*. This explains the grammaticality of (11a). However, when a pronominal theme follows the goal, as in (11b), the theme is an SO. This results in a potential contradiction: As an SO, the theme cannot have personal *a*, but it needs personal *a* because it is still an accusative pronoun. Object pronouns, then, unlike other NPs, must have personal *a*. Because SOs cannot have personal *a*, this excludes pronouns from being SOs in Spanish. Therefore pronoun objects cannot follow the goal of a ditransitive, accounting for the ungrammaticality of (11b).

Independent Evidence: Personal *a* in Relative Clauses

Our analysis of the rigid word order exemplified in the contrast between (11a) and (11b) rests on the PO *a*-marking hypothesis. A theme that follows a goal is an SO, and that is why it cannot be marked by *a*. This, in turn, excludes pronominal themes from the position that follows the goal, as pronouns must be marked by *a*. The evidence we have used to argue that a complement is an SO, however, comes primarily from word order facts. Nonetheless, to use the constraints on SOs to explain word order restrictions in Spanish puts our argumentation in danger of being circular. To avoid this risk, we provide independent evidence for the status of *a*-marked DOs as POs (for the claim that SOs cannot be marked by *a*), based on relativization.

The key data are presented in (12). As (12a) shows, a goal can be relativized in a ditransitive relative clause, but only if the theme does not have the personal *a*. The theme, on the other hand, can always be relativized, as shown in (12b).

(12) a. *Ésta es la niñera a la que Miguel le entregó (*a) sus hijos.*

   This.fem is the nanny to the which Miguel 3.sg.dat give.past (*anim) his children

   "This is the nanny Miguel gave her children to."

   b. *Éstos son los niños que Miguel le entregó a la niñera.*

   These.masc are the children that Miguel 3.sg.dat give.past to the nanny

   "These are the children that Miguel gave to the nanny."

The antidative analysis of Spanish ditransitives accounts for this fact in a natural way. Dryer argues that many grammatical rules are sensitive to the scale PO < SO. As an example he cites passivization in Yindjibarndi: In this language, DOs can be turned into the subject of a passive in monotransitives but not in ditransitives. In the latter, it is the IO that becomes the subject of the corresponding passive (Dryer 1986, 830, and references therein). That is, Yindjibarndi POs outrank SOs as candidates for promotion to subject in passives. The consequence we draw from this is that there may be constructions and syntactic rules that are sensitive to the scale S < PO < SO < Obl.

We suggest that relativization is a perfect candidate to show the effect of this scale for a couple of reasons. First, relativization is known to be sensitive to hierarchical distinctions among grammatical relations (Keenan and Comrie 1977). Second, relative pronouns are typically topics. A conflict may potentially arise, then, in languages that allow for relativization of DOs but not IOs, as IOs are more topical than DOs. When the higher degree of topicality of the IO over the DO is grammaticalized in the PO/SO distinction, it is only natural that a language will develop a relativization rule sensitive to the S < PO < SO < Obl scale instead of to the S < DO < IO < Obl scale proposed in Keenan and Comrie (1977).

We can now account for the restriction on relativization in (12a). If the theme has the personal *a,* it must be a PO. The goal, then, is not a PO in that case, having been demoted to the functional equivalent of a *chômeur* (in other terms, the goal is less topical than the theme). In (12a), the presence of personal *a* on the theme renders the sentence ungrammatical because the goal must be a PO to be relativized. This requires the theme to be an SO and therefore unable to have the personal *a*. Thus, *chômeurs* are below the threshold for relativization in Spanish. (12b), conversely, shows that the theme can be relativized. This seems to run contrary to the claim that SOs cannot be relativized if there is a PO in the clause. In such a case, the antidative rule comes in to fix the problem: The theme in (12b) is in fact the PO while the goal is a demoted PO.

The constraints on relativization of ditransitives, then, give independent evidence for the antidative analysis of Spanish personal *a*.

The Applicative Accounts of Spanish Ditransitives

There are some recent analyses of Spanish ditransitives suggesting that Spanish has a rule of dative shift. The problem those analyses present is that the applicative interpretation on which they are grounded concerns itself with the apparent optional doubling of the IO by a dative clitic pronoun, as shown in (13).

(13) a. *Di libros a los niños.*
　　　1.give.past books to the children
　　　"I gave books to the children."
　　b. *Les di libros a los niños.*
　　　3.sg.dat 1.give.past books to the children
　　　"I gave books to the children."

Cuervo (2003), for example, assumes that the Spanish ditransitive sentences that present dative clitic doubling [as in (13b)] are derived from those that do not have it [as in (13a)]. She postulates that sentence (13b) is parallel to the English double object construction *I gave the children books* and that the theme in (13a) is a DO. Furthermore, in her study Cuervo states that *a los niños* is a locative prepositional phrase (PP) in (13a) and presumes that, as such, PP cannot be doubled by any dative clitic in the same way that the locative constituent *a Barcelona* in (14) cannot be doubled by dative *le:*

(14) *(*Le) mandé libros a Barcelona.*

    (*3.sg.dat) 1.send.past books to Barcelona

    "I sent books to Barcelona."

Her premise is that a dative clitic only doubles a goal when it has been promoted to DO. Yet her view presents a problem: In sentences with dative reduplication [as in (13b)], it falls short of explaining why—upon considering the goal to be a final DO—the dative clitic [*les* in (13b)] is the clitic doubling the full "accusative" complement, not the accusative clitic *los,* as expected in full accusative arguments:

(15) *(*Los) di libros a los niños.*

    (*3.pl.masc.acc) 1.give.past books to the children.masc

    "I gave books to the children."

In the strictest terms, the impossibility of sentences like (13) to be doubled by accusative *los* and their possibility to be doubled by dative *les* [as in (13b)] poses a contradiction to the fact that the goal *a los niños* in (13b) is, for Cuervo, a final DO.

Conversely, in the antidative analysis of Spanish, the goals *a los niños* of (13a) and (13b) are IOs. This fact accounts for the licit clitic doubling of such goals, even if the theme follows the goal:

(16) *(Les) di a los niños libros.*

    (3.pl.dat) 1.give.past to the children books

    "I gave the children books."

The themes *libros* of (13a) and (13b) are newly advanced POs that are derived from the promotion of a previous SO in (16), a sentence of the basic V-IO-DO order. Therefore the compatibility of the goals in (13b) and in (13a) to allow for clitic doubling signals that both of these goals are IOs. In short, what distinguishes the antidative account of Spanish ditransitives from the applicative analysis mentioned earlier is that it treats sentences (13a) and (13b) as two equivalent constructions in respect to the grammatical relations of their objects. Thus our interpretation of sentence (13a) is that its goal is not a DO but a PO *chômeur* that still remains an IO. Although our analysis says nothing about the optionality of clitic doubling, it is possible that the presence or absence of the dative clitic is also sensitive to the PO/SO distinction, that is, that clitic doubling (or the absence thereof) is a sign of antidative. This is left for future research.

Conclusions

In this chapter we have proposed an analysis of word order variation among the complements of Spanish ditransitives based on Dryer's (1986) antidative analysis. We claimed that whichever complement immediately follows the verb (be it the theme or the goal) is the PO of the clause. The argument that follows the PO may be an SO (if the PO is the goal) or a demoted PO (if the PO is the theme). The latter case is derived by application of the antidative rule, a rule promoting the SO to PO. We offered two pieces of evidence in support of this analysis. First, the distribution of personal *a* on themes is restricted to those that occur immediately after the verb. This can be accounted for under the antidative analysis by a constraint that excludes marking by personal *a* from SOs. Second, we showed that goals cannot be relativized when the theme is marked by personal *a*. This follows from our claim that the goal is not a PO in these cases, but a demoted PO, and the assumption that only those arguments at the top of the relational hierarchy S < PO < SO < Chô can be relativized. Both pieces of evidence address phenomena that are sensitive to the information structure of the clause in Spanish. Personal *a* marks complements that are highly topical (human NPs, pronouns, definite complements), and relativization also targets topics over foci. If Dryer's suggestion that the PO/SO distinction is a grammaticalization of the functional notion of secondary topic, then it makes sense to state the constraints on personal *a* and on relativization in terms of the PO/SO distinction.

A corollary of our analysis is that a surprising exception to the word order flexibility among ditransitive complements in Spanish is explained in a natural way. Pronominal themes cannot follow the goal because they need to be introduced by personal *a,* but as SOs they cannot do so. We are able to account for this restriction on word order without postulating any sort of rule that changes grammatical relations, such as the applicative rules proposed in Cuervo (2003). The advantage of this approach is that it does not require us to stipulate any exceptions to the general rule that doubles IOs with dative clitics. Our study, then, highlights the importance of "little words" such as Spanish *a* for the study of grammatical relations and syntactic structure at large. The function of little words is often to make visible the unobservable processes in the grammar, marking on the surface the results of abstract syntactic rules. In this case, personal *a* tells us that Spanish may be on its way to become a PO/SO language or that it has already arrived there.

NOTES

We are tremendously indebted to Míriam Hernández-Rodríguez, of the University of California, Davis, for providing us with the spontaneous data of Spanish ditransitives that motivated this study.

1. In his study, Dryer postulates that in direct object languages, the patient patterns with the theme in ditransitives and that in primary object languages, the goal patterns with the DO of monotransitives.
2. Because the initial PO is demoted to oblique in the final stratum, it is not considered a functional object anymore. This allows for the initial SO to advance to PO in the final stratum because it is the only object argument in the final stratum, when the initial PO becomes an oblique.
3. Our claims are supported by the behavior of Spanish personal *a* (the accusative animacy marker) in ditransitive environments, whose behavior is not an instance of free variation but a predictable phenomenon, and by the pronominalization restrictions of Spanish complements.
4. In sum, what is expected in this Antidative account of Spanish ditransitives is the deletion of personal *a* from SOs and its optional presence in POs:

   (1) a. *Les describí (a) el profesor a los alumnos.*
          3.sg.dat 1.describe.past (anim) the professor to the students
          "I described the professor to/for the students."
       b. *Les describí a los alumnos (*a) el profesor.*
          3.sg.dat 1.describe.past to the students (*anim) the professor
          "I described the professor to/for the students."

The surface evidence of Spanish presented in (1) corroborates the prediction that the theme in version (1a) may take personal *a* because of its status as a PO, while in version (1b) it cannot because of its status as an SO.

REFERENCES

Cuervo, María Cristina. 2003. Structural asymmetries but same word order: The dative alternation in Spanish. In *Asymmetry in grammar,* vol. 1, *Syntax and semantics,* ed. Anna Maria Di Sciullo, 117–44. Amsterdam: Benjamins.

Demonte, Violeta. 1995. Dative alternation in Spanish. *Probus* 7:5–30.

Dryer, Matthew. 1986. Primary objects, secondary objects, and antidative. *Language* 62:808–45.

Keenan, Edward, and Bernard Comrie. 1977. Noun phrase accessibility and universal grammar. *Linguistic Inquiry* 8:63–99.

Larson, Richard K. 1988. On the double object construction. *Linguistic Inquiry* 19:335–91.

Perlmutter, David, and Paul Postal. 1983. Some proposed laws of basic clause structure. In *Studies in relational grammar I,* ed. David Perlmutter, 81–128. Chicago: University of Chicago Press.

Semantics

11

▨ Predicting Argument Realization from Oblique Marker Semantics

JOHN BEAVERS
The University of Texas at Austin

▨ **THIS CHAPTER DISCUSSES** the role of adpositions and oblique cases (which I group under a single category P, excluding structural cases and their adpositional equivalents) in determining argument realization patterns across languages. Consider the Japanese data in (1) and their English translations, where English *clear* and Japanese *katazukeru*, "clear," both take agent, theme, and source arguments, yet differ in how these arguments may be realized. In (1a) the theme is the object and the source is an oblique marked by *from* in English and *–kara*, "from," in Japanese. In (1b) the source is the object, but only in English can the theme be realized as an oblique, marked by *of.*

(1) a. *Ueetaa-wa syokutaku-kara syokki-o   katazuketa.*
    waiter-TOP table-from   dishes-ACC cleared
    "The waiter cleared the dishes from the table."

  b. *Ueetaa-wa syokutaku-o (*syokki-de/kara/ni)   katazuketa.*
    waiter-TOP table-ACC   (*dishes-INST/from/DAT) cleared
    "The waiter cleared the table (of the dishes)." (Japanese; Kageyama 1980, 38)

Why should English and Japanese differ in this way? The simplest answer is to blame it on verbal polysemy: *clear* and *katazukeru* both have a variant subcategorized for a theme object and an oblique source, but only *clear* has a variant selecting for a location object and a theme oblique [even though (1b) entails the existence of a theme]. However, this misses significant generalizations about why languages differ in terms of verbal argument structure. A common alternative is to assume that both Vs and Ps can determine clause structure but in different contexts, yielding different realization patterns (following in the tradition of Hale and Keyser 1993). For example, Folli and Harley (2004) propose that change-of-state predicates decompose into a light verb *v* and a small clause headed by whatever head (V or P) describes the result. On this approach we might analyze (1b) and its translation as in (2) (following Harley's [2005], 62, analysis of *smear*-type locative verbs), where dyadic *of* predicates a separation relation between the theme and the source, while monadic *katazukeru* predicates a "cleared" state of the source (where the English manner root *clear* is independently incorporated onto *v* via manner incorporation, represented by parentheses).

(2) a. [$_{vP}$ [$_{DP}$ the waiter] [$_{v'}$ v_0+(clear) [$_{PP}$ [$_{DP}$ the table] [$_{P'}$ of [$_{DP}$ the dishes]]]]]

    b. [$_{vP}$ [$_{DP}$ *Ueetaa-wa*] [$_{v'}$ [$_{VP}$ [$_{DP}$ *syokutaku-o*] ~~*katazukeru*~~] *katazukeru*+v_0]]

While this approach admits a role for P semantics, it has the counterintuitive side effect that Vs with similar meanings across languages have radically different functions in the clause. Indeed, Harley (2005, 54) analyzes the translation of (1b) more along the lines of (2b) (modulo word order) with the *of*-PP as a complement to the *clear* root, meaning different locative verbs have different analyses even in English. I advocate a more symmetric approach wherein all clauses always have a V-head and all obliques have a P-head. However, following Beavers (2006a), Gawron (1986), and Wechsler (1995), I argue that V and P are subject to an *implicational compatibility relationship,* where the role assigned to the argument by V is a strictly more specific version of the role assigned by P, which I refer to as the Oblique Selection Principle (see Beavers 2006a, 129–32):

(3) *Oblique Selection Principle (OSP):* The role θ_V assigned by V to oblique argument x in event e must imply the role θ_P assigned by P to x in *e,* that is, $\forall x \forall e[\theta_V (e, x) \rightarrow \theta_P(e, x)]$.

A quick look at the data shows that both V and P contribute semantic components to any clause, consistent with the OSP. First, certain aspects of the role of any oblique argument are determined solely by V, as the "same" obliques have different roles with different Vs, as in (4).

(4) a. Sandy loaded the wagon *with the hay.*   (Theme; loaded)

    b. Sandy cut the bread *with the knife.*   (Instrument; inserted)

    c. Sandy chipped the rock *with the chisel.*   (Instrument; hit bluntly)

Clearly each *with*-oblique has a role determined by V. In (4a) it is a theme, in (4b) it is an instrument that moves toward the patient like a theme and then penetrates it, and in (4c) it is an instrument that moves into blunt contact with the patient. These differ from instrument adjuncts (e.g., *Sandy ate the grits with a fork*) in that they are entailed to exist by the V. Nonetheless, there is commonality across all of these *with*-obliques: they are all "causally intermediate" between the agent and the patient in the force-dynamic structure of the event (following Croft 1991, 178). This suggests a unified semantics for (at least one use of) *with* that subsumes themes and instruments, including all of those given in (4). Crucially, the V semantics is always more specific than the P semantics (if Sandy loads the wagon with hay she first acts on the hay and then on the wagon, etc.), supporting the OSP as a general constraint on V + P combinations.

This makes two predictions. First, unsurprisingly, only semantically compatible V + P combinations are possible; for example, *I loaded the wagon above hay* is infelicitous because *about* does not encode causal intermediacy and does encode things not entailed by *load*. However, the OSP is not a sufficiency condition: Some putatively synonymous Ps may not occur marking the same oblique arguments, for example, *Sandy loaded the wagon with/*by/*via hay* (assuming *with, by,* and *via* mark causal intermediacy). This suggests that in addition to the OSP there may still be c-selectional requirements for specific V + P combinations.

The second, more interesting prediction, which I explore in depth, is that the presence/absence of certain Ps in a language determines the possibility of oblique realization of certain arguments of certain verbs. Thus the contrast between (1b) and its translation may simply reflect the independent presence of a class of *of*-obliques in English that Japanese systematically lacks. This will involve demonstrating that English *of* is semantically contentful and that Japanese has no corresponding postposition. There is in fact evidence for this, as English *of* is historically derived from Old English ablative *æf* (cf. *off*). Hook (1983) calls its use with *clear* the "abstrument": an in*strument* in an *ab*lative context, that is, a theme that is moved away from something. In fact, *of* is even more general than this. While *from* marks only sources, *of* can mark both abstruments as in (5) *and* sources as in (6), that is, *either* side of a separation relation.

(5) a. The government robbed/deprived them of/*from their jobs.

    b. The doctor cured him of/*from his nail biting.   (Marking abstruments)

(6) a. He partook of/?from the salad.

    b. We desired it of/from him.   (Marking sources)

The difference between English and Japanese is that Japanese lacks an abstrument marker: *-de* marks instruments and *-kara* marks sources, but neither marks an abstrument. In particular, translations of (5a) follow the pattern in (1), while translations of (5b) involve a possessive similar to *cure his disease* (Mika Hama, p.c.):

(7) *Isha-ga   kare-no byoki-o   naoshita.*
    doctor-NOM he-GEN disease-ACC cured
    "The doctor cured his disease." (= cured him of his disease)   (Japanese)

Thus we can assume that the Japanese and English sentences in (1b) have the same clause structure (modulo word order), but English allows a PP theme because it has the P *of,* while Japanese does not because it does not have an equivalent P. Unfortunately, I have no deeper explanation for the absence of an abstrument P in Japanese except that its presence in English is a historical oddity. However, in the next two sections I turn to two cases of systematic variation in argument realization across languages and show that in each case the variation is correlated with the independent presence/absence of certain Ps in the relevant languages. Moreover, I show that this can often be reduced to independent typological variation across these languages, suggesting that these differences are systemic rather than arbitrary. I also show how in many cases other properties of the languages may provide alternative means consistent with the OSP for capturing some of the functionality of the missing argument realization pattern, thus further validating this hypothesis.

Encoding of Goals—Possibilities and Impossibilities

A classic case study of cross-linguistic variation in argument marking is the typology of Talmy (2000) for how languages encode directed motion, based on how the notions *path of motion* and *manner of motion* are encoded in a single clause. The crucial distinction is between S(atellite)-framed languages (e.g., English, Russian), in which manner is characteristically encoded in the V and path in some satellite to V, and V(verb)-framed languages (e.g., French, Japanese), where path is characteristically encoded in the V, and manner in some satellite, illustrated in (8).

(8) a. John limped into the house.   (English; S-framed)

    b. *Je suis entré   dans la maison (en boitant).*

    I am entered in   the house in limping

    "I entered (into) the house (limping)."   (French; V-framed)

    (cf. *#J'ai boité dans la maison.*)

    Traditionally, this distinction has been analyzed in terms of Vs (Talmy 1975, 1985): In V-framed languages manner Vs are not compatible with path obliques, while in S-framed languages they are. However, an alternative view is that this contrast instead reflects cross-linguistic, motion-independent variation of (among other things) inventories of Ps (Beavers, Levin, and Wei 2008; Folli and Ramchand 2002; Talmy 2000; Son 2007). For example, in S-framed languages, path/goal Ps (e.g., *[in]to*) often have very general uses, even occurring with Vs that do not inherently select for them:

(9) a. John crossed to the other side of the river. (V implies motion to a goal)

    b. John walked/ran/promenaded (in)to the

       store.   (V implies motion but no goal)

    c. Ted scrubbed/polished his shoes to a

       healthy shine.   (V implies process to a result)

    d. James rubbed the finish to a dull luster. (V implies process but no result)

    Thus these Ps are more like semantic allative Ps. If the V does not entail a goal/result as in (9b) and (9d) the oblique adjunctively contributes this semantics, while if the V does entail a goal/result as in (9a) and (9c) the oblique further specifies it. Conversely, in V-framed languages, goals/results are marked by dative/locative Ps [*dans*, "in" in (8b)], but only when the V selects for a goal/result. They may not occur adjunctively on these readings. This is illustrated in (10) for Japanese *-ni*, which has a range of uses marking arguments of Vs (e.g., causees in derived causatives, logical subjects of passives, recipients of ditransitives; Kuno 1973; Sadakane and Koizumi 1995) but not adjuncts:

(10) a. *John-wa eki-ni   itta/modotta/?(?)hashitta/??aruita.*

     John-TOP station-to went/went-up/ran/walked

     "John went (up)/walked/ran to the station."   (Entailed vs. nonentailed goal)

    b. *Mary-ga   doresu-o pinku-ni someta.*

     Mary-NOM dress-ACC pink-DAT dyed

     "Mary dyed the dress pink."   [Entailed result; Washio 1997, 5, (13b)]

    c. *John-ga   kinzoku-o   petyanko-ni tataita.

       John-NOM metal-ACC flat-DAT   pounded

       "John pounded the metal flat."   [Nonentailed result; Washio 1997, 5, (16b)]

Thus distributionally -*ni* is not comparable to *to*, and this is so for other putative goal/path Ps in V-framed languages (Beavers, Levin, and Tham 2008). Instead, -*ni* is more akin to a dative than an allative, marking nonnominative, nonaccusative verbal arguments, that is, something entailed to exist and possibly directly subcategorized for by the V. So the V/S-framed distinction may derive not from differences in V inventories but differences in P inventories: S-framed languages have allative Ps, and V-framed languages do not. The lack of allative Ps in turn follows from the more general lack of secondary predication in most V-framed languages, whereas V-framed languages tend to lack productive resultative constructions altogether, including adjectival or adpositional resultatives (see Aske 1989, on Spanish; and Washio 1997, on Japanese; although see Son 2007). Thus while the absence of an abstrument P in Japanese may be just a lexical quirk, the absence of the class of allative Ps in V-framed languages ties in to a much broader typological parameter, with the result that certain ways of realizing an entire class of arguments is disallowed.

However, there is a curious and very telling exception to the generalization that V-framed languages disallow S-framed encoding, but one that conforms to and supports the OSP. It is seldom noted that V-framed languages often *do* have one P that can realize goals with manner Vs, namely the P meaning "until." This is shown in (11) for the Japanese P -*made* (similar data is attested in other V-framed languages, including Spanish, French, and Turkish; Beavers 2008).

(11) *John-wa   kishi-made/*ni oyoida/tadayotta.*

     John-TOP shore-until/to swam/drifted

     "John swam/drifted to the shore."   [Japanese; Beavers 2008, 284, (1b)]

Until-markers are of course not unique to motion constructions but have a range of uses for marking temporal and numerical boundaries:

(12) a. *Ohiru-made kore-o   shite-kudasai.*

       noon-until   this-ACC do-please

       "Please do this until noon."

     b. *Yuka-kara yane-made nan-meetoru   arimasu ka?*

       floor-from roof-until how-many-meters are   QUES

       "How many meters from the floor to the roof?"

                            [Kuno 1973, 108–10, (1a), (6)]

Beavers (2008) analyzes such markers as delimiter, adjunctively predicating an endpoint on some participant in the event/state. A goal of motion, however, is crucially just the endpoint of a path of motion. Thus what -*made* is doing in (11) is predicating the endpoint of the path, which has the indirect effect of specifying what the goal of motion is. More crucially, *until*-markers also show up with path verbs, which select for a goal argument, exactly as expected by the OSP:

(13) *John-wa   eki-made/ni   itta/modotta.*
    John-TOP station-until/to went/went-up
    "John went/went up to the station."   [Beavers, 2008, 284, (1a)]

Note that *until* in English is rarely acceptable as a goal marker (cf. #*John walked until the store*). This is not a counterexample to the OSP, as it is not a sufficiency condition. But in this case there is a simple explanation: English, an S-framed language, has a host of specific goal-marking Ps that presumably block the use of the far more general *until*. Thus what we see is that the independent presence of a compatible P in V-framed languages opens up the possibility of otherwise disallowed realization options, something such languages can exploit to get around the absence of allative Ps in a way consistent with the OSP.

Dative Alternations

Following on the goal-marking use of *to*, English allows a dative alternation in which a recipient may be realized either as the first object of a ditransitive V or as a *to*-oblique:

(14) a. Kim gave/sent/tossed *Sandy* the ball.
    b. Kim gave/sent/tossed the ball *to Sandy.*

As has long been noted, there are often information structural constraints on the alternation, where the element that comes first tends to be more topical (Wasow 2002). There is also an interesting semantic effect in this alternation. The first object must be capable of possession, whereas the corresponding *to*-oblique may be interpreted as a (purely locational) goal. This is demonstrated in (15), where inanimate London cannot be a first object unless it is interpreted as capable of possession, for example, "the London Office" (Beavers 2006a, 188; Green 1974, 103–4).

(15) a. #John sent London a letter.   (OK on "London Office" reading)
    b. John sent a letter to London.   (OK on "London Office" or goal reading)

Note that the relevant notion is the *capability* of possession, not actual possession, which is often (though not always) an implicature, for example, *John sent Mary a letter, but it never arrived.* Other languages have similar alternations. In German the contrast is between a dative DP and a DP marked by some allative P such as *zu* or *nach,* "to," whereas in Greek the relevant contrast is between agenitive (or accusative) DP and an oblique marked by a goal-marking P *se* (Anagnostopoulou 2003). The general shape of the alternation is always between direct and oblique realization, however manifested in a given language. However, not all languages allow both variants. For example, in Finnish the typical way to realize a goal/recipient argument of a ditransitive V is with the allative case; there is no dative in Finnish, nor is there genitive object or double object constructions (Kaiser 2002):

(16) *Minä   annoin miehelle   kirjan.*
    I.NOM gave   man.ALL book.ACC
    "I gave the man a book."   [Finnish; Kaiser 2002, (4b)]

Conversely, in Japanese the goal/recipient must be realized by dative *-ni;* as noted earlier there is no allative in Japanese, following from the more general lack of secondary predication:

(17) *Masao-ga   Akira/Tokyo-ni   syasin-o   okutta.*

Masao-NOM Akira/Tokyo-DAT picture-ACC sent

"Masao sent a picture to Akira/Tokyo." [Japanese; cf. Beavers 2006a, 189, (11)]

In each case the lack of a variant corresponds to the independent absence of some class of Ps in the language. Interestingly, the information structural and semantic functionality of dative alternations is accomplished through other means in these languages. For example, in both languages the relatively free word order encodes the relative topicality of the theme and goal/recipient arguments rather than a morphological alternation (see Kaiser 2002, on Finnish; and Miyagawa and Tsujioka 2004, on Japanese). For the semantic contrast the data are more complicated but very telling. Both Finnish and Japanese in fact *do* have alternations of sorts, of a different form than English or German, yet consistent with the P and structural case inventories of each language. In Finnish a goal can also be realized in the illative "into" case:

(18) *Minä   lähetin kirjan   Suomeen.*

I-NOM sent book-ACC Finland.ILLAT

"I sent a/the book to Finland."   [Finnish; Kaiser 2002, (a), fn.2]

In general the allative encodes capability of possession while the illative is appropriate for locations, mirroring the first object/oblique contrast in English (Paul Kiparsky, Elsi Kaiser, p.c.). However, the allative/illative contrast differs from the English contrast in that it is an oblique/oblique contrast, though one that is consistent with the presence in Finnish of a great number of locational semantic cases, some of which are compatible with the semantics selected for by ditransitive verbs.

In Japanese a similar effect can be observed through an interesting contrast in the relative obliqueness of *-ni* in different contexts. The contrast between structural and oblique Ps in Japanese can be probed through a variety of means (see Sadakane and Koizumi 1995), including their variable behavior under the topic-marking P *-wa.* When a nonoblique argument is *-wa* marked, the corresponding structural case (i.e., nominative *-ga* or accusative *-o*) is deleted and replaced by *-wa* as in (19a). But when an oblique is *-wa* marked, the P may not be dropped (Beavers 2006a, 190–91, and 2008, 304–5). Interestingly, if we *-wa* mark the *-ni* marked recipients in (17) as in (19b), dropping *-ni* is optional, but when it is dropped the "London Office" effect obtains as in the following:

(19) a. *John-wa   eki-ni   itta.*

John-TOP station-to went

"As for John, he went to the station." (*-ga* deleted under topic-marking *-wa*)

b. *Tokyo-ni-wa/#Tokyo-wa   Masao-ga   syasin-o   okutta.*

Tokyo-DAT-TOP/Tokyo-TOP Masao-NOM picture-ACC send

"As for Tokyo, Masao sent a picture to it/#sent it a picture."   (OK on "Tokyo Office" reading)

This suggests that -*ni* can be more or less oblique in this construction, forming an alternation quite similar to the dative alternation (see also Miyagawa and Tsujioka 2004; and Sadakane and Koizumi 1995), though whether this corresponds to two different -*ni* morphemes or one polysemous morpheme is a murkier question.

However, there is one potential problem. So far I have claimed that recipients are a more specific type of goal (and thus may be realized by goal-marking Ps), and goals are a more specific type of limit (and thus may be realized by limit marking *until*-markers). Thus by the OSP we should expect that recipients can be realized by *until*-markers. As far as I am aware no language marks recipients with an *until*-marker, contrary to this prediction. This is not a counterexample to the OSP per se, as again the OSP is not a sufficiency condition. It could simply be that no language has taken up this option. However, I suggest that this is ruled out on more principled grounds. As discussed in Beavers (2008), *until*-markers mostly occur with durative predicates, while Beavers (2006a, 2006b) note that nearly all ditransitives (in English at any rate) allow only punctual readings. If this is the case, the absence of ditransitive + *until* combinations may be due to independent semantic incompatibility. Tellingly, however, Danish *til,* "to," historically connected to *until,* is used in *both* allative/dative and *until* contexts (Allan, Holmes, and Lundskær-Nielsen 1995, 420–25), with both punctual and durative readings, suggesting the validity of the correlation between *until*-markers and allative Ps.

The Case of Default Ps

Another potential problem involves so-called default Ps that mark arguments of heads that are unable to check/assign Case (Chomsky 1981, 49ff). The most common candidate is English *of,* which marks complements of nouns (e.g., *the founding of Rome*) and adjectives (e.g., *fond of Kim*), traditionally thought of as unable to assign Case, as well as complements of certain Ps (e.g., *off of the rock*) and Vs (e.g., *spoke of him*). Default Ps are presumably meaningless (because in principle they can mark *any* Caseless argument), and thus any argument of any V could be realized by this P according to the OSP. This predicts that we might expect a wide range of direct argument/default P alternations, as well as arguments in canonical Caseless positions (e.g., internal arguments of unaccusatives and passivized verbs) being realized via default Ps. For example, in addition to *The vase broke,* where *the vase* merges first as a sister to V and then raises to [Spec,TP] to check Case and the EPP feature on tense (T), we might expect to find something like **It was broken of the vase,* where *of* is inserted to check Case for the vase and an expletive is inserted to check the extended projection principle (EPP) feature of T. However, we do not find such examples, and they are conspicuous in their absence.

I suggest here a simple explanation for this: Default Ps do not exist, at least not in the verbal domain (following Beavers 2005 on argument/oblique alternations). Crucially, all uses of *of* in the verbal domain correspond to a very limited set of thematic roles (as a glance through the *Oxford English Dictionary* suggests), including abstruments and sources [as shown in (5) and (6)], material/topic of discussion (e.g., *I wrote of/about him, I was notified of/about his plans*), and basis of comparison (e.g., *This soup tastes of/like mutton, He reminds me of a peacock*). This suggests that while *of* is a few ways polysemous in the verbal domain, it is not semantically vacuous (and therefore **It was broken of the vase*, even if grammatical, could not mean *The vase was broken*). As much as it is a default in the (ad)nominal domain, it is essentially a direct argument marker (nonverbal objective case) and thus is not subject to the OSP. The use of *of* to mark complements of Ps seems primarily restricted to a small class of spatial Ps [e.g., *off (of) the table, out (of) the house*] and might best be viewed as a remnant of a re-analysis of such Ps from earlier status as adverbs/particles (which do not assign/check case). Thus there does not appear to be any evidence for a truly default P in English in the verbal domain, and I am not aware of any such evidence in other languages.

Conclusion

Both V and P assign thematic roles to oblique arguments, but they are constrained by the OSP, which enforces semantic compatibility between them. This predicts not just which V + P combinations will surface in a language but also that certain combinations possible in one language will be impossible in another due to the absence of the appropriate P, a factor that may in turn be reducible to independent typological properties of a given language. What is crucial, therefore, is that the relevant P or class of Ps has a semantics that can be independently identified across a range of constructions. Of course, the evidence presented here is tentative; future work will involve a more systematic view of a range of oblique realization options/inventories across languages.

REFERENCES

Allan, Robin, Philip Holmes, and Tom Lundskær-Nielsen. 1995. *Danish: A comprehensive grammar.* London: Routledge.

Anagnostopoulou, Elena. 2003. *The syntax of ditransitives: Evidence from clitics.* Berlin: Mouton.

Aske, John. 1989. Path predicates in English and Spanish: A closer look. *Proceedings of the Berkeley Linguistics Society* 15:1–14.

Beavers, John. 2005. A semantic analysis of argument/oblique alternations in HPSG. In *HPSG 2005,* ed. Stefan Müller, 28–48. Stanford, CA: CSLI Publications.

———. 2006a. *Argument/oblique alternations and the structure of lexical meaning.* PhD diss., Stanford University.

———. 2006b. The aspectual behavior of ditransitives in English. Talk given at the 80th annual meeting of the LSA, Albuquerque, NM, January 5.

———. 2008. On the nature of goal marking and delimitation: Evidence from Japanese. *Journal of Linguistics* 44:283–316.

Beavers, John, Beth Levin, and Tham Shiao Wei. 2007. The typology of motion events revisited. Unpublished ms.

Chomsky, Noam. 1981. *Lectures on government and binding.* Dordrecht: Foris.

Croft, William. 1991. *Syntactic categories and grammatical relations: The cognitive organization of information.* Chicago: University of Chicago Press.

Folli, Raffaella, and Heidi Harley. 2004. Consuming results: Flavours of little-*v.* In *Aspectual enquiries,* ed. Paula Kempchinsky and Roumyana Slabakova, 1–25. Dordrecht: Kluwer.

Folli, Raffaella, and Gillian Ramchand. 2002. Event structure composition: The case of goal of motion and resultative constructions in Italian and Scottish Gaelic. In *Proceedings of Perspectives on Aspect Conference,* ed. Henk J. Verkuyl, 81–106. Utrecht: OTS.

Gawron, Jean Mark. 1986. Situations and prepositions. *Linguistics and Philosophy* 9:327–82.

Green, Georgia. 1974. *Semantic and syntactic regularity.* Bloomington: Indiana University Press.

Hale, Ken, and Samuel J. Keyser. 1993. On argument structure and the lexical expression of syntactic relations. In *The view from building 20: Essays in linguistics in honor of Sylvain Bromberger,* ed. Ken Hale and Samuel J. Keyser, 53–109. Cambridge, MA: MIT Press.

Harley, Heidi. 2005. How do verbs get their names? Denominal verbs, manner incorporation, and the ontology of verb roots in English. In *The syntax of aspect,* ed. Nomi Erteschik-Shir and Tova Rapoport, 42–64. Oxford: Oxford University Press.

Hook, Peter. 1983. The English abstrument and rocking case relations. In *Papers from the nineteenth regional meeting,* 183–94. Chicago: Chicago Linguistics Society.

Kageyama, Taro. 1980. The role of thematic relations in the *spray paint* hypallage. *Papers in Japanese Linguistics* 7:35–64.

Kaiser, Elsi. 2002. The syntax-pragmatics interface and Finnish ditransitive verbs. In *ConSOLE IX,* ed. Mario van Koppen, Erica Thrift, Erik van der Torre, and Malte Zimmermann, www.sole.leidenuniv .nl/index.php3?m=14&c=6 (accessed October 12, 2008).

Kuno, Susumu. 1973. *The structure of the Japanese language.* Cambridge, MA: MIT Press.

Miyagawa, Shigeru, and Takae Tsujioka. 2004. Argument structure and ditransitive verbs in Japanese. *Journal of East Asian Linguistics* 13:1–38.

Sadakane, Kumi, and Masatoshi Koizumi. 1995. On the nature of the "dative" particle *ni* in Japanese. *Linguistics* 33:5–33.

Son, Minjeong. 2007. Event (de-)composition of directed motion in Korean and English. Talk given at GURT 2007, Georgetown University, March 9.

Talmy, Leonard. 1975. Semantics and syntax of motion. In *Syntax and semantics,* vol. 4, ed. J. P. Kimball, 181–238. New York: Academic Press.

———. 1985. Lexicalization patterns: Semantic structure in lexical forms. In *Grammatical categories and the lexicon,* ed. Timothy Shopen, 57–149. New York: Cambridge University Press.

———. 2000. *Toward a cognitive semantics: Typology and process in concept structuring.* Cambridge, MA: MIT Press.

Washio, Ryuichi. 1997. Resultatives, compositionality, and language variation. *Journal of East Asian Linguistics* 6:1–49.

Wasow, Thomas. 2002. *Postverbal behavior.* Stanford, CA: CSLI Publications.

Wechsler, Stephen. 1995. *The semantic basis of argument structure.* Stanford, CA: CSLI Publications.

12

Aspect Selectors, Scales, and Contextual Operators: An Analysis of *by* Temporal Adjuncts

MICHAEL F. THOMAS AND LAURA A. MICHAELIS
University of Colorado at Boulder

MANY TEMPORAL ADJUNCTS select for specific aspectual classes; these adjuncts include measure adverbials such as *for an hour* and interval adverbials such as *in an hour*. While such adjuncts have traditionally served as diagnostics of telicity, it is only relatively recently that aspectual theorists have elucidated the relationship between the scalar-semantic meanings of these adjuncts and the internal structure of the event representations to which they apply (see Dowty 1979; Herweg 1991; Krifka 1998, among others). Krifka (1998) proposes that both measure adverbials and interval adverbials operate on representations that involve motion along a path. It seems entirely plausible that these adverbials should have path-based meanings, as they concern the "run times" of processes. It is less clear whether path schemas can be applied to the semantics of aspectually sensitive temporal adverbs in general, and particularly those that denote time points. One such adverbial is the *by* time adverbial (BTA), which will be the focus of our attention in this chapter. An example of the BTA is given in (1):

(1) But at least Burger King has signed on, and says that *by year end* it won't be
    using any shell eggs.   (*Wall Street Journal*)

In (1), the year's end represents a point at which a state (absence of shell eggs) is subject to verification. In the semantic analysis that we propose here, the BTA resembles another aspectually sensitive temporal adverb, *still* (Michaelis 1993). Both adverbial types have apparently paradoxical behavior: They denote time points but have interval-based semantics. The paradox disappears when we assume that the BTA, like adverbial *still,* denotes a point and presupposes an interval, specifically, a path schema. In the case of the BTA in particular, we will argue, these path schemas represent conventional sequences of development, for example, schedules. We will use corpus data to survey the variety of discourse contexts in which such sequences are invoked. In this way we further substantiate Krifka's claim that aspectual meaning involves path structures that represent both movement through space and qualitative changes in entities over time.

We explore patterns of BTA use by examining tokens from the *Wall Street Journal* (WSJ) corpus (Marcus, Santorini, and Marcinkiewicz 1993).[1] One fact that is initially puzzling about the corpus data is that while, for example, English pedagogical grammars (Fuchs and Bonner 2006, 32–40; Van Zante et al. 2000, 65) focus on its use in past-perfect predications, perfect-form predications, as in (2), account for only 4 percent of the BTA tokens in the WSJ:

(2) Baron Elie de Rothschild, the family's elder spokesman, explains that *by the end of the 19th century,* Berlin had replaced Frankfurt as Germany's financial center.   (WSJ)

Other contexts in which BTAs occurred are as follows. Seven percent occurred in simple past-tense predications, both stative and dynamic, as in (3) and (4), respectively:

(3) The airports in San Jose and Oakland were both fully operational *by noon* yesterday, the Federal Aviation Administration said.   (WSJ)

(4) And *by late Friday afternoon,* actually after the close, we decided that was the wrong tone to take.   (WSJ)

Two percent occurred in past-tense progressive predications, as in (5):

(5) Japanese stocks dropped early Monday, but *by late morning* were turning around.   (WSJ)

Sixteen percent occurred in gerunds and event nominals, as in (6) and (7), respectively:

(6) Some projections show Mexico importing crude *by the end of the century.*   (WSJ)

(7) Mr. Ehrlich predicted unprecedented famine *by 1980.*   (WSJ)

Thirty-six percent occurred in *to*-marked infinitival complements, as in (8):

(8) Hughes said it expects the sale to close *by year end.*   (WSJ)

Finally, 31 percent occurred in complements of modal verbs, including *will,* as in (1). Such examples raise three questions. First, how can we reconcile the BTA's apparently wide combinatoric potential with the presumption that it selects for a specific aspectual class? Second, what accounts for the prevalence of modal and infinitival predications, as in (1) and (8), respectively, which collectively account for 67 percent of the BTA tokens? Third, why should an author ever use a BTA when there are more specific forms of time reference available, in particular, adverbial expressions such as *on Monday* or *in the afternoon*? We will argue that adequate answers to these questions require reference to lexical and grammatical aspect (Bickel 1997), frame semantics (Fillmore 1985), pragmatic scales (Kay 1990), and coercion (De Swart 1998). We claim that the BTA takes a state predication as its argument and that it denotes a sampling point located just after the potential or actual inception of this state. Further, we propose, this state is understood in relation to a contextually evoked path schema, construed as either a schedule or a natural course of development. As a consequence, we suggest, BTAs are contextual operators, in the sense of Kay (1997).

The remainder of this study is structured as follows. In the first section we discuss the sense of *by* at issue here. The second section discuss the usage patterns that reference and pedagogical grammars predict for BTAs and how the corpus data fail to conform to those predictions. In the third section we propose that BTAs select for the class of states. The fourth section shows that we can assimilate apparently nonstative BTA tokens to stative examples by regarding them as cases of stative coercion. In the fifth section we argue that BTAs are discourse-indexical expressions, insofar as they induce the interpreter to retrieve an event sequence or schedule that includes the denoted state. The last section contains brief concluding remarks.

Which Sense of *by*?

The second edition of the *Oxford English Dictionary* (OED) lists thirty-nine adverbial senses of the preposition *by*. The sense of interest here is the twentieth sense, in which *by* takes a nominal denoting a time point as its argument and the resulting prepositional phrase (PP) means "no later than." This sense is distinct from that listed as the seventeenth sense of *by* in the OED, in which the *by*-phrase indicates "extent," as in (9):

(9) In point of fact, this catharsis was overdue *by decades.*   (WSJ)

In (9), the *by*-headed PP indicates degree of difference, just as the measure expressions *two inches* and *five dollars* do in the comparative expressions *two inches taller* and *five dollars cheaper.* As it happens, the *by*-headed PP in (9) was erroneously given the part-of-speech tag PP-TMP by a Treebank II tagger rather than the appropriate tag, PP-EXT. This error is understandable, as in both cases the complement of *by* is a time expression, but on closer inspection it is obvious that the two *by*-adverbials not only have distinct types of complement daughters (time-point noun phrases [NPs] in the case of BTAs and coextensive-measure NPs in the case of *by*-adverbials of extent) but also combine with different types of predicates: Extent-measure *by*-adverbials combine with "predicates of surpassing," for example, comparative adjectives, whereas BTAs do not.

How Are BTAs Used?

As mentioned earlier, pedagogical grammars tend to associate the BTA with the past-perfect construction. Certainly, the BTA and the past perfect interact in a transparent and compositional way: Assuming the Reichenbachian representation of the past perfect (Reichenbach 1947; Hornstein 1990), one would say that the BTA marks the R point (reference time) that follows an E point (event time). But the use of a past-perfect predication is neither a necessary nor sufficient condition for BTA use. That it is not necessary is shown by the fact that of 315 BTA tokens examined, only 12 were found in perfect-form predications. That it is not sufficient is shown by the fact that there are otherwise acceptable past-perfect sentences that do not welcome BTAs. One such sentence is the attested (10), found in a Google search. The past perfect in this example is a continuative perfect: The sentence asserts the existence of a state phase (that of unwillingness) whose terminus is 1983:

(10) Until 1983, France . . . had been unwilling to extradite ETA members to Spain.
(Google)

If we replace the time adverbial *until 1983* with a comparable BTA, the result is anomaly, as shown by (10'):

(10') *By 1983, France had been unwilling to extradite ETA members to Spain.

Why is (10') anomalous? The reference grammars give some clues. Quirk et al. (1985, 692) describe BTAs as expressing "the time at which the result of an event is in existence." If BTAs mark resultant states, then we can easily explain the anomaly in (10') by observing that the state of unwillingness is not resultant state and that it therefore does not satisfy the BTA. At the same time, however, resultant states cannot be the whole story. As mentioned in the previous section, a plurality (36%) of BTA tokens appear in infinitival complements. Further, in the vast majority of such cases, these infinitival clauses are complements of control and raising verbs that presuppose a desired or expected event, for example, *require, order, want, hope, expect,* and *plan.* An additional trend suggesting a close association between the BTA and futurity is that involving modal verbs. As mentioned in the previous section, the second largest group of BTA tokens consists of those with modal head verbs, as in (11) and (12):

(11) That should happen *by today,* he said.   (WSJ)

(12) Then it turned up, and by one estimate the number will be up to about 109,000
regulators *by next year.*   (WSJ)

Thus it would appear that BTAs select states that are not only resultant states but also desired or predicted states. The latter condition is in fact captured by Huddleston and Pullum's (2002, 655) characterization of BTAs as coding "time deadlines." The fact that many BTA tokens express literal deadlines seems to validate this characterization:

(13) He said Chrysler fully expects to have them installed across its light-truck line
by the Sept. 1, 1991, deadline.   (WSJ)

(14) Mr. Bush has called for an agreement *by next September* at the latest.   (WSJ)

Frequently, however, it is difficult to characterize the BTA as denoting a deadline. In (15), for example, the BTA appears instead to encode the final state of a process of accretion:

(15) Some atmospheric scientists think that even if CFCs were released into the
atmosphere at an accelerating rate, the amount of ozone depletion would be
only 10% *by the middle of the next century.*   (WSJ)

That state of ozone depletion is not one subject to direct human control; thus it seems inaccurate to characterize *the middle of the next century* as a deadline. While it might be accurate to characterize it instead as a point at which the state in question is expected (by atmospheric scientists) to be in force, the expectations of the participants described play a limited role in examples like (16) through (18):

(16) The incentives boosted sales for a while, but the pace had cooled *by last month.* (WSJ)

(17) *By the early 1980s,* its glory had faded like the yellow bricks of its broad façade. (WSJ)

(18) Shearson Lehman Hutton Inc. *by yesterday afternoon* had already written new TV ads. (WSJ)

In (16) through (18), the BTAs appear to denote author-selected rather than participant-selected sampling points. For example, *last month* and *the early 1980s* in (16) through (17), respectively, are mentioned simply because they are reference times that are relevant to the narratives in question, not because anyone is aiming to ensure that the denoted states (slow sales, faded glory) are in force at those times. Further, while in (18) Shearson Lehman Hutton Inc. might have intended to have new TV ads at the time described as *yesterday afternoon,* they need not have so intended: Yesterday afternoon is the author's sampling point and not necessarily a time that figured in any participant's planning. Such sampling points have a retrospective quality to them in that they are located within a state of aftermath following the occurrence of an event or event series; this state of aftermath is that denoted by perfect-form predications, whether they are existential perfects, as in (16), or resultative perfects, as in (17) through (18) (Herweg 1991; Michaelis 2004). However, the BTA sample is not necessarily taken after the fact, as shown by (19) through (21):

(19) U.S. oil supplies, however, had peaked in 1970 and 1971 and *by 1973* were declining. (WSJ)

(20) Stunned, Mr. Breeden turned to his market-monitoring computer, which *by then* was next to his desk. (WSJ)

(21) And *by the early 1980s* U.S. capitalists had ample reason to welcome junk bonds, to look the other way. (WSJ)

In (19) through (21), the BTA denotes a point located within, rather than subsequent to, a process (19) or state [(20) through (21)]. Thus a BTA need not select a state of aftermath. In addition, as we have seen, the BTA need not denote a time point that figured in any participant's schedule. Instead, we propose, the BTA denotes the first point at which some observer—whether the author or a participant—got, expects to get, or hopes to get a positive answer to the question *Is state x in force?*

BTAs as State Selectors

In describing the truth conditions on English progressive predications, Dowty (1977) proposes the "bet test," a version of which runs as follows. Say that I wager with a friend that at midnight it will be snowing, and we later find out that midnight was the *first* moment at which it was snowing. Have I won my bet? For Dowty, the answer is no, because the semantics of the progressive require reference time to be located *during* the process denoted by its gerundial complement. The same "noninitial moment" condition appears to apply to BTAs, but because of the deontic nature of many BTA uses, it seems fitting to replace the bet with a curfew in the test scenario. Say, for example, that a soldier is ordered to be back on base by midnight and at midnight is seen returning to base. Has the soldier violated curfew? We believe that the answer is yes. Thus what the progressive construction and the BTA have in common is that both constructions locate reference time within the situation denoted by the lexical verb, prohibiting reference time from being the *first* moment of that situation. And in both cases, we submit, this constraint follows from a central property of state predications: States include the reference times for which they are asserted to hold (Partee 1984).

The progressive and the BTA differ in that the former is a *stativizer,* while the latter is a *state selector.* What does it mean to call the progressive a stativizer? Following De Swart (1998) and Herweg (1991), we assume that the progressive shifts dynamic eventualities to states. This characterization is supported by the fact that progressive predications pass numerous stativity diagnostics, including various tests involving temporal overlap (Michaelis 2004). The same can be said of perfect predications, and thus we assume that the perfect denotes a state—that state which follows the occurrence of the event denoted by the participial complement (Herweg 1991; Michaelis 2004).

If the BTA is a state selector, then it stands to reason that it should combine with progressive predications, as in (19), perfect predications [(16) through (18)], and simplex state predications [(20) through (21)]. But one puzzle remains: Why should the BTA combine with verbs that neither denote states nor have undergone stativization? Three such combinations are exemplified in (22) through (24):

(22) A slight recovery in the stock market gave currency traders confidence to push
     the dollar higher before the unit dropped back *by day's end.*   (WSJ)

(23) The big futures buying triggered stock-index buy programs that eventually
     trimmed the Dow's loss to 31 points *by 11 a.m.*   (WSJ)

(24) That index . . . gained 17.97 % *by Sept. 30 this year.*   (WSJ)

In (22) through (24), BTAs modify the perfective predicates *drop back, trim,* and *gain,* respectively. If the BTA is in fact a state selector we would expect that the verb forms in question would be past-perfect forms (e.g., *had dropped*) or perhaps progressive forms (e.g., *was dropping*). A similar problem is raised by the infinitival complements that collectively account for the majority of BTA tokens in the WSJ corpus: These tend to be perfective predicates, as in (11): *That should happen by today.* What then allows for the appearance of nonstativized perfective verbs in clauses containing BTAs? A clue is provided by *after*-clauses. In *after*-clauses such as that in (25), the past-perfect and simple-past forms are free variants:

(25) After she (had) caught sight of him, she crossed the street.

In temporal discourse, an *after*-clause establishes an interval during which the main clause event takes place, but in order to do so, the *after*-clause must encode a state, because only a state can overlap a next-mentioned event. Thus the *after*-clause in (25) denotes a state that starts at a time just after the time of the event of her catching sight of him. In other words, when *after* combines with a dynamic verb like *catch sight of,* that verb expresses the initiating event of the *after*-clause state. A similar analysis can be applied to the perfective BTA examples in (22) through (24). In the case of (24), for example, the combination of a perfective verb and the BTA induces the interpreter to recover a state that starts just after the time at which the index gained 17.97 percent. The time point expressed by *Sept. 30 this year* is then understood as located within this inferred state. In the next section, we discuss the mechanism by which such inferences take place, coercion, and discuss the evidence that supports our contention that BTAs are stative coercion triggers.

Coercion

Coercion effects are semantic enrichments that interpreters perform in order to resolve conflict between the semantic type selected for by a given operator (construction) and the semantic type expressed by the lexical item with which that operator has combined in a given context (De Swart 1998; Jackendoff 1997, chap. 3). Coercion is an interpretive procedure that like presupposition is triggered by linguistic form. Via coercion, all aspectual-class selectors are also potential aspectual-class shifters. Examples of coercion include those in which event-denoting predicates are interpreted as states and vice versa. For example, the state predication *I knew the answer* receives an inceptive-event reading in combination with the event-selecting adverbial *suddenly* (De Swart 1998, 359). Conversely, as argued by Michaelis (1996, 2004), the event verb *eat* gets a resultant-state reading in combination with the state-selecting adverbial *already* in (26). Compare the preterite-form sentence with (27), in which a stativizing construction, the perfect, compositionally yields the stative type sought by *already,* and no coercion is required:

(26) I already ate. (coerced state)

(27) I've already eaten. (compositionally derived state)

We propose that perfective predications containing BTAs, whether they are tensed, as in (22) through (24), or tenseless, as in imperatives and infinitival complements, have coerced resultant-state interpretations identical to that in (26). This proposal unifies BTA uses that otherwise require distinct analyses: BTAs in stative predications, progressive predications, perfect predications, and perfective predications, both tensed and infinitival. In addition to this argument from parsimony, there is linguistic evidence that supports the stative coercion proposal. This evidence comes from constraints on present-time adverbial reference in simple-past tense perfective predications, as illustrated in (28) through (29):

(28) You probably already heard this *(*by) now.* I found out earlier this afternoon.

(Google)

(29) If you're a frequent reader, you probably noticed *(*by) now* that I'm a
    passionate guy.   (Google)

The grammaticality contrasts in (28) through (29) show that the BTA *by now* does something that the adverb *now* by itself would not: It imposes a present-perfect reading on a predication that would otherwise have a past-tense perfective reading. This present-perfect reading shifts reference time to the present, thereby allowing for present-time adverbial reference. If we presume that the BTA is a state selector, we can explain why (28) through (29) have present-perfect readings when the BTA *by now* is present, but not otherwise: The BTA selects for a resultant state, and when such a state is lacking in the verb's Aktionsart representation, the interpreter adds one in the interest of semantic-conflict resolution.

BTAs as Contextual Operators

We have already addressed the first of the three questions we raised in the introduction: How can we reconcile the apparently wide combinatoric potential of the BTA with the claim that it is a state selector? Our answer is that the BTA is not only a state selector but also a stative coercion trigger. In this section, we address the second and third questions: What accounts for the strong association between the BTA and futurate (modal and other infinitival) contexts? Why do speakers use BTAs when time-denoting PPs headed by *at* provide more precise temporal specifications and are equally compatible with state predications? As a first step toward answering these questions, let us consider the contrast in (30) and (31):

(30) At midnight, I was lying on the couch.

(31) By midnight, I was lying on the couch.

While both (30) and (31) assert that a state held at midnight, only (31) requires us to view that state as one of a series of causally connected states. Thus, we propose that a BTA instructs the interpreter to map the denoted state to a point on a canonical time scale. This point is the first feasible sampling point described in the third section. By *canonical* we mean whatever granularity of intervals the situation requires (e.g., days, hours, etc). These intervals are associated with situations, each of which represents a stage within an event series. The event-series characterization applies even in cases of deontic meaning such as imperatives, for example, *Be home by midnight.* What is the event series in this case? It could be the process that culminates in return to one's point of origin, which might entail, for example, hailing a cab at 11:30 PM, or a sequence of hypothetical returns by the addressee, each of which occurs at a different time prior to midnight. In either case, midnight represents a first feasible sampling point for the state of being at home. Of course, the speaker who uses the imperative *Be home by midnight* intends not merely to observe the time of return but also to influence it. Because tracking emergent states of affairs generally subserves planning, it stands to reason that futurate predications, both modal and desiderative, should be prevalent in the BTA data.

The sampling point denoted by a BTA might be one that, in the speaker's view, is seen by most as infeasible (i.e., unlikely to yield a positive result for the state in question). Thus one potential implicature of an assertion containing a BTA is that the state is early with respect to some canonical developmental sequence. This is shown by the following sentences, the latter of which comes from the Switchboard corpus of conversational English (Godrey, Holliman, and McDaniel 1992):

(32) But while traffic was heavy early in the commute over the Golden Gate, *by 8 a.m.* it already had thinned out.   (WSJ)

(33) Speaker A: Well then, it will be mostly reruns, I guess.

Speaker B: And *by the end of February,* the way they do it nowadays.

(Switchboard)

As indicated by his use of *already,* the author of (32) believes that his readers will be surprised to learn that Golden Gate Bridge traffic is light at 8 AM. Whether or not they actually are, they will interpret (32) against a frame in which states of traffic density are associated with times of day. In (33) Speaker B asserts that, perhaps contrary to the expectations of Speaker A, February is a point at which a television viewer will find programming that consists largely of reruns. Again, whether or not February strikes Speaker A as an early eventuation point for this state of affairs, she must still assess (33) against a canonical developmental sequence—in this case, one involving the broadcast industry's normal patterns of program production. Both commuting and television broadcasting cycles are frames, in the sense of Fillmore (1985), that enable the interpreters of these sentences to evaluate them against the appropriate developmental sequences.

In light of these findings, we propose that BTAs belong to the class as *contextual operators,* as described by Kay (1990, 1997). These are lexical items and grammatical constructions whose "semantic value consists, at least in part, of instructions to find in the context a certain kind of information structure and place the information presented by the sentence within that information structure" (Kay 1997, 159). Examples of contextual operators include *even,* which instructs the hearer to interpret the asserted proposition as an extreme case along a scale of eventualities (Kay 1990); *already,* which instructs the hearer to interpret the denoted state as one that holds prior to the inception of a process that typically brings it about (Michaelis 1996); and *let alone,* which instructs the hearer to interpret the asserted proposition as more informative than a contextually given proposition within a scalar model (Fillmore, Kay, and O'Connor 1988).

Kay (1990) argues that one can regard the meanings of contextual operators as conventional implicatures, insofar as they do not alter truth conditions. For example, as Kay points out, appending *even* to the front of the sentence *John swims in winter* does not change its truth conditions but rather instructs the hearer to evaluate the proposition against a scalar model of likely swimmers and place the argument "John" at the low end of this scale (Kay 1990, 53–56). It is debatable whether the BTA can be treated in a similar vein, as triggering a conventional implicature. If it could be treated in this manner, it would presumably add its implicature to the meaning expressed by *at*-headed PPs such as *at midnight.* However, (34) and (35) actually do seem to differ truth conditionally:

(34) She gave the signal at midnight.

(35) She gave the signal by midnight.

Whereas (34) would be false if she had given the signal at, say, 11 PM, (35) would be true in this situation, as the BTA *by midnight* merely places an upper bound on signal-giving times.[2] We leave open the question of whether the meaning of the BTA is properly treated as a conventional implicature, but in the meantime we will continue to assume that it is appropriately treated as a contextual operator, as BTA-bearing predications require interpreters to retrieve or construct frames containing time series. Like other contextual operators, in particular its fellow state selector *already* (Michaelis 1996), the BTA can be regarded as pragmatically ambiguous in the sense of Horn (1989): Its semantic structure is schematic in comparison to the rich array of implications it can have in context. BTAs locate a state relative to a canonical time scale, and there are a variety of reasons for which one might do this. Thus the sampling point denoted by a BTA might be an earlier than expected point of eventuation, as in (32) through (33), a deadline, as in (36), the culmination point of a process, as in (37), or a retrospective assessment point located within a state of aftermath, as in (38), repeated from (16):

(36) *Deadline:* Such legislation must be enacted *by the end of the month.*   (WSJ)

(37) *Culmination point:* A dollar invested in the stock market in 1926 would have grown to $473.29 *by the end of last June,* according to Laurence Siegel, managing director at Ibbotson Associates Inc.   (WSJ)

(38) *Assessment point:* The incentives boosted sales for a while, but the pace had cooled *by last month.*   (WSJ)

These uses are not distinct at the semantic level but are instead contextual implications of BTAs.

Conclusion

As Binnick notes, "time adverbials have just begun to be studied" (1991, 300). We have suggested that one way to advance this field of study is to use corpus data, because corpus examples help us understand why speakers choose the time adverbs they do. We have shown that intuitions about the use of BTAs found in reference and pedagogical grammars are at odds with BTA use patterns in the *Wall Street Journal* corpus. We have offered a more comprehensive account of the BTA's function in which it denotes a sampling point located just after the potential or actual inception of a state. To account for those examples in which the BTA combines with a perfective rather than stative verb, we have proposed that it is a coercion trigger: If the predicate with which the BTA combines is nonstative, it is augmented up to a resultant-state predication. Beyond simply expressing the time at which a given state holds, BTAs instruct the hearer to interpret the situation described as the end state of a sequence of causally connected states. This case study substantiates two general claims about the meanings of grammatical constructions and the "little words" that they contain: aspectually sensitive constructions may index contextually available knowledge structures (Michaelis 1996), and such constructions, despite having etiologies that involve semantic "bleaching," may have rich frame-semantic content (Goldberg 1995).

NOTES

The authors gratefully acknowledge advice and constructive criticism provided by Martha Palmer, Alan Bell, and an anonymous reviewer.

1. The WSJ data used in this study were retrieved from the Penn Treebank II corpus by means of the search tool Tgrep. Treebank II supplements standard syntactic tags (NP, PP, S, etc.) with functional tags that express argument-adjunct relations. The Tgrep string used defined BTAs as PPs headed by *by* that also bear the functional tag TMP, for "time adverbial."

2. We presume that BTAs, like interval adverbials, are upward entailing and "downward compatible" (Herweg 1991). For example, the sentence *She finished the job in two hours* entails upward to *She finished the job in three hours,* and is downward compatible (via suspension of its lower-bounding implicatum) with the assertion *In fact, she finished the job in one hour.* Similarly, the assertion *She got home by midnight* entails upward to *She got home by 1 AM* and is downward compatible with the assertion *In fact, she got home by 11 PM.*

REFERENCES

Bickel, Balthasar. 1997. Aspectual scope and the difference between logical and semantic representation. *Lingua* 102:115–31.

Binnick, Robert. 1991. *Time and the verb.* New York: Oxford University Press.

De Swart, Henriette. 1998. Aspect shift and coercion. *Natural Language and Linguistic Theory* 16:347–85.

Dowty, David. 1977. Toward a semantic analysis of verb aspect and the English "imperfective" progressive. *Linguistics and Philosophy* 1:45–77.

———. 1979. *Word meaning and Montague grammar: The semantics of verbs and times in generative semantics and in Montague's PTQ.* Dordrecht: Kluwer Academic.

Fillmore, Charles J. 1985. Frames and the semantics of understanding. *Quaderni di Semantica* 6:222–54.

Fillmore, Charles J., Paul Kay, and Mary C. O'Connor. 1988. Regularity and idiomaticity in grammatical constructions: The case of *let alone. Language* 64:501–38.

Fuchs, Marjorie, and Margaret Bonner 2006. *Focus on grammar 4: An integrated skills approach* (3rd ed.). New York: Pearson Education.

Godfrey John, Ernest Holliman, and Jane McDaniel. 1992. SWITCHBOARD: Telephone speech corpus for research and development. *Proceedings of ICASSP-92.* San Francisco, 517–20.

Goldberg, Adele. 1995. *Constructions: A construction grammar account of argument structure.* Chicago: University of Chicago Press.

Herweg, Michael. 1991. A critical account of two classical approaches to aspect. *Journal of Semantics* 8:362–403.

Horn, Laurence. 1989. *A natural history of negation.* Chicago: University of Chicago Press.

Hornstein, Norbert. 1990. *As time goes by: Tense and universal grammar.* Cambridge, MA: MIT Press.

Huddleston, Rodney, and Geoffrey Pullum. 2002. *The Cambridge grammar of the English language.* Cambridge: Cambridge University Press.

Jackendoff, Ray. 1997. *The architecture of the language faculty.* Cambridge, MA: MIT Press.

Kay, Paul. 1990. Even. *Linguistics and Philosophy* 13:59–111.

———. 1997. *Words and the grammar of context.* Stanford, CA: CSLI Publications.

Krifka, Manfred. 1998. The origins of telicity. In *Events and Grammar,* ed. Susan Rothstein, 197–235. Dordrecht: Kluwer Academic.

Marcus, Marcus, Beatrice Santorini, and Mary Ann Marcinkiewicz. 1993. Building a large annotated corpus of English: The Penn Treebank. *Computational Linguistics* 19:313–30.

Michaelis, Laura. 1993. The polysemy of adverbial *still. Journal of Semantics* 10:193–237.

———. 1996. On the use and meaning of *already. Linguistics and Philosophy* 19:477–502.

———. 2004. Type shifting in construction grammar: An integrated approach to aspectual coercion. *Cognitive Linguistics* 15:1–67.

Partee, Barbara. 1984. Nominal and temporal anaphora. *Linguistics and Philosophy* 7:243–86.

Quirk, Randolph, Sidney Greenbaum, Geoffrey Leech, and Jan Svartvik. 1985. *A comprehensive grammar of the English language.* London: Longman.

Reichenbach, Hans. 1947. *Elements of symbolic logic.* New York: Macmillan.

Van Zante, Janis, Debra Daise, Charl Norloff, Randee Falk, and M. Kathleen Mahnke. 2000. *Grammar links 3: A theme-based course for reference and practice.* New York: Houghton Mifflin.

13

Distributive Effects of the Plural Marker –*tul* in Korean

JONG UN PARK
Georgetown University

THE PLURAL MARKING PARTICLE –*tul* in Korean has drawn much attention in the literature because of its puzzling distributions. First, the particle basically attaches to a noun, as in (1), whose role is similar to the English plural suffix –*s* in that it indicates the plural entities denoted by that noun.[1]

(1) a. Ai-*tul*-i   hakko-ey ka-ss-ta.
      Child-PL-Nom school-to go-Past-Dec
      "The children went to school."

   b. Ku   yeca-ka   ai-*tul*-kwa   hakko-ey ka-ss-ta.
      Dem woman-Nom child-PL-with school-to go-Past-Dec
      "That woman went to school with children."

Second, unlike the English plural suffix –*s,* the Korean plural marker –*tul* can also attach to an adverb and a postpositional phrase (PP), as in (2a) and (2b), respectively. Because it is attached to categories other than nouns, the particle -*tul* appearing in these environments is often called the non-nominal plural marker.

(2) a. Haksayng-tul-i   tosekwan-eyse yelsimhi-*tul*   kongpwu-hay-ss-ta.
      Student-PL-Nom library-in   laboriously-PL study-do-Past-Dec
      Lit. "The students studied laboriously in the library."

   b. Hakasying-tul-i   tosekwan-eyse-*tul* yelsimhi   kongpwu-hay-ss-ta.
      Students-PL-Nom library-in-PL   laboriously study-do-Past-Dec

One might think that the particle –*tul* attached to the adverb and the PP in (2) is a morphological realization of syntactic agreement with a plural subject in number. A number of researchers (cf. Kuh 1987; Lee 1991; Park and Sohn 1993; Yim 2003, among others) have made such a claim, although the way in which the category hosting the non-nominal –*tul* establishes agreement with the plural antecedent varies depending on the theoretical framework they adopt. If the syntactic agreement approach were correct, however, we would end up saying that Korean may fall under languages with syntactic agreement, which is not an uncontroversial conclusion. Furthermore, as will be discussed in the second section of this chapter, even though the syntactic agreement approach correctly captures a syntactic locality condition imposed on the non-nominal marker –*tul* (henceforth NNM –*tul*) and its plural antecedent, a close examination of data suggests that the syntactic agreement approach is not sufficient to account for semantic effects triggered by the NNM –*tul*.

This chapter will thus claim that the NNM –*tul* is not simply a reflex of syntactic agreement with subject in number but signals the existence of a plural subject as well as that of a plural event (in other words, multiple occurrence of an event) denoted by a predicate (cf. Kim 2005; Park 2005; Song 1997). Particularly, I argue that two types of distributive readings are available in a sentence with the NNM –*tul*, an "argument distributive" and "event distributive" reading, respectively (cf. Oh's [2002] similar distinction about distributive readings by –*ssik*, "each," in Korean), but each type of reading has a different source. On the one hand, the argument distributive reading is made possible, regardless of the existence of the NNM –*tul*, when a distributive operator optionally introduced by a plural noun phrase (NP) distributes each subpart of the plural subject over subparts of an event denoted by a predicate (contra Kim 1994 and Lee 1991, who claim that the NNM –*tul* itself is a distributive operator). On the other hand, the event distributive reading is due to the NNM –*tul* and arises when variables in the denotation of the NNM –*tul* are valued by a given context (cf. Kim 2005).

This chapter is organized as follows. Section 1 reviews a syntactic licensing condition regulating the distribution of the NNM –*tul*. Section 2 examines some data that show systematic patterns of distributive effects, which are derived by the NNM –*tul* and the type of predicate that it interacts with. In section 3, under a neo-Davidsonian event semantics, I provide a formal analysis of how the NNM –*tul* yields each interpretation in a compositional manner. Section 4 offers some conclusions.

1. Syntactic Licensing Condition on the Non-nominal –*tul*
Unlike the English plural suffix –*s*, the Korean plural marker –*tul* can attach not only to countable nouns but also to elements other than nouns. However, the distribution of the NNM –*tul* is not arbitrary. To begin with, as in (3), the NNM -*tul* in italic cannot be used unless a subject to which it relates is plural. However, if we look at the sentences in (4), it turns out to be insufficient to simply say that the NNM –*tul* should take a plural subject as its antecedent.

(3) a. Haksayng-<u>tul</u>-i   kongpwu-lul yelsimhi-*tul*   hay-ss-ta.
       Student-PL-Nom study-Acc   laboriously-PL do-Past-Dec
       "The students studied laboriously."

   b. *Han haksayng-i   kongpwu-lul yelsimhi-*tul*   hay-ss-ta.
       One student-Nom study-Acc   laboriously-PL do-Past-Dec
       "One student studied laboriously."

(4) a. John-i [haksayng-<u>tul</u>-i   chayk-ul yelsimhi-*tul*   ilk-ess-ta]-ko
       J.-Nom [student-PL-Nom book-Acc laboriously-PL read-Past-Dec]-
       Comp mal-hay-ss-ta.
       words-do-Past-Dec
       "John said that the students read books laboriously."

b. *Haksayng-<u>tul</u>-i [John-i chayk-ul yelsimhi-*tul*   ilk-ess-ta]-ko

Student-PL-Nom [J.-Nom book-Acc laboriously-PL read-Past-Dec]-

Comp mal-hay-ss-ta.

words-do-Past-Dec

"The students said that John read books laboriously"   (Park and Sohn 1993)

Therefore a first hypothesis that can be made from the two data here would be that in order for the NNM —*tul* to be licensed, at least two conditions should be met; that is, an element suffixed with —*tul* must have a plural subject, and they must be in the same clause.

Notice, however, that although a plural pronominal subject is in the same clause as a PP *hakkyo-ey,* "at school," in (5), the NNM —*tul* cannot be licensed. The ungrammaticality of (5) suggests that the antecedent that is responsible for licensing the NNM —*tul* should not only appear in the same clause but also be able to c-command it.

(5) *Wuri* ai-ka   hakkyo-ey(-**tul*) iss-ess-ta.

Our   child-Nom school-Loc-PL   exist-Past-Dec

"Our child was at school."   (Yim 2003)

All in all, the three sets of data thus lead us to propose the syntactic licensing condition in (6), and any sentence with the NNM —*tul* that fails to satisfy it will become ungrammatical.

(6) *Syntactic Licensing Condition*

A constituent to which the non-nominal plural marker —*tul* attaches must be in the same clause as a plural subject that c-commands it.

2. Semantic Effects of the Non-nominal —*tul*
2.1 Distributive Effects and Event Plurality

Whether or not the syntactic agreement approach is pursued, most researchers have commonly observed that the NNM marker —*tul* gives rise to distributive effects (Kim 1994; Kim 2005; Lee 1991; Park 2005; Park and Sohn 1993; and Song 1997, among others). Section 2.1 shows that the non-nominal use of —*tul* presupposes the existence of a plural event, which cannot be captured solely by the syntactic licensing condition in (6).

Let us first look at the data in (7). Following Kim (1994), Park and Sohn (1993) suggest that the third-person singular pronoun *kukes,* "it," can be used as a diagnostic for detecting a distributive reading. That is, the legitimate use of the pronoun *kukes* in (7a) presupposes the availability of a "collective" reading in the preceding sentence, while the prohibition of the same pronoun in (7b) implies that only a "distributive" reading can be obtained.

(7) a. Bill-kwa Mary-ka kutul-uy sensayngnim-kkey senmwul-ul kongsonhi

B.-and   M.-Nom they-Gen teacher-Dat   gift-Acc   politely

tuli-ess-ta.   Kukes/Kukestul-un sikyey-iess-ta.

give-Past-Dec It-Top/They-Top   watch-be.Past-Dec

Lit. "Bill and Mary gave a gift to their teacher. It was a watch/they were watches"

(i) Col: ✓"Bill and Mary *together* gave a gift."

(ii) Dist: ✓"Bill and Mary *each* gave a gift to their teacher."

b. Bill-kwa Mary-ka kutul-uy   sensayngnim-kkey senmwul-ul kongsonhi-*tul*

B.-and   M.-Nom they-Gen teacher-Dat   gift-Acc   politely-PL

tuli-ess-ta.   *Kukes-un/Kukestul-un sikyey-iess-ta.

give-Past-Dec It-Top/They-Top   watch-be.Past-Dec

(i) Col: ✗"Bill and Mary *together* gave a gift."

(ii) Dist: ✓"Bill and Mary *each* gave a gift to their teacher."

                                                        (Park and Sohn 1993)

Unlike (7a) in which the preceding sentence can be interpreted ambiguously, when the NNM *–tul* is attached to the manner adverb *kongsonhi,* "politely," as in (7b), the singular pronoun *kukes* cannot be used, suggesting that a collective reading is not available in the preceding sentence. The contrast (7a) and (7b) leads Park and Sohn (1993) to a claim that the NNM *–tul* gets rid of a collective reading but preserves a distributive reading.

Consider another pair of sentences, in (8), with an inherently collective predicate *gurwup,* "group" (see Dowty 1987 for a relevant test, in which the author suggests that the incompatibility of *all,* a trigger of distributive subentailments, indicates the property as a collective predicate). Notice that if the NNM *–tul* is attached to the modifier *kacang,* "most," the sentence becomes unnatural, as in (8b).

(8) a. Wuri pan   haksayng-<u>tul</u>-i   hakkyo-eyse kacang kun gurwup i-ess-ta.

     Our class student-PL-Nom school-Loc most   big group be-Past-Dec

     Lit. "Students in our class was the most big group."

  b. #Wuri pan   haksayng-<u>tul</u>-i   hakkyo-eyse kacang-*tul* kun gurwup i-ess-

     Our   class student-PL-Nom school-Loc most-PL   big group be-

     ta.

     Past-Dec

Sentence (8b) obviously satisfies the syntactic licensing condition but is nevertheless semantically anomalous. The unacceptability of (8b) should be attributed to another source, and I suggest that it is due to a semantic property of the predicate *gurwup,* "group," that does not allow a plural event (cf. Landman 2000; Lasersohn 1995; and Oh 2002 for the argument that an event can be plural).

If it is the case that the availability of a distributive reading entails the multiple occurrence of an event, as shown in (7) and (8), it follows that a predicate co-occurring with the NNM *–tul* should be able to denote a plural event. Therefore a conclusion can be made that the non-nominal use of *–tul* is allowed only when the requirements of both a plural subject and a plural event are obeyed.

2.2 Generalized Patterns of the Semantic Effects of the Non-nominal –tul

If the semantic function of the NNM –*tul* is to yield a distributive reading, eliminating a collective reading, one might predict that it cannot appear with a collective predicate. In section 2.2, however, we will see that this prediction does not hold for every sentence with a collective predicate. I will instead argue that when combined with some collective predicates, the NNM –*tul* yields another type of distributive reading, which is distinguished from a distributive reading of the kind observed in (7b). As briefly mentioned in the introduction, on the one hand, in the latter type of distributive reading (i.e., the argument distributive reading), each of individuals who are members of the plural subject is distributed over subparts of an event by the distributive operator. On the other hand, in the former type (i.e., the event distributive reading), it is the property of a category to which the NNM –*tul* attaches that is distributed over a "plural individual" who is a participant of subevents of an event denoted by a predicate (cf. section 3.1 for relevant discussion).

Consider (9), where a conjoined noun is predicated of an inherently collective verb *mannata*, "meet." As shown in (9b), unlike the prediction made earlier, the NNM –*tul* does not make the sentence ungrammatical or semantically anomalous.

(9) a. Bill-kwa Mary-ka tosekwan-eyse manna-ss-ta.

    B.-and   M.-Nom library-in   meet-Past-Dec

    "Bill and Mary met in the library."

    (i)   Collective: ✓"Bill and Mary met each other in the library."

    (ii) Argument distributive: ✗"Bill and Mary each met somebody else."

  b. Bill-kwa Mary-ka tosekwan-eyse-*tul* manna-ss-ta.

    B.-and   M.-Nom library-in-PL   meet-Past-Dec

    (i)   Collective: ✗ "Bill and Mary met each other in the library."

    (ii) Argument distributive: ✗ "Bill and Mary each met somebody else."

    (iii) Event distributive: ✓ "There was an event of Bill and Mary's meeting each other and the event of their meeting was repeated *more than once in the library.*"

A closer examination of possible interpretations from (9b) enables us to see why the NNM –*tul* can still co-occur with the inherently collective predicate. First, because the predicate is a collective one, we can naturally expect to get a collective reading from (9a), namely, "There was a single event where Bill and Mary met together"; however, if the NNM –*tul* is attached to the locative phrase, the collective reading disappears, as in (9b). Thus we are tempted to conclude that the role of the NNM –*tul* is a distributive marker that eliminates a collective reading. However, this conclusion does not seem to hold because the presence of the NNM –*tul* in (9b) does not allow a prototypical distributive reading (called the "argument distributive" reading) either; that is, we cannot get a reading "Each of John and Mary is distributed over meeting events that took place in the library." By contrast, it is not difficult to see another type of distributive reading (called the "event distributive" reading) arise, as in (9b,iii); in other words, the NNM –*tul* makes it possible to obtain a reading where the property of the locative phrase that the marker combines with is distributed over subparts of the plural subject. Therefore I argue that it is the event distributive reading that makes the use of the NNM –*tul* compatible with the collective predicate in (9b).[2]

Second, look at another pair of examples, where a conjoined subject is predicated of a verb *hwacangha-*, "put on makeup," that can be classified as an "inherently distributive" predicate.

(10) a. Mary-wa Jane-un ppalli   hwacang-ul   hay-ss-ta.

     M.-with   J.-Top   quickly make.up-Acc do-Past-Dec

     Lit. "Mary and Jane put on makeup quickly."

     (i)   Collective: ✗"Mary and Jane *together* put on makeup quickly."

     (ii) Argument distributive: ✓"Mary and Jane *each* put on makeup quickly."

   b. Mary-wa Jane-un ppalli-*tul*   hwacang-ul   hay-ss-ta.

     M.-with   J.-Top   quickly -PL make-up-Acc do-Past-Dec

     (i)   Collective: ✗"Mary and Jane *together* put on makeup quickly."

     (ii) Argument distributive: ✓"Mary and Jane *each* put on makeup."

     (iii) Focus: ✓"It was *quickly* that an event of Mary's and Jane's putting on makeup each took place."

Because of the inherent property of the distributive predicate, it is correctly predicted that while an argument distributive reading is available, as in (10a,ii), a collective reading is not, as in (10a,i). Notice also that even when we attach the NNM –*tul* to an adverb *ppalli*, "quickly," no change appears to arise, at least regarding a collective or an argument distributive reading, as in (10b,i) and (10b,ii). What is more important is that unlike the inherently collective verb *manna-*, "meet," in (9b), the inherently distributive predicate *hwacangha-* fails to induce an event distributive reading even in the presence of the NNM –*tul,* and (10b) thus cannot be read as "There was an event of Mary and Jane's putting on makeup together and the event took place quickly more than once." Instead, the sentence triggers a focus reading, as given in (10b,iii). I suggest that the reason for which an event distributive reading is absent from (10b) is that the distributive effect of the plural marker –*tul* becomes vacuous due to the semantic property of the inherently distributive predicate (similar to how Fox's [2000] *Scope Economy* works).

Third, one more set of sentences where both a collective reading and a distributive reading are available in the absence of the NNM –*tul* can make the same point; for convenience's sake, I will call this class of verbs "ambiguous" predicates although they are the residue of inherently collective or inherently distributive predicates. Given the patterns that are found in the first two sets of examples in (9) and (10), we would predict that the use of the NNM –*tul* gets rid of a collective reading while it allows an event distributive reading. This prediction turns out to be correct, as illustrated in (11).

(11) a. John-kwa Mary-ka tosekwan-eyse nonmwun-ul sse-ss-ta.

     J.-and   M.-Nom library-Loc   paper-Acc   write-Past-Dec

Lit. "John and Mary wrote a paper in the library."

(i) Collective: ✓"John and Mary *together* wrote a paper in the library."

(ii) Argument distributive: ✓"John and Mary *each* wrote a paper in the library."

b. John-kwa Mary-ka tosekwan-eyse-*tul* nonmwun-ul sse-ss-ta.

    J.-and   M.-Nom library-Loc-PL   paper-Acc   write-Past-Dec

(i) Collective: ✗"John and Mary *together* wrote a paper in the library."

(ii) Argument distributive: ✓"John and Mary *each* wrote a paper in the library."

(iii) Event distributive: ✓"There was an event of John and Mary's writing a paper together, and the event was repeated *more than once in the library.*"

On the one hand, in sentence (11a) without the NNM –*tul,* either a collective or a distributive reading is available. In sentence (11b) with the NNM –*tul,* on the other hand, the argument distributive survives, but the collective reading cannot. More important, besides the argument distributive reading, we can get another interpretation from (11b), that is, an event distributive reading, which is described in (11b,iii).

The three sets of data in section 2.2 confirm the long-standing observation that the NNM –*tul* gives rise to distributive effects. In particular, the data led me to suggest that the distributive effects appear in two different forms: The first type corresponds to an argument distributive reading and another type to an event distributive reading. At first glance, both types of distributive readings appear to be due to the existence of the NNM –*tul.* With a closer look at the data, however, one can easily see that the event distributive reading comes from the NNM –*tul,* while the argument distributive reading has another source.

To sum up, it has been revealed in section 2 that, along with the syntactic requirement of a plural subject, the requirement of a plural event must be satisfied in order for the NNM –*tul* to generate distributive effects. I have particularly shown that there are two types of distributive readings, an argument distributive reading and an event distributive reading, and the availability of the latter is determined by the interaction of the NNM –*tul* with the type of predicate. Because many of the previous analyses fail to capture these facts, we need to find out an alternative approach, which necessarily combines the syntactic perspective with the semantic one. I will take up this issue, advancing an eclectic approach to the behaviors of –*tul,* in section 3.

3. Two Types of Distributivity Revisited

3.1 Basic Assumptions

Recall that the purely syntactic agreement approach adopting (6) fails to capture the distributive effects triggered by the NNM –*tul,* and the previous semantic approach does not distinguish an argument distributive reading from an event distributive one. Therefore I claim that both approaches should be combined to account for both the syntactic distribution of the NNM –*tul* and the generalized patterns of its semantic interpretations as reported in section 2.2.

As a preliminary step to explain the distributive effects by the NNM plural marker *–tul,* this chapter makes a couple of assumptions. First, an analysis that I advance here is based on a neo-Davidsonian event semantics, which treats every verb as a one-place predicate taking an event argument (cf. Parsons 1990). Unless events are included in semantic representations, it would be hard to explain how distributive effects are derived.

Second, regarding the notion of plurality, this chapter assumes with Link (1983) that a plural noun is similar to a mass noun in that both are cumulative. For example, if α is water and β is water, then the sum of α and β is also water. Likewise, if *animals* in a certain barn are horses and *animals* in another barn are horses, then the sum of the entities in both barns are also *animals* (cf. Link 1983, 303). This cumulative property can be represented in the following way (where a symbol $\cup_I$ stands for cumulation of individuals): $[[\textbf{animals}]] = \{x, y, z, x\cup_I y, x\cup_I z, y\cup_I z, x\cup_I y\cup_I z\}$. In particular, the plurality defined in terms of cumulativity will be called "individual plurality." Furthermore, if the notion of plurality is defined by cumulativity, then it is possible to extend this notion to conjoined nouns, regardless if each conjunct is singular or plural. For example, a conjoined noun phrase *John and Mary* can be represented as follows, as it denotes not only two individuals but also one cumulative entity called "plural individual": $[[\textbf{John and Mary}]] = \{$John, Mary, John$\cup_I$Mary$\}$ where the former two members are atomic parts (which is not an uncontroversial assumption, as the reviewer points out).

Third, it is assumed that every plural NP, including bare plurals or conjoined nouns, can optionally induce a distributive operator D_{Op} (cf. Kim 2005; Link 1983; Park 2005), which will be defined in the following way: $[[\textbf{D}_{\textbf{Op}}]] = \lambda P\lambda x\lambda e\forall y[y \leq x \rightarrow \exists e'[e'\leq e\wedge P(e')(y)]]$. Recall that there are two types of distributive readings, an argument reading and an event distributive reading, and that the latter is due to the NNM *–tul,* while the former has to do with the occurrence of the distributive operator. In particular, the argument distributive reading is a byproduct of scope interactions between a distributive operator and a plural subject. To be more specific, the argument distributive reading is obtained when atomic parts of a plural subject can be distributed by the distributive operator over an event that is denoted by the whole predicate.

Fourth, I suggest that as defined in (12), the plural marker *–tul* consists of a null pro_1 whose referent is determined by a c-commanding plural subject and a context-dependent variable R_2 whose referent is fed by a context-sensitive variable assignment g_c (cf. Cooper's [1979] analysis for E-type pronouns, and Kim's [2005] analysis for the NNM *–tul*). In (12), R_2 represents the relation between subparts of a plural subject and the property of an event.

(12) $[[\textbf{\textit{tul}}]] = \exists R\ \forall z[z\leq pro_1 \rightarrow R_2(z)]$.

Building on the assumptions made here, I provide a compositional analysis of how the generalized patterns of the semantic effects of the NNM *–tul* can be derived in section 3.2.

3.2 A Compositional Analysis of Distributive Effects

3.2.1 Interpretation patterns of ambiguous predicates.   Let us consider how interpretation patterns from an ambiguous predicate can be explained under the current analysis. For this

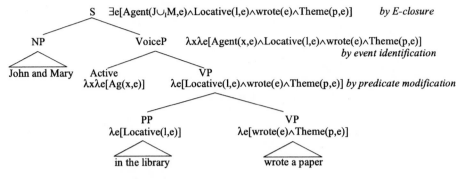

※ Figure 13.1 Representation for (11a,i)

purpose, I analyze the examples in (11), which will not be repeated here due to space issues. As observed in section 2.2, the ambiguous predicate *ssu-*, "write," allows both a collective and an argument distributive reading even in the absence of the NNM −*tul*, as in (11a,i) and (11a,ii), respectively. As in (11b), when the NNM −*tul* is added, a collective reading disappears, but an argument distributive reading is preserved, which lends support for the current claim that an argument distributive reading does not come directly from the NNM −*tul*. Figure 13.1 illustrates the abstracted syntactic structure as well as the semantic representation for the collective reading in (11a,i). Notice that, following Kratzer (1996), I assume that an agent argument is not part of the meaning of a predicate but is introduced by a separate node labeled VoiceP and that when the VoiceP combines with the external argument, the rule *event identification* applies.

The representation in figure 13.1 can be read as "There was an event of John and Mary's writing a paper together in the library." In particular, as discussed in section 3.1, in order for the collective reading to be available, the external argument should behave like a plural individual, that is, *John∪₁Mary;* otherwise, the sentence becomes pragmatically anomalous. Note, however, that the collective reading will disappear when the NNM −*tul* attaches to the PP *in the library,* as in (11b,i), because the meaning of the NNM −*tul* alters the collective reading into an event distributive one, which will be discussed shortly.

Let us see how the argument distributive reading in (11a,ii) is obtained. As emphasized earlier, it is not the NNM −*tul* but the distributive operator that gives rise to an argument distributive reading. In particular, the reading arises when the distributive operator applies to the VoiceP, distributing each individual over subparts of an event, as in (13).

(13) "John and Mary *each* wrote a paper in the library." [= (11a,ii)]

   a. $[[\mathbf{D_{Op}}]]([[\mathbf{VoiceP}]])$

     $= \lambda P\lambda x\lambda e\forall y[y \leq x \rightarrow \exists e'[e' \leq e \wedge P(e')(y)]](\lambda x\lambda e[Agent(x,e)$
     $\wedge Locative(l,e)\wedge wrote(e)\wedge Theme(p,e)])$

     $= \lambda x\lambda e\forall y[y \leq x \rightarrow \exists e'[e' \leq e \wedge \lambda x\lambda e[Agent(x,e)\wedge Locative(l,e)$
     $\wedge wrote(e)\wedge Theme(p,e)](e')(y)]]$

$= \lambda x \lambda e \forall y [y \le x \rightarrow \exists e'[e' \le e \wedge Agent(y,e') \wedge Locative(l,e') \wedge wrote(e')$
$\wedge Theme(p,e')]]$

$= \lambda x \lambda e \forall y [y \le x \rightarrow \exists e'[e' \le e \wedge Agent(y,e') \wedge Locative(l,e') \wedge wrote(e')$
$\wedge Theme(p,e')]]$

b. $[[(13a)]]([[John\ and\ Mary]])$

$= \lambda x \lambda e \forall y [y \le x \rightarrow \exists e'[e' \le e \wedge Agent(y,e') \wedge Locative(l,e') \wedge wrote(e')$
$\wedge Theme(p,e')]](\{John,\ Mary\})$

$= \lambda e \forall y [y \le \{John,\ Mary\} \rightarrow \exists e'[e' \le e \wedge Agent(y,e') \wedge Locative(l,e')$
$\wedge wrote(e') \wedge Theme(p,e')]]$

$= \exists e \forall y [y \le \{John,\ Mary\} \rightarrow \exists e'[e' \le e \wedge Agent(y,e') \wedge Locative(l,e')$
$\wedge wrote(e') \wedge Theme(p,e')]]$

(13a) is the step-by-step derivation that shows the way in which the distributive operator D_{Op} applies to the VoiceP. After that, the result obtained from (13a) is combined with the plural individual *John and Mary*, as in (13b), and what we get in the last line is the argument distributive reading in (11a,ii). Because the NNM *–tul* has nothing to do with an argument distributive reading, the argument distributive reading in (11b,ii) will be derived in the same way as in (11a,ii).

Turning to an event distributed reading, given the current assumption that it is due to the NNM *–tul,* the event distributive reading in (11b,iii) can be obtained by valuing the two variables, *pro_1* and R_2, which are components of the denotation of the NNM *–tul* in (12). On the one hand, the plural subject *John and Mary* will determine the value of *pro_1,* because the former can c-command the latter, thereby establishing the syntactic binding relation between them. On the other hand, the variable R_2 whose denotation is given in (14a) should represent a relation between a plural subject and the property of an event that is denoted by the part of a predicate. In particular, a function f in (14a) denotes the meaning of a category to which the NNM *–tul* attaches, and another function P corresponds to the meaning of VoiceP from which f is excluded. The step-by-step derivation for the meaning of the NNM *–tul* is illustrated in (14b).

(14) "There was an event of John and Mary's writing a paper together, and the event was repeated *more than once in the library.*" [= (11b, iii)]

a. $[[\mathbf{R_2}]] = g_{C2} = \lambda P \in D_{<s,t>} \lambda f \in D_{<s,t>} \lambda x \in D_e \exists e'[\forall e'[e' \le e \wedge P(e')(x) \rightarrow f(e')]]$ $(|e| > 1)$

b. $[[\textit{\textbf{tul}}]] = \exists R \forall z[z \le pro_1 \rightarrow R_2(z)]$

$= \exists R \forall z[z \le J \cup_1 M \rightarrow R(z)]$

$= \forall z[z \le J \cup_1 M \rightarrow \lambda P \in D_{<s,t>} \lambda f \in D_{<s,t>} \lambda x \in D_e \exists e[\forall e'[e' \le e \wedge P(e')(x) \rightarrow f(e')]](z)]$

$= \forall z[z \le J \cup_1 M \rightarrow \lambda P \in D_{<s,t>} \lambda f \in D_{<s,t>} \exists e[\forall e'[e' \le e \wedge P(e')(z) \rightarrow f(e')]]]$

$= \forall z[z \le J \cup_1 M \rightarrow \lambda f \in D_{<s,t>} \exists e[\forall e'[e' \le e \wedge \lambda x \lambda e[Agent(x,e) \wedge wrote(e) \wedge Theme(p,e)](e')(z) \rightarrow f(e')]]]$

$= \forall z[z \le J \cup_1 M \rightarrow \lambda f \in D_{<s,t>} \exists e[\forall e'[e' \le e \wedge Agent(z,e') \wedge wrote(e') \wedge Theme(p,e') \rightarrow f(e')]]]$

$$= \forall z[z \leq J\cup_l M \rightarrow \exists e[\forall e'[e' \leq e \wedge Agent(z,e') \wedge wrote(e') \wedge Theme(p,e') \rightarrow \lambda e[Loc(l,e)](e')]]]$$

$$= \forall z[z \leq J\cup_l M \rightarrow \exists e[\forall e'[e' \leq e \wedge Agent(z,e') \wedge wrote(e') \wedge Theme(p,e') \rightarrow Loc(l,e')]]]$$

What is obtained in the last line in (14b) is the event distributive reading in (11b,iii), which can be read as "For all z that is part of the plural individual *John and Mary*, there was an event of z's writing a paper such that it took place in the library more than once." Notice also that just like the case of the collective reading in (11a,i), the plural subject *John and Mary* should not be treated as atomic subparts but as a plural individual.

3.2.2 *Interpretation patterns of collective predicates.*   Turning to the interpretation patterns of the NNM *–tul* occurring with a collective predicate, let us consider the examples in (9), which will not be repeated here. First, the collective reading in (9a,i) whose representation is given in (15) disappears when the NNM *–tul* is attached to the PP *in the library*, as in (9b,i). This is because a variable pronoun *pro* in the denotation of the NNM *–tul* requires a nonatomic plural subject, forcing an event distributive reading.

(15) $\exists e[Agent(B\cup_l M,e) \wedge Locative(l,e) \wedge met(e)]$ [= (9a,i)]

Second, regardless of the appearance of the NNM *–tul*, the argument distributive reading whose representation is given in (16) is not available in both (9a) and (9b).

(16) ✗$\exists e \forall x[x \leq B\cup_l M \rightarrow \exists e'[e' \leq e \wedge Agent(x,e') \wedge Locative(l,e') \wedge met(e')]]$

Recall our assumption made in section 3.1 that the argument distributive reading is derived from the distributive operator, distributing subparts of the plural subject over subevents denoted by the whole predicate. As shown in (16), however, the inherently collective predicate *manna-*, "meet," by definition, requires its plural subject *Bill and Mary* to be a plural individual *Bill$\cup_l$Mary*, so the distributive operator cannot distribute the plural subject. That is why the argument distributive reading is unavailable in both (9a) and (9b).

Third, when we add the NNM *–tul* to the PP, the event distributive reading, which is represented in (17), becomes available, as in (9b,iii).

(17) ✓$\forall z[z \leq B\cup_l M \rightarrow \exists e[\forall e'[e' \leq e \rightarrow Agent(z,e') \wedge met(e') \rightarrow Locative(l,e')]]]$
[= (9b,iii)]

Observe that the sentence in (9b) satisfies the syntactic requirement of a plural subject, and its counterpart without *–tul* in (9a) basically allows a collective reading. Therefore nothing is incompatible with the meaning of the NNM *–tul*, which is defined in (12), and once the two variables *pro₁* and R_2 are valued, the event distributive reading can be obtained.

3.2.3 *Interpretation patterns of distributive predicates.*   Finally, consider the examples in (10), which will not be repeated here, to see how the interpretation patterns of a distributive predicate with the NNM *–tul* are derived. First, the collective reading whose representation is given in (18) can be obtained in neither (10a) nor (10b), as the inherently distributive predicate, by definition, does not allow that reading. Recall that the inherently distributive predicate requires its plural subject to be atomic, while the collective reading is possible only when an event denoted by the whole predicate is distributed over a plural individual.

(18) ✗∃e[Agent({M, J},e)∧quickly(e)∧put-on-makeup(e)]

Second, the argument distributive reading, represented in (19), can be obtained in both (10a) and (10b), regardless of whether the NNM –*tul* attaches to the adverb.

(19) ✓∃e∀x[x ≤ {M, J} → ∃e'[e' ≤ e ∧Agent(x,e')∧quickly(e)∧put-on-makeup(e')]] [= (10a/b,ii)]

Notice that the inherently distributive predicate by definition requires its plural subject to be atomic, so the distributive operator can distribute the atomic parts of the plural subject *Mary and Jane* over an event denoted by the whole predicate, that is, the event of putting on makeup quickly.

Finally, even when the NNM –*tul* attaches to the adverb *ppalli*, "quickly," the event distributive reading, which can be represented as in (20), is not available, as shown in (10b,iii).

(20) ✗∀z[z ≤ {M, J} → ∃e[∀e'[e' ≤ e → Agent(z,e')∧put-on-makeup(e') → quickly(e')]]]

The unavailability of the event distributive reading in (10) immediately follows from the current analysis. To begin with, in order for an event distributive reading to arise, the predicate should be able to allow a collective reading, but the inherently distributive predicate *hwacangha-*, "put on makeup," does not obviously allow such a reading. Furthermore, as mentioned in section 2.2, the distributive effect of the NNM plural marker –*tul* becomes vacuous due to the semantic property of the inherently distributive predicate. Instead, a focus reading is imposed on the category to which the NNM –*tul* attaches.

4. Conclusion

This chapter provided the generalized patterns of interpretations that are drawn from the NNM –*tul* and its interactions with different types of predicates. In particular, I showed that there are two distinct types of distributive effects, an argument reading and an event distributive reading, and that only the latter is due to the presence of the NNM plural marker –*tul*, while the former is due to the distributive operator introduced by a plural subject. In order to explain the generalized patterns, I proposed the eclectic approach under the neo-Davidsonian event semantics, which combines both the syntactic agreement approach and the semantic approach.

NOTES

An earlier version of this chapter was presented at the Linguistic Society of America (LSA) 2007 annual meeting. I am very grateful to Michael Diercks, Sun Hee Hwang, Elena Herburger, and Raffaella Zanuttini for their helpful comments and encouragement. My thanks go to the audiences at both the LSA and GURT conferences and, particularly, to an anonymous reviewer of *GURT '07 Proceedings* for pointing out many unclear issues. All remaining errors are mine.

1. Note that other categories such as VPs and CPs host the non-nominal –*tul* in Korean, but our discussion will be limited to the cases where the marker attaches to adverbs or PPs.
2. Brisson (2003) classifies collective predicates into collective I and collective II in terms of whether they contain direct objects (DO) in their event composition where a distributive operator resides. The former include collective activity and accomplishment predicates that allow the distributive operator to be inserted either in a DO subpart (that triggers a collective reading) or in a verb phrase (VP) part (that yields a distributive reading). The latter include collective state and achievement ones, and because they do not contain DO in their event composition, a distributive reading is obligatory. Notice, however, that when a conjoined subject is predicated of a verb falling into Brisson's collective I in Korean, only a collective reading survives. This chapter does not have an appropriate account of such disparity and will disregard Brisson-style subclassification of collective predicates.

REFERENCES

Brisson, Christine. 2003. Plurals, all, and the nonuniformity of collective predication. *Linguistics and Philosophy* 26:129–84.

Cooper, Robin. 1979. The interpretation of pronouns. In *Syntax and semantics,* vol. 10, *Selections from the third Groningen round table,* ed. Frank Heny and Halmut Schnelle, 61–92. New York: Academic Press.

Dowty, David. 1987. A note on collective predicates, distributive predicates, and all. In *Proceedings of the third ESCOL,* ed. Fred Marshall: 97–115.

Fox, Danny. 2000. *Economy and scope interpretation.* Cambridge, MA: MIT Press.

Kim, Chong-Hyuck. 2005. The Korean plural marker tul and its implications. PhD diss., University of Delaware.

Kim, Yookyung. 1994. A non-spurious account of "spurious" Korean plurals. In *Theoretical issues in Korean linguistics,* ed. Young-Key Kim-Renand, 303–23. Stanford, CA: CLSI Publication.

Kratzer, Angelika. 1996. Severing the external argument from its verb. In *Phrase structure and lexicon,* ed. Johan Rooryck and Laurie Zaring, 109–37. Dordrecht: Kluwer.

Kuh, Hakan. 1987. Plural copying in Korean. In *Harvard studies in Korean linguistics,* vol. 2, ed. Susumu Kuno, Ik-Hwan Lee, John Whitman, Sung-Yun Bak, and Young-Se Kang, 239–50. Seoul: Hanshin.

Landman, Fred. 2000. *Events and plurality.* Dordrecht: Kluwer.

Lasersohn, Peter. 1995. *Plurality, conjunction and events.* Dordrecht: Kluwer.

Lee, Han-Gyu. 1991. Plural marker copying in Korean. In *Harvard studies in Korean linguistics,* vol. 4, ed. Susumu Kuno, Ik-Hwan Lee, John Whitman, Joan Mailing, Young-Se Kang, and Young-joo Kim, 513–28. Seoul: Hanshin.

Link, Godehard. 1983. The logical analysis of plural and mass term: A lattice theory approach. In *Meaning, use and interpretation of language,* ed. Rainer Bäuerle, Christoph Schwarze, and Arnim von Stechow, 302–23. Berlin: de Gruyer.

Oh, Sei-Rang. 2002. Distributivity in an event semantics. Paper presented at SALT XI, May 13, 2001.

Park, Myung-Kwan, and Keun-Won Sohn. 1993. A minimalist approach to plural marker licensing in Korean. In *MITWPL 20,* 193–208. Cambridge, MA: MITWPL.

Park, So-Young. 2005. So-called plural marking –*tul* and distributivity. Paper presented at Harvard International Symposium on Korean Linguistics, August 6.

Parsons, Terence. 1990. *Events in the semantics of English.* Cambridge, MA: MIT Press.

Song, Jae Jung. 1997. The so-called plural copy in Korean as a marker of distribution and focus. *Journal of Pragmatics* 27:203–24.

Yim, Changguk. 2003. Subject agreement in Korean: Move F, attract F, or agree? In *TLS 5 Proceedings,* ed. William Earl Griffin, 147–56. Austin: Texas Linguistics Forum.

Pragmatics

14

▨ The Pragmatics of the French Discourse Markers *donc* and *alors*

STÉPHANIE PELLET
Wake Forest University

▨ **SPOKEN FRENCH** relies heavily on a vast array of discourse markers, small words that help speakers in situating discourse at the referential, structural, interpersonal, and cognitive levels (Maschler 1998) and illustrating the import of pragmatics in interactions. This study focuses on the two French discourse markers *donc* and *alors* (both equivalent to the English *so* in some contexts) in native speaker conversations. Highly frequent in spontaneous speech, *donc* and *alors* represent important means of managing conversation. While several studies have shown that *donc* and *alors* express various discourse functions, the underlying assumption has been that they both broadly express consequence (i.e., conclusions and results), as in (1):

(1) [nf1 speaks about her lack of experience with the American way of life][1]

NF1: J'suis pas là d'puis longtemps *alors / donc* y'a des choses

NF1: I've not been here for very long, so there are things

In this utterance, taken from the native corpus used for the study, there is no way of saying, from the outset, that either discourse marker is preferable. In fact, past research emphasizes the functional overlap between *alors* and *donc*. According to Hansen (1997), the fact that the two markers may occur together indicates "partially overlapping distributions" (162). Barnes (1998) also sees common discourse functions between *alors* and *donc*. In her second language (L2) study, she asserts that "*donc* and *alors* mark a relation of consequence or a discourse transition" (193); specifically, "both *alors* and *donc* may mark a shift from one level of the discourse to another, for example, from descriptive background or commentary to the main story line" (193). For Barnes, *donc* and *alors* are so functionally identical that, at least in this second language acquisition (SLA) research, she collapses them into one category: marking consequence and transition. Finally, in a Canadian French L2 study, Rehner (2002) grouped together *donc, alors, ça fait que* (an expression typical of this variety of French), and *so,* suggesting that they are form-function equivalents. In fact, she assigns the same function labels to *donc* and *alors* (organizational/transitional, clarification/expansion, turn-yielding signal, emphasizer, and punctor).

I argue that these two French discourse markers are not functional equivalents in conversations and that a form-function analysis of recorded interactions between pairs of native speakers reveals that, to a large extent, *donc* and *alors* occur in complementary distribution. Specifically I argue that *donc* is used to assert the validity of a speaker's viewpoint and occurs within a turn-at-talk (monologal use). By contrast, *alors* is used to preface a reaction to new information usually presented by the interlocutor and tends to occur turn-initially (dialogal use). In other words, *donc* marks continuity, whereas *alors* marks a shift and indexes a reactive move.

Discourse Markers and Analytical Frameworks

Discourse markers do not have propositional meaning and do not explicitly contribute new information (Brinton 1996; Jucker and Ziv 1998). Neither content words nor function words, they fulfill two main pragmatic functions in spoken discourse: First, discourse markers guide the interlocutor toward a correct interpretation of the propositional content of an utterance as well as indicate the speaker's position with regard to the utterance (epistemic orientation). They also play an important role in sequence structuring and turn management. Analytically, binary approaches essentially distinguish between a discourse content function and a discourse management function (Brinton 1996; Moeschler 2002; Rehner 2002).[2] Other approaches can be viewed as "multiplane": Schiffrin's (1987) five-plane model; Östman's (1982) tripartite model (anchoring vs. implicitness vs. expressiveness); Roulet's (1997) modular model applied to French; or Maschler's (1998) four-domain approach (referential, structural, interpersonal, and cognitive) applied to Israeli Hebrew. While binary approaches may help to sort functions more easily, multiplane approaches better address overlapping and gray areas that arise because of the typical multifunctionality of discourse markers. Hence I find that Maschler's framework best categorizes the different pragmatic functions of discourse markers.[3]

Because discourse markers are said not to contribute new information, narrow definitions exclude them from having any referential function. Within the referential domain, they express logical relationships (causal, coordinative, disjunctive) between utterances. In other words, when *donc* marks a consequence, it functions as a grammar word (conjunction of coordination) not a discourse marker.[4] Nonetheless, to sort out the referential and nonreferential (or literal vs. pragmatic) uses of *donc* and *alors* with respect to one another, their referential use must be included: although a distinction exists between connectives (referential function) and other "pragmatic" functions of the same linguistic form, it is situated at an abstract plane. The functions are not clearly distinguished in the minds of the speakers—in fact, the distinction is made post facto by linguists. Thus it is possible to hypothesize some sort of interaction between the unique form of a discourse marker and its different functions.

The Corpus

This study is based on an analysis of a corpus of three pairs of native speakers (three men, three women) who discussed two topics for ten minutes, for a total of one hour of recordings. The native-speaker data was part of a larger study involving language learners; therefore the task and type of interaction were designed to serve that purpose. The main criterion for the study design was to obtain conversational data. Because discourse markers are a trademark of informal oral expression, creating an informal context would be more conducive to their production and allow the participants equal opportunities to use them at different conversational points, for instance, embedded in a question or prefacing an answer to a question. In fact, both *alors* and *donc* are used at these junctures with specific speaker intent. If the data do not qualify as "naturally occurring" (participants volunteered for the study and did not choose the topics for their semiguided interaction), the study situation did resemble a natural conversation in that there was no interviewer/interviewee structure, which often leads to unequal participation and power issues.

The topics for the two conversational tasks tapped into everyday situations, requiring no specific knowledge: participants were first led to express their opinions on French perceptions of Americans; they then had to plan a trip to France together. The two tasks provided some degree of cross-task validation (see Chaudron 2003) and created more opportunities for openings and closings, typically signaled by discourse markers (Andersen et al. 1999).

Results

The results of the distribution of *donc* and *alors* with respect to their turn position are given in table 14.1. The numeric results confirm at least the position component of the hypothesis for the corpus under analysis: *alors* occurs more often at the beginning of a turn (thirteen out of nineteen occurrences), and *donc* more often within a turn (forty-nine out of fifty-nine occurrences). A striking result is the three times greater frequency of *donc* over *alors,* which held not only overall but also across participants, despite individual variation, as indicated by table 14.2.[5] The study's small sample cannot address individual variation, but the nature of the task (conversation)

Table 14.1
Distribution of *alors* and *donc* with Respect to Turn

Marker	Turn Initial (dialogal %)	Within Turn (monologal %)	**Total**
alors	13 (68)	6 (32)	19
donc	10 (17)	49 (83)	59

Table 14.2
Distribution of *alors* and *donc* per Participant

Marker	Nf1	Nm1	Nf2	Nm2	Nf3	Nm3	Total
alors	2	1	2	2	9	3	19
donc	20	14	3	4	8	10	59

may explain the differential frequency: *alors,* because it can mark sequentiality, is particularly important in oral narratives, which usually follow a chronology, whereas *donc* is likely to dominate interactions.

Alors

According to the hypothesis, *alors* is preferred at the beginning of a turn to preface a reaction to newly received information. There were nineteen occurrences of *alors* in the native corpus under study; thirteen occurred at the beginning of a turn, with only six occurring within a turn.

Alors turn-initial (thirteen occurrences).   When *alors* is turn-initial, its discourse functions fall into two broad categories. First, it fulfills the function of "attaque de discours" (Bouacha 1981), or discourse opening, for which *donc* is never used in my data. This function is illustrated in examples (2) and (3):

(2) *Alors,* les vacances en France . . .

   So, vacation in France . . .

(3) *Alors* . . . Sur le matérialisme des Américains . . . ben . . . c'est vrai . . .

   So . . . About the materialism of the American people . . . well . . . it's true . . .

Because *alors* opens the discursive sequence, it is obviously turn-initial. It shifts the interlocutors from [0] (i.e., no discourse) to [purpose for the interaction]. There cannot be continuity here as there is no preceding discourse.

Second, *alors* is a reactive marker and functions as an anaphoric to reprise the information just given by the interlocutor to present a different perspective or an alternative proposal, or to take issue with the interlocutor's position or information. For instance, in (4) Nm3 presents an alternative:

(4) NF3: Je veux partir, je veux voir aut'chose.

   NM3: Ben *alors* pourquoi pas dans l'Nord?

   NF3: I want to leave, I want to see somethin' else.

   NM3: Well then why not in the North?

The reactive aspect of *alors* is particularly evident in the English equivalent, which better translates the marker as *then* rather than *so.* As it occurs at the beginning of the turn, *alors* emphasizes that the alternative proposal (here, going to northern France) directly derives from the information just shared by the interlocutor.

Taking up an issue after just-shared information is often reinforced with the co-occurrence of the contrastive marker *mais.* There were three such instances in this corpus, as in (5):

(5) NF3: /attends/ si on prend l'autoroute A-un . .

   NM3: Ben voilà.

   NF3: c'est direct y'a deux heures.

   NM3: Ben voilà. On est en Normandie sans problème.

NF3: Ouais *mais alors* c'est pareil en Normandie va y'avoir tous les touristes pour le D-day pour euh la plage du débarquement . . .

NF3: /wait/ if we take the highway A-one . . .

NM3: Well there you go.

NF3: It's direct it's two hours.

NM3: There you go. We're in Normandy without any problem.

NF3: Yeah but <u>then</u> it's the same thing in Normandy there's going to be all the tourists for the D-day for uh the landing beach . . .

In fact, the preferred format of response with *alors* at the beginning of the turn is with another marker. The sequence can comprise up to three markers preceding *alors* and forming one single intonation unit: (1) a "receptive" marker (receiving or taking in the information); (2) an optional phatic marker; with (3) a contrastive marker, followed by *alors,* as, for example, (6):

(6) NF3: Après euh . . . toi tu t'occupes de l'organisation?

NF3: *Ben ouais mais alors* comment j'fais moi pour trouver un gîte?

NM3: After uh . . . you, you take care of the organization?

NF3: <u>Well yeah but then</u> how do I do, me, to find lodging?

Ben ouais forms a subunit that sets the stage for marking the speaker's different perspective. Its apparent function is to signal that the interlocutor's contribution (a cooperative move in surface) is taken into account. At the same time, *ben* specifically indexes the contribution as containing evident information, or information that does not give a complete perspective. Affirmative *ouais* (as opposed to standard *oui*) is not a neutral phatic response but signals the speaker's mitigated attitude, which is confirmed when the speaker brings up the issue of lodging. *Mais alors* forms the second subunit and prefaces the upcoming disagreement with, or at least objection to, the information just received by the speaker. *Alors* anaphorically evokes and reacts to the information by marking the speaker's distancing from its propositional content.

Example (7) represents an exception. The speaker presents her interlocutor with a problem following just-heard information, yet *alors* is utterance-final:

(7) NF3: On a la forêt, on a le lac, on va faire une petite randonnée en vélo.

NF3: On va pouvoir prendre les vélos *alors*?

NM3: We've got the forest, we've got the lake, we're going to a little bike ride.

NF3: We're going to be able to take the bikes <u>then</u>?

In fact, example (4) could be rephrased as (4′) yet carry out the same pragmatic function:

(4′) NF3: Je veux partir, je veux voir aut'chose.

NM3: Ben pourquoi pas dans l'Nord *alors*?

NF3: I want to leave, I want to see somethin' else.

NM3: Well why not in the North <u>then</u>?

Although *alors* is utterance-final in (7), it is still dialogical: It occurs at a point of turn taking and is uttered by the speaker who regains the floor. This question has a yes/no answer, and as is typical of spoken French, the speaker resorts to intonation rather than subject-verb inversion to signal the interrogative value. Because there is no interrogative word, I believe that moving *alors* to the end of the utterance reinforces the rising intonation pattern associated with a question. One more reason to consider (7) dialogal is that a question inherently, if briefly, returns the floor to the interlocutor. In (7), *alors* shifts the focus from the interlocutor's proposal of riding bikes to taking bikes. By contrast, (4') does contain a question word, so there is no need to mark the interrogative pattern. *Alors* does not have to carry that burden (signaling a question), and (4) is therefore preferred. Note that in (4') *ben* and *alors* are split, which certainly occurs in conversations but may not be the preferred format.

In sum, *alors* used at the beginning of a turn is a reactive marker that presents the interlocutor with a problem that he or she had not taken into account but that derives from his or her newly presented information. In this sense, the discursive *alors* does not represent a consequence or conclusion but a new perspective, often involving a problem. *Alors* allows the speaker to realize a shift of focus.

Alors within a turn (six occurrences).   In my data, *alors* within a turn fell into three categories. First, it marked a shift to a new topic, as in (8):

> (8) NF3: enfin . . . c'est un petit peu comme ça. *Alors* après on nous demande . . .
> [continues]
>
> *NF3: I mean . . . it's a little bit like that. <u>So</u> after we're being asked . . .*
> *[continues]*

Second, in a narrative, it marked a return to the foreground (another type of shift), as in (9):

> (9) NF1: Et j'étais chez des amis, et le 31 d . . . le 31 au soir . . . *alors* on sort et tout euh . . .
>
> *NF1: And I was at a friend's place, and the 31st d . . . the 31st in the evening . . . <u>so</u> we got out and all uh . . .*

Third, in *if* constructions, *alors* introduced the apodosis (a consequence and/or conclusion), a function that cannot be assumed by *donc* (Hansen 1997), so no overlap is possible.

> (10) NF3: Bon déjà <u>si</u> les Américains sont très conformistes, une conclusion serait peut-être: la vie aux Etats-Unis est artificielle *alors*. *Mais alors* est-ce que ça aussi/
>
> *NF3: OK for one thing is the Americans are very conformists, a conclusion could be: life in the United States is artificial <u>then.</u> <u>But then</u> does that too/*

The second instance of *alors* (co-occurring with the contrastive marker *mais*) is not functionally identical and indexes a focus shift. This time, the speaker is reacting to what she just said. In all three instances, *alors* functions anaphorically, as it often does, to refer back to a newly presented (potential) situation. More important, *alors* marks a shift in focus: In (10), although we don't know exactly what Nf3 is about to say, the question marker "est-ce que" indicates that she is considering a new perspective. In other words, *alors* does not entail continuity here but rather a rupture (a shift).

In sum, when *alors* occurs within a turn, it usually marks a shift to a (sub)topic and, in narration, to the next chronological event (sequencing). In the only instance when *alors* marked a conclusion (*if* constructions), *donc* could not be used, so there is no overlap with *donc*.

Donc

The argument made for *donc* is that, because of its ability to index continuity, it preferentially appears within a turn to assert the validity of a speaker's viewpoint (discourse content function). By extension, *donc* is also used to keep the floor (discourse management function), although at times it can be used to relinquish it. Its forty-nine within-turn occurrences out of fifty-nine indicate that the native speakers of this corpus markedly prefer this placement (monologal use), and the difference between dialogal (turn-initial) and monologal occurrences is even more marked (in the reverse direction) than for *alors*.

Donc turn-initial (ten instances).   The marked preference for the monologal use of *donc* finds an unexpected confirmation in a particular set of turn-initial occurrences: where the initial use of *donc* marked a new turn, five of the ten occurrences should be reanalyzed as instances of monologal use. There, the interlocutor gives a phatic response to encourage the speaker to pursue, which is exactly what happens:

(11) NM3: En France on aime beaucoup plus se poser contre ce qu'on nous dit

   NF3: Mmm

   NM3: *Donc euh* /dans c'cas-là/ y'a p't-être moins d'conformisme

   NF3: /Mais pas forcément . . . /

   NM3: In France we like much better to take an opposing stance to what we're told

   NF3: Mmm

   NM3: <u>*So uh*</u> */in that case/there may be less conformism*

   NF3: /But not necessarily . . . /

By indexing topic continuity, *donc* legitimizes the speaker's regaining the floor with, in the previous instance, the blessing of the interlocutor.

Donc is therefore used at two levels: Its discourse content function marks topic continuity through the indexing of a consequence, and, more strategically, its discourse management function allows the speaker to keep the floor. To some degree, *donc* overtly marks topic continuity as a connector, but pragmatically, as a discourse marker, it operates somewhat covertly as a conversational strategy. Native speakers may not be conscious of it, but their use of *donc* demonstrates that playing off its overt/covert functions is part of their pragmatic competence (Svartvik 1979).

The cumulating of the two functions is apparent in the next instance, where the two speakers compete to gain the floor:

(12) NM1: ouais ouais mais bon /j'veux dire/

    NF1: /donc/ après y'a une distance [inaudible] ils créent un cercle d'amis

    NM1: yeah yeah but well /I mean/

    NF1: /<u>so</u>/ after there's a distance [inaudible] they create a circle of friends

The speaker using *donc* does get the floor; its ability to index continuity asserts the right of the speaker to pursue his idea.

    Donc turn-initial can have a dialogal function when used to mark a confirmation request:

(13) NF1: Enfin tout l'sud quoi j'connais pas l'nord.

    NM1: Ouais.

    NF1: *Donc* toi tu . . . t'organises toi?

    NF1: Well the entire South DM I don't know the North.

    NM1: Yeah.

    NF1: <u>So</u> you . . . you . . . you organize, you?

Donc again expresses topic continuity—checking whether the interlocutor's assertion and the speaker's understanding of it match. *Donc* can also be used to mark a recapitulation, the effect of which is to verify agreement between the interlocutors (here, planning a vacation in France) before moving on.

(14) NF1: Ouais d'accord.

    NM1: Bon. *Donc* Marseille. Oui mais d'la Corse, euh ok

    NF1: Yeah all right.

    NM1: Ok. <u>So</u> Marseille. Yes but from Corsica, uh ok

Therefore not only is *donc* turn-initial rare in my data, but also it is used as a conversational strategy to regain the floor through its ability to index continuity rather than mark a consequence. Conceptually, consequence and continuity are not unrelated, which explains how *donc* can take on discourse functions such as prefacing confirmation requests and recapitulations.

Donc within a turn (forty-nine occurrences).   *Donc* was overwhelmingly used within a turn (83%). It was used argumentatively to mark conclusions and results in 50 percent of the cases, which means that in the other half, it was used for other functions, giving even less ground for functional overlap with *alors*. The ability of *donc* to index continuity is reinforced by its use to stress the truth condition of the utterance with *et, c'est vrai que, finalement,* and *c'est clair que* (*and, it's true that, finally,* and *it's clear that,* respectively), as in examples (15) and (16):

(15) NF1: On a cette idée-là par rapport à l'image en fait que les Etats-Unis veulent
        véhiculer d'eux au reste du monde. *Donc c'est vrai que* le système de
        santé, ben euh, il est permissible

NF1: We have this idea with respect to the image in fact that the United States want to present to the rest of the world. <u>So it's true that</u> the health system, well uh, it's permissible

(16) NM3: En plus là on est en train d'parler d'vacances d'été *donc c'est clair que* euh . . . [laughs] y'aura du monde partout [pause] y'a qu'chez soi où y'a personne finalement!

NM3: *In addition here we're talking about summer vacation <u>so it's clear that</u> uh . . . [laughs] it will be crowded everywhere [pause] there's only at home that there's no one in the end!*

Such terms also reinforce the validity of the speaker's point of view. The use of the contrastive marker *mais* as a repair strategy after using *donc* is an indirect confirmation that *donc* indexes topic continuity or validation of the viewpoint, as in (17):

(17) NF1: Ah oui parce que les Parisiens sont plus . . . sont plus à Paris *donc finalement mais* euh . . .

NM1: Y'a qu'des touristes! Y'a qu'des touristes, américains entre autres euh ou allemands

NF1: *Ah yes because the Parisians are no longer . . . are no longer in Paris <u>so finally but</u> uh . . .*

NM1: *There are only tourists! There are only tourists, American among others uh or German*

In this example, *finalement* is in line with *donc* and marks continuity of the argument, whereas the adjacent *mais* allows the speaker to back out of this continuity. In fact, the interlocutor fills in the counterargument that is missing in Nf1's turn.

Donc can also preface a recapitulation (Hansen 1997; Pellet 2005) at the beginning of a turn and within a turn. By marking that a decision has been reached, the speakers may progress toward the completion of their conversational agenda, as in (18):

(18) NM3: C'est pas un problème. Euh bon ben *donc* on a décidé le gîte. On peut p't-être aller visiter quelques châteaux . . .

NM3: *That's not a problem. Uh ok well <u>so</u> we decided on the lodging. We can maybe go and visit a few castles . . .*

Within a frameshift, as in example (19), *donc* reestablishes topic continuity after the disjunctive or contrastive marker *mais* and thus establishes the speaker's right to continue.[6] The use of the interactive marker *tu vois* encourages the interlocutor to share the speaker's viewpoint:

(19) NM1: C'est une région qu'est extrêmement belle au point de vue nature c'est une région qu'est pas plate parce que j'en ai marre des régions plates *mais donc tu vois* c'est un peu vallonné y'a des . . . euh des pas des précipices y'a des huh des p'tites montagnes, des collines . . .

NM1: *It's a region that's extremely beautiful nature-wise it's a region that's not flat because I'm sick of flat regions <u>but so you see</u> it's a little hilly there are . . . uh some not canyons there are uh small mountains, hills . . .*

Finally, *donc* is used to signal that the speaker is engaged in a cognitive process (see Schourup 2001 for *well*) with the practical result of allowing the speaker either to retain or to yield the floor. *Donc* marks the speaker's intention to pursue a thought that is not yet formulated. In fact, the speaker may give up on further elaboration, and in this case, the use of *donc* followed by either a pause or a hesitation particle offers the interlocutor a point of entry, as (20) illustrates:

(20) NM1: Parce que qu'tu prennes euh que tu prennes un hôtel et que tu restes dans
         cet hôtel pendant huit jours ou qu'tu prennes des hôtels différents et qu'tu
         . . . ça r'vient à peu près au même prix *donc euh* . . .

      NM1: Because whether you take uh whether you take a hotel and you stay in
         this hotel for eight days or whether you take different hotels and you . . .
         it comes more or less to the same price so uh . . .

This processing use of *donc* within turn (twelve instances in the corpus, or 25%) may be viewed as an exceptional case. *Donc* seems to occur at the end of a turn, but the interlocutor is indirectly encouraged to fill in with the unstated but obvious conclusion. The concluding thought "*va de soi*," that is, "goes without saying," is acted out here literally. Besides this discourse content function, processing *donc* may simultaneously have the discourse management function of a yield signal. Note that the English *so* functions similarly.

Conclusion: *Alors donc*

In this corpus, French native speakers strongly associate *donc* with marking the validity of their own viewpoint because it indexes continuity through its core value of inferential evidential; that is, it asserts that something logically follows from what has just been said. The corollary is that it can assume a discourse management function by indexing (logical) continuity. *Donc* can be and is used to keep the floor, and argumentative *donc* is therefore used within a turn-at-talk, which explains why, in (21), *donc* is possible but not *alors:*

(21) C'est le cousin de ma femme, et *donc / *alors* mon cousin par alliance
                                        (from Jayez 1988, 136, cited in Hansen 1997)
     He is my wife's cousin, and so my cousin by marriage.

By contrast, native speakers associate *alors* with the processing of just-heard information. *Alors* manifests a change of orientation following an assessment of the interlocutor's newly shared perspective on a topic in progress. At the discourse content level, *alors* allows the speaker to index a reactive move or even to mark a distancing from the interlocutor's position. At the conversation management level, the marker gives the speaker an opportunity to interject and (or in order to) get the floor, and thus *alors* is favored in a dialogal context, at the beginning of a turn, which explains why, in (22), *alors* is possible but not *donc:*

(22) Tu sais tout, *alors / * donc* donne-moi le tiercé   (from Roulet 1997, 151)
     You know everything so give me the three winning numbers for the
     horse-race

There were no instances of the compound form *alors donc* in my data, and the compound is far less frequent than each individual marker. It is a known fact that *donc alors* cannot occur, but why? I contend that when the markers occur together, *alors* functions at the structural level, while *donc* functions at the content level. In other words, *alors* operates sequentially to mark forward movement, whereas *donc* marks the end of a previous aside and continuity with the previous topic. The latter is important because it justifies the speaker's going on. Therefore *alors* must occur before *donc*. As there were no instances of *alors donc* in my corpus, I explored the DELIC corpus (www.up.univ-mrs.fr/delic/corpus/index.html) for *alors donc* and found that it occurs more frequently within turn (sixteen out of twenty-seven occurrences) than at the beginning (twelve out of twenty-seven occurrences).

The corpus used for this study was limited in sample size and duration of interaction. The pair format also favored a cleaner interactional pattern. With multiple speakers, the turn-taking dynamics would change, and the conversational structure, fairly linear with two speakers, would likely become messier.[7] More competition to get the floor might lead to cooperation issues among speakers and to the possible emergence of a dominant speaker. Nonetheless, the semantics and patterns of the use of *donc* as a marker indexing continuity, evidentiality, and inferentiality should hold true, just as *alors* is foremost a marker indexing sequentiality and focus shift.

NOTES

1. Nf1 reflects the coding system used: N stands for native speaker, f for female, and the number simply reflects the order of recording sessions.
2. More recently, Netz and Kuzar (2007) also make the case for content versus management discourse functions beyond discourse markers.
3. Maschler relies on single form-function equivalences to explain her model, while of course, in reality, each discourse marker fulfills several, usually related discourse functions.
4. The distinction between function and content words is not helpful here because discourse markers obviously fulfill functions at the pragmatic level.
5. Individual variation along with age (see Andersen 2001) and gender (see Brinton 1996) characterize the use of discourse markers.
6. "Frameshift" is a term usually associated with narratives, meaning that the speaker returns to the main point of the story or ends a digression, both of which are signaled with a marker.
7. Each speaker implicitly recognizes that the turns will alternate.

REFERENCES

Andersen, Elain S., Maquela Brizuela, Beatrice DuPuy, and Laura Gonnerman. 1999. Cross-linguistic evidence for the early acquisition of discourse markers as register variables. *Journal of Pragmatics* 31:1339–51.

Andersen, Gisle. 2001. *Pragmatic markers and sociolinguistic variation: A relevance-theoretic approach to the language of adolescents.* Amsterdam: John Benjamins.

Barnes, Betsy K. 1998. The acquisition of connectors in French L2 narrative discourse. *French Language Studies* 8:189–208.

Bouacha, Ali. 1981. Alors dans le discours pédagogique: Epiphénomène ou trace d'opérations discursives? *Langue Française* 50:39–52.

Brinton, Laurel. 1996. *Pragmatic markers in English: grammaticalization and discourse functions.* New York: Mouton de Gruyter.

Chaudron, Craig. 2003. Data collection in SLA research. In *The handbook of second language acquisition,* ed. Catherine J. Doughty and Michael H. Long, 762–828. Oxford: Blackwell.

Hansen, Maj-Britt. 1997. *Alors* and *donc* in spoken French: A reanalysis. *Journal of Pragmatics* 28:153–87.

Jayez, Jacques. 1988. *Alors:* Description et paramètre. *Recherches Pragmatiques sur le Discours* 9:133–75.

Jucker, Andreas, and Yael Ziv. 1998. Discourse markers: Introduction. In *Discourse markers: Description and theory,* ed. Andreas Jucker and Yael Ziv, 1–12. Amsterdam: John Benjamins.

Maschler, Yael. 1998. Rotsè lishmoa kéta? "Wanna hear something weird/funny [lit. 'a segment']"?: The discourse markers segementing Israeli Hebrew talk-in-interaction. In *Discourse markers: Description and theory,* ed. Andreas Jucker and Yael Ziv, 13–60. Amsterdam: John Benjamins.

Moeschler, Jacques. 2002. Pragmatics and linguistic encoding: Evidence from the conceptual/procedural distinction. www.unige.ch/lettres/linge/moeschler/publication_pdf/pragmatics.pdf (accessed October 15, 2004).

Netz, Hadar, and Ron Kuzar. 2007. Three marked theme constructions in spoken English. *Journal of Pragmatics* 39 (2): 305–35.

Östman, Jan-Ola. 1982. The symbiotic relationship between pragmatic particles and impromptu speech. In *Impromptu speech: A symposium,* ed. Nils E. Enkvist, 147–77. Abö: Abö Akademy.

Pellet, Stéphanie. 2005. The development of competence in French interlanguage pragmatics: The case of the discourse marker "donc." PhD diss., University of Texas, UMI.

Rehner, Katherine. 2002. The development of aspects of linguistic and discourse competence by advanced second language learners of French. PhD diss., University of Toronto, UMI.

Roulet, Eddy. 1997. A modular approach to discourse structures. *Pragmatics* 7 (2): 125–46.

Schiffrin, Deborah. 1987. *Discourse markers.* Cambridge: Cambridge University Press.

Schourup, Lawrence. 2001. Rethinking well. *Journal of Pragmatics* 33 (7): 1025–60.

Svartvik, Jan. 1979. *Well* in conversation. In *Studies in English linguistics for Randolph Quirk,* ed. Sidney Greenbaum, Geoffrey Leech, and Jan Svartvik, 162–77. London: Longman.

15

▨ "Little Words" in *Small Talk:* Some Considerations on the Use of the Pragmatic Markers *man* in English and *macho/tío* in Peninsular Spanish

LAURA ALBA-JUEZ
Universidad Nacional de Educación a Distancia

▨ PRAGMATIC MARKERS are linguistic forms that are very common and frequent in spontaneous conversation, and, as Carranza (1997) points out, they can signal not only some kind of attitude on the part of the speakers toward their interlocutor(s) but also the limits and relationships between different parts of the text or discourse.

In this chapter I present, discuss, and analyze (both qualitatively and quantitatively) the different uses and discourse functions of the pragmatic markers *man* in English (E) and *macho tío* in Peninsular Spanish (PS), including some reflections on and analysis of their feminine counterpart (*tía* and "*macha*") in Spanish.

The corpus used for the analysis has been taken from different sources, such as the online concordances of oral language of the *British National Corpus* (BNC) in *Variation in English Words and Phrases* (VIEW; Davies 2005) and *US TV Talk,* as well as some American radio interviews and movies. For Spanish, the main source has been the oral section of the *Corpus de Referencia del Español Actual* (CREA), which includes television and radio shows, telephone conversations, and face-to-face oral interactions among friends, workmates, or members of a family. The recording and transcriptions of some conversations in Spanish, carried out by the researcher and author of this article, have also been made use of.

Following Fraser's (1996, 2006) taxonomy, we could label the markers *man* (E) and *macho/tío* (PS) as parallel pragmatic markers, "whose function is to signal an entire message in addition to the basic message" (1996, 21). I also follow Fraser in his view of pragmatic markers as expressions that occur as part of a discourse segment but are not part of the propositional content of the message conveyed and that do not contribute to the meaning of the proposition *per se.*

Within parallel markers, *macho/tío* (PS) and *man* (E) belong to the subclass of vocatives, but, as will be shown with examples in the following sections, they can also be found fulfilling the functions of any of the other three subclasses in Fraser's taxonomy, namely *speaker displeasure markers, solidarity markers,* and *focusing markers.*

Other authors, such as Gille (2006) refer to these markers as a kind of "conversational appendix," a term defined as a mechanism that is typically conversational in nature and that is used in order to modify the original, basic message or to make sure that the appropriate interactive effect is conveyed. Within the class of conversational appendices, Gille classifies the Spanish *macho* as an "intersubjectivity appendix" (*apéndice de intersubjetividad*), which is a kind of appendix that addresses the interlocutor(s) and consequently regulates the ongoing interaction.

As authors like Gili Gaya (1970) or Martín Zorraquino (1998) point out, pragmatic markers[1] can be associated to different communicative registers. Some markers are normally associated with the written registers and others with the spoken ones. The markers being analyzed herein (*man* [E] and *macho/tío* [PS]) are normally found in spoken, informal registers in both English and Spanish, and, as the results of this study show, they very frequently form part and are features of the so-called small talk. The underlying perspective of small talk in this study adheres to that of Coupland (2000) and many other authors who, far from considering this kind of talk as "small," view it as a useful tool in helping individuals accomplish social goals such as building solidarity and connection with their interlocutors, putting people at ease, or winning the listener's approval of their own perspective (among other functions). Small talk then acts as a catalyst for "big talk," also called (according to Tracy and Naughton 2000) "information exchange," "formal remarks," or "real business" (63).

An important feature of small talk is the fact that, in some way or another, the speakers always tend toward the use of conversational strategies that entail a certain degree of solidarity. As will become apparent, the markers studied herein very frequently carry a solidarity message that is independent from, but at the same time accompanies, the basic propositional message of the utterance. This fact makes the study of these markers a fertile ground for their analysis from the linguistic politeness perspective. In the examples found in the corpus, these markers tend to be used within positive politeness strategies (Brown and Levinson 1987), in order to mark the affiliation (Bravo 1999) bonds between the interlocutors. However, on some occasions they may also become markers of a greater or lower degree of impoliteness (in the sense given to it by Kaul de Marlangeon 1995; Culpeper 1996; or Alba-Juez 2006, 2007), as well as of disapproval or disbelief.

Another interesting function of the markers *man* (E) and *macho/tío* (PS) is their turn-changing function (Sacks, Schegloff, and Jefferson 1974), that is, they are very frequently found at the beginning or end of an utterance, where they clearly mark the change of a turn in the ongoing conversation. This function is related to the above-mentioned view (Gille 2006) of these markers as interaction regulators.

It is interesting and important to point out that these expressions, as well as any other pragmatic markers, are versatile, multifunctional, and polysemous, for they communicate not only one message but also different and various messages, depending on the context and situation in which they are found.

Some similarities and differences between the use of *man* in English and *macho/tío* in Spanish will be commented on as well, although I do not intend to arrive at definitive or final contrastive conclusions.

Man (E) and Macho/Tío (PS) as Parallel Pragmatic Markers

When used as pragmatic parallel markers, the "little words" *man* (E) and *macho/tío* (PS) may occur in initial, middle, or final position in the utterance, as illustrated in table 15.1.

According to Fraser (1996), there are a number of small classes of parallel markers, of which he presents the following four: (a) vocative markers, (b) speaker displeasure markers, (c) solidarity markers, and (d) focusing markers. It is evident that the markers *man* (E) and *macho/tío* (PS) belong to class *a*, that is, to the class of vocative markers. However, apart from being clearly vocative, in some situations they can also be classified as speaker displeasure, solidarity, or focusing markers. Examine the following examples:

(1) (Scene: in the limousine)
Lee and Carter land in the back. Slam into their seats and try to catch their breath. The TWO MEN START TO LAUGH when they realize they're alive!

CARTER: We made it, *man.*

LEE: No problem.

(Movie Script: *Rush Hour 2,* by Jeff Nathanson)

Example (1) is one of many instances where the marker *man* has been found to be used not only as a vocative but also as a solidarity marker. Here both men are happy because they finally beat their enemies, and therefore the language and expressions they use are an explicit sign of solidarity and friendship.

But many other times this vocative marker can be used with a very different, almost opposite, meaning, as is the case in example (2), where Lucy Lawless shows her anger after the New Orleans floods in 2005:

(2) *LUCY :* You know the best thing to come out, the only good thing that can come out of this, is this is our wake up call to consciousness, *man;* you gotta be awake for what's coming. Consciousness is going to stop us all being lazy, intellectually, emotionally, in our

Table 15.1

Examples of the Different Markers in Initial, Middle, and Final Position

Marker	Initial Position	Middle Position	Final Position
Man (E)	**Man,** I'm scared!	We were, er . . . **man,** accused of robbery.	Watch out, **man!**
Macho/tío (PS)	**Tío/macho,** ¿qué te pasa?	Te digo, **macho/tío,** que te calles la boca.	Cállate, **macho/ tío!**

relationships with our neighbors. Also politically, socially, stopping lazy, let's stop anaesthetizing ourselves with BeniFer or Michael Jackson or Nancy Grace in my case.

HARRISON: [chuckles] At least you admit it, that's step 1.

LUCY: Yeah, *man,* recognize your own shit. I think that's really important. We can't fix anything while all this disinformation, all the nonsense about "let's not point the finger" moment. BS! *Man,* you are going to use your anger to springboard you into action. THERE'S NO HOPE WITHOUT ACTION. So get off our arses and start making a difference in our own lives and everyone else.

(Interview with Lucy Lawless on *Harrison on the Edge* radio show, September 18, 2005, AUSXIP)

The three occasions on which Lucy uses the marker *man* are instances in which she shows her deep anger and displeasure, and, even though we may say that *man* is a vocative and she is addressing Harrison, in fact her anger is directed toward the government and the desperate situation of the city at that moment. Thus we may place the marker *man* into the speaker displeasure category here, and, at least in the last instance where it is used ("Man, *you are going to use your anger to springboard you into action*"), we may also classify it as a focusing marker, because Lucy is trying to incite the listeners to take action. In addition, it is worth noticing that this is one of few instances in the corpus where a woman uses the marker *man,* which, according to the findings of this study, seems to be much more widely used by men in general, as shown by the quantitative analysis results in table 15.2.

Man may also co-occur with other vocatives (as in *John man, please shut up!*), with other classes of pragmatic markers or with other subclasses of parallel marker. Examine (3):

(3) SARAH: Look, I'll show you, right. It's right to save, yeah. Nationwide that . . . *wow, see man,* that's, that's just, just what, that's what I put in and take out do you get me. Hi you see, you know er . . . how much are you taking out?   (BNC, 3691 KPY)

Here *man* is used together with an interjection (*wow,* a lexical basic marker) and another parallel marker of the *focusing* type (*[you] see*):

Table 15.2
Use of the Marker *man* according to Gender (%)

Occurrence in the English Corpus	
Male addressing male	85.6
Male addressing female	1.8
Female addressing male	10.8
Female addressing female	1.8

In Spanish, *macho* or *tío* may also co-occur with other pragmatic markers, such as *pues*[2] and *mira* (4). *Mira* functions here in a way similar to Fraser's focusing parallel markers in English:

(4) . . . ¿De dónde la has sacado? ¡De mis contactos! *¡Pues, macho mira,* me lo pidió Diseprosa. Entonces una cosa, una cosa dime. . . .

(CREA, párrafo n° 5, Conversación telefónica en una empresa, 20/03/91)

Solidarity and Gender

As pointed out in the introductory remarks, the analysis made through the concordances of the markers *macho* and *tío* in the CREA corpus (as well as that of the marker *man* in the English corpus) sheds light on the fact that, in the majority of cases, these little words are used as markers of solidarity. In most of these cases, the solidarity message is given from a man to another man or boy, but there are a few instances in which a woman uses the markers when she addresses men. When women address other women in Spanish, they can use the feminine *tía,* which is not an uncommon feature of Peninsular Spanish. Also, in everyday conversation in Spain, I have been able to observe that some women are now using the marker *macho* when addressing other women, which sounds surprising when first hearing it, considering the feature of masculinity attached to the meaning of the word. Probably that is the reason why, mainly among female teenagers, one can sometimes hear utterances like (5), which still sound a bit contradictory, for the feminine of *macho* in Spanish is *hembra.* However, *hembra* would sound rude or rough to the ears of a native speaker, because it is normally associated with animals, not people.

(5) A: *"Macha,* ¿te vienes conmigo o te quedas?"

Table 15.3 shows the percentages of occurrence of all these possibilities in the Spanish corpus used for this study. As can be observed, of all occurrences, the marker *macho* used by men addressing men is the most frequent (33.7%). Second in order of frequency is the use of the marker *tía* used by women addressing women (20.4%). Thus *macho* seems to be the most frequent choice for men, and *tía* for women, leaving the use of *tío* in second place for men and *macha* for women. In instances of men addressing women, *tía* seems to be the preferred option (10.2%) and *tío* the most common choice for women addressing men (7.14%), in cases where they decide to use a marker of the kind.

▒ Table 15.3
Use of the Different Markers in Spanish according to Gender (%)

	macho	macha	tío	tía
Male addressing male	33.7	0	14.3	0
Male addressing female	0	4.08	0	10.2
Female addressing male	1.02	0	7.14	0
Female addressing female	3.06	5.1	0	20.5

The Use of These Markers as Elements of Small Talk

Because of the inherent spoken/colloquial quality of the markers in question, they are very frequently found within episodes of small talk in both English and Spanish. As stated previously, small talk is a type of talk that helps the interlocutors achieve certain social goals, such as building rapport, putting people at ease, or winning power, approval, or support. In the corpora examined, it is clear that the use of the markers *man* (E) and *macho/tío* (PS) is a strategy that contributes to these goals, in combination with other strategies of small talk, such as (a) use of narratives of personal experience/use of the vernacular language, (b) deviation from the norm in the use of journalistic talk (conversationalization [Fairclough 1995] of journalistic talk), (c) joking (humor and irony), (d) gossiping, and (e) cursing/use of impoliteness markers.

We very frequently find instances of the use of the markers *man* (E) and *macho/tío* (PS) in combination with, or as substrategies of, one or more of the above-mentioned strategies. Example (6) presents an instance of *tío* (PS) used in a radio program in Spain, within a kind of talk that has been conversationalized and consequently does not strictly follow the norms of formal journalistic discourse. We can also observe a certain degree of gossiping and humor in the conversation, and thus it can be said that there is a combination of strategies b, c, and d:

(6) A: Bueno, pero lo que te he dicho, que hoy les voy a tener que dar esquinazo a las periquitas. Porque tengo mucha prisa que esta tarde tengo una boda. Que me han dicho los novios que estás invitado.

B: Pero, pero si no sé ni quiénes son los novios, no los conozco, ni sé si los conozco, ni sabía nada de esta boda.

A: Pero yo pero, pero **tío,** ellos a ti sí te conocen, sí. Además yo te he hablado de la novia ¿sí? Si te he hablado en otras emisiones ¿sí? Te he hablado de la novia que es la madre de mi amigo el orejones López. ¡Anda! Que no, que no parece una madre porque está superbuena.

B: Mira **tío,** ésa no es manera de hablar de las madres de un amiguito.

(Adapted from CREA, párrafo nº 4, *A vivir que son dos días,* Madrid, 02/11/96, Cadena SER)

Example (7) contains an instance of the marker *man* used within a narrative of personal experience (strategy *a*), where the vernacular language (Labov 1972) is used:

(7) Then we had bayonet practice. And er, then, we was all sorted out, this was the staple for the Home Guard, we was sorted out er to go to er, er *man,* the guns at Sutton-on-Sea, the er, girder rockets. And er I was er one that was sorted out to go, but they wouldn't let me go because er, I couldn't get , they couldn't get me.
(Adapted from BNC, 279 FY2)

In spite of the fact that *man* (E) and *macho/tío* (PS) are normally markers of a high degree of solidarity and rapport, on some occasions they may accompany some curse words and rude language. However, even when used with rude language, they may be markers of solidarity or rapport, by showing that the speakers have a high degree of familiarity or closeness with their interlocutors, which makes them feel comfortable enough to allow for the use of a kind of language that would otherwise be used in private or intimate conversations.

The data analyzed exhibit innumerable cases of these markers within the informal context and language of small talk. The examples in this section are only a small sample illustrating the fact and making the point that *man* in English and *macho* or *tío* in Spanish are also used as strategic markers that fulfill important discursive functions, to which I now turn.

Discourse Functions

The study of the different and numerous occurrences of the markers *man* (E) and *macho/tío* (PS) in the corpora has shed light on the fact that these markers are normally used in one or more of the following three ways: (a) as markers of (im)politeness, (b) as markers of turn change (interaction regulators), and (c) as alerters (focusing or warning function).

  a) Markers of (im)politeness: These markers always show a given attitude on the part of the speakers toward their interlocutor(s), and consequently some degree of politeness force can always be ascribed to them. In the majority of occurrences studied in the corpora, both in Spanish and in English, these markers are used within a positive politeness context (Brown and Levinson 1987) showing some kind of affiliation (Bravo 1999), where the speakers are willing to express feelings or emotions such as rapport, encouragement, admiration, or bewilderment (91% of occurrences in English and 84.7% in Spanish; see table 15.4), as illustrated in (8) and (9).

  (8) 75 WINSTON: Oh, you were brilliant, *man*!

     DAVID: Nah, not really

     (Adapted from *US TV Talk* 26:871)

  (9) A: Venga, elijan lo que más les guste, señores, Oye, guarda, guarda. El conejito o el perrito pon-pon. El de los lunares. Toma, *tío*, para la colección. Mira, mira, así, venga, y sorteamos. Toma, figuritas. Para toda aquella persona que no tenga.

     B: No me ha tocado nada, *tía*.

     (Adapted from CREA, párrafo n° 39, Conversación en Talleres de *Inspección Técnica de Vehículos,* Madrid, 23/12/91)

Table 15.4
Frequency of Use of the Different Markers according to Discourse Function (%)

	Markers of (Im)politeness		Interaction Regulators	Focusing Function
	Rapport	Impoliteness		
Man (English)	91	9	53.2	35.1
Macho/a // tío/a (Spanish)	84.7	15.3	42.9	44.9

As stated earlier, these vocative parallel markers can also be used to indicate some degree of impoliteness (9% of occurrences in English and 15.3% in Spanish; see table 15.4), conveying some negative thoughts or feelings such as threat, warning, disapproval, disappointment, or disbelief, as examples (10) and (11) show:

(10) BOBBY: You're dead, *man,* you're dead!

   (*US TV Talk,* 52:604)

(11) A: ¿Negocio? ¡Me cago en la puta! Chungo, tío, me he limpiado nada más que un coche en todo el día!

   B: Limpia, que me has dejado aquí una caca de pájaro! Pero, ¿cómo es posible, hombre? ¡Si tienes aquí el negocio del siglo!

   A: ¿Qué negocio? ¡Pero si todo el mundo baja y me da de hostias! ¿Qué no puedo limpiar ni un coche, *macho*! Pero, quítate de ahí, me cago en la puta! Venga hombre, con el cubo, hostia!

   Mira, mira, mira el pie, me han chafado veinticinco veces ya . . .

   (Adapted from CREA, párrafo n° 22, *No te rías que es peor,* Madrid, 19/12/91, TVE 1 A)

   b) Markers of turn change/Interaction regulators: One very noticeable and frequent function of the markers *man* in English and *macho/tío* in Spanish is the function of regulating the interaction by marking turn change. Consider example (12):

(12) (Conversation about a video game):

   A: Oh this is so rubbish, *man.*

   B: You can only see like his back, his legs an, and the back of running. They're copycats, *man.*

   A: So shit, *man.*

   B: Mm, Sega's better. Sega are blatantly better.

   (BNC, 3248 KNV)

The marker *man* is found at the end of each turn except for the last, where the culmination of the term is marked by *yeah,* a lexical basic marker expressing agreement (Fraser 1996). In some of the conversations analyzed this is taken to such an extent that we find repeated instances of the marker at the end of almost every tone group uttered by the same person, in which case the function is not marking turn change but change of tone group, as in (13):

(13) Get your knees under the table and 'move them, '*man.* You take up all the 'space, '*man.* 'Yeah, dark 'horse. 'Right.

   (BNC, 4108 KSN)

Table 15.4 shows that *man* is used as an interaction regulator in 53.2 percent of occurrences in the English corpus, and *macho/a* or *tío/a* in Spanish are used in 42.9 percent of occurrences in the Spanish corpus fulfilling the same function, which makes it the second most frequent function in English and the third most frequent in Spanish. As we shall see, the focusing function (see following discussion) occurs slightly more frequently in Spanish, and many times both interaction regulation and focus can be attributed to the same marker in the same instance.

    c) Alerters/Focusing function: The markers *man* (E) and *macho/tío* (PS) are also used on occasions at the beginning of an utterance with the intention of calling the attention of the speaker to focus on the message. Many times the marker also carries a threatening tone, the meaning behind the marker being something like "pay attention to what I'm going to say or else," as is the case with Lucy Lawless in (14):

(14) LUCY: Yeah *man,* recognize your own shit. I think that's really important. We can't fix anything while all this disinformation, all the nonsense about "let's not point the finger" moment. BS! *Man,* you're going to use your anger to springboard you into action. THERE'S NO HOPE WITHOUT ACTION. So get off our arses and start making a difference in our own lives and everyone else.

(Interview with Lucy Lawless on *Harrison on the Edge* radio show, September 18, 2005, AUSXIP)

    Of all three functions, the use of these expressions as markers of positive politeness (rapport) is by far the most frequent, the least frequent being their use as markers of impoliteness (9% for *man* and 15.3% for *macho/a or tío/a*). Table 15.4 displays these results, as well as the fact that on most occasions the marker is fulfilling more than one function at a time (considering that the sum of the subtotals is higher than 100%).

Conclusions and Comparison

Both the qualitative and quantitative findings of this study suggest that there are probably more similarities than differences between the use of the marker *man* in English and the markers *macho* and *tío* in Spanish. In both cases they are characteristic of oral, colloquial, and informal conversation, and consequently they are common features of small talk. The three markers in question may appear at the beginning, middle, or end of an utterance and can be classified as parallel pragmatic markers that carry out important functions in discourse, such as building solidarity and rapport, changing turn or regulating the interaction, or, when at the beginning of the utterance, focusing on or alerting the speaker about some aspect of the ongoing discourse.

    In spite of all the similarities, the use of *macho* and *tío* in Spanish might be qualified as "more colorful" and varied than the use of *man* in English, due to the fact that both Spanish words have the possibility of undergoing grammatical gender change, however ridiculous the word *"macha"* might sound to anyone's ears. The fact is that *macha* is nonetheless used, especially among adolescents or very young people in general. I do not have any records of the word *woman* used in English as a pragmatic marker in the same way as *man* is. The word *girl,* however, could be considered as the feminine counterpart in this case. Also, the different examples of *man* in the corpus show that both women and men may use the marker *man* when addressing men or women indistinctly.

The present study has only been an initial approach to the study of these markers, and therefore they have been analyzed in a very general way, without taking into account other variables that might intervene in their use, such as, for instance, social class or race. The results have shed some light on the influence of the gender, strategy, and discourse function variables, as shown by the examples analyzed and the quantitative analysis results in tables 15.2, 15.3, and 15.4.

In addition, I am conscious of the fact that *man* in English and *macho/a* and *tío/a* in Spanish are not the only markers of this kind that are in use nowadays. These were chosen for being the most general and standard, but many interesting conclusions could be drawn if we also researched (and made comparisons among) similar markers, such as *dude* in English or *tronco* in Spanish, which, at first sight, seem to belong exclusively to the younger people's repertoire.

NOTES

1. Notice, however, that neither of these authors uses the term "pragmatic marker": Gili Gaya writes about "partículas" (particles), and Martín Zorraquino speaks of "marcadores del discurso" (discourse markers), the latter being more in agreement with Schiffrin's (1987, 2001) view of the phenomenon.
2. The marker *pues* has been labeled differently by different authors. Bello (1847) refers to it as a "continuative particle."

REFERENCES

Alba-Juez, L. 2006. Some pragmatic markers of impoliteness in British English and Peninsular Spanish. In *A pleasure of life in words: A festschrift for Angela Downing,* ed. Marta Carretero, Laura Hidalgo Downing, Julia Lavid, Elena Martínez Caro, JoAnne Neff, Soledad Pérez de Ayala, and Esther Sánchez Pardo, 403–19. Madrid: Universidad Complutense.
———. (2007). On the impoliteness of some politeness strategies: A study and comparison of the use of some pragmatic markers of impoliteness in British English and American English, Peninsular Spanish and Argentine Spanish. Chap. 2 in Pilar Garcés-Conejos, Manuel Padilla Cruz, Reyes Gómez Morón, and Lucía Fernández Amaya, eds., *Studies in intercultural, cognitive and social pragmatics.* New Castle upon Tyne, UK: Cambridge Scholars.
Bello, Andrés. 1847. *Gramática de la lengua castellana destinada al uso de los americanos.* Con las notas de Rufino José de Cuervo. Estudio y edición de Ramón Trujillo. 2 vols. Madrid: Arco Libros, 1988.
Bravo, Diana. 1999. ¿Imagen "positiva" vs. Imagen "negativa"?: Pragmática socio-cultural y componentes de face. *Oralia. Análisis del Discurso Oral* 2:155–84.
Brown, Penelope, and Stephen Levinson. 1987. *Politeness: Some universals in language usage.* Cambridge: Cambridge University Press.
Carranza, Isolda. 1997. *Conversación y deixis de discurso.* Córdoba, Argentina: Universidad de Córdoba.
Coupland, Justine, ed. 2000. *Small talk.* London: Pearson Education.
———. 2003. Small talk: Social functions. *Research on Language and Social Interaction* 36:1–6.
Culpeper, J. 1996. Towards an anatomy of impoliteness. *Journal of Pragmatics* 25:349–67.
Davies, Mark. 2005. *VIEW* (Variation in English Words and Phrases). Salt Lake City: Brigham Young University. Concordances from the BNC. http://view.byu.edu/.
Fairclough, Norman. 1995. *Critical discourse analysis: The critical study of language.* Harlow: Longman.
Fraser, Bruce. 1996. Pragmatic markers. *Pragmatics* 6 (2): 167–90.
———. 2006. Towards a theory of discourse markers. In *Approaches to discourse particles,* ed. K. Fischer, 189–204. Bremen: Elsevier.

Gili Gaya, Samuel. 1970. *Curso superior de sintaxis Española.* Barcelona: Biblograf.

Gille, Johan. 2006. "Este hombre se debe de mover, vamos": Un primer acercamiento a los apéndices conversacionales. *Actas del XVI Congreso de Romanistas Escandinavos.* CD-ROM.

Kaul de Marlangeon, Silvia. 1995. "La fuerza de cortesía-descortesía y sus estrategias en el discurso tanguero de la década del '20." *Revista de la Sociedad Argentina de Lingüística* 3:7–38.

Labov, William, ed. 1972. The transformation of experience in narrative syntax. In *Language in the inner city,* 354–405. Philadelphia: University of Pennsylvania Press.

Martín Zorraquino, María Antonia. 1998. Los marcadores del discurso desde el punto de vista gramatical. In *Los marcadores del discurso: Teoría y análisis,* ed. María Antonia Martín Zorraquino, and Estrella Montolío Durán, 19–53. Madrid: Arco Libros.

REAL ACADEMIA ESPAÑOLA: Banco de datos (CREA) [online]. Corpus de referencia del español actual. www.rae.es (accessed October 24, 2006).

Sacks, Harvey, Emanuel Schegloff, and Gail Jefferson. 1974. A simple systematics for the organization of turn-taking in conversation. *Language* 50 (4): 696–735.

Schiffrin, Deborah. 1987. *Discourse markers.* Cambridge: Cambridge University Press.

———. 2001. Discourse markers: Language, meaning, and context. In *The handbook of discourse analysis,* ed. Deborah Schiffrin, Deborah Tannen, and Heidi Hamilton, 54–75. Malden, MA: Blackwell.

Tracy, Karen, and Julie M. Naughton. 2000. Institutional identity-work: A better lens. In *Small talk,* ed. Justine Coupland, 62–83. London: Pearson Education.

Web Concordancer: US TV Talk & BNC. 2005. WorldNet entries for *man.* www.lextutor.ca/concordances/concord_ehtml (accessed October 26, 2006).

16

Little Words That Could Impact One's Impression on Others

Greetings and Closings in Institutional E-mails

SIGRUN BIESENBACH-LUCAS
Georgetown University

IN ACADEMIC INSTITUTIONS, much of the interaction between students and professors occurs face-to-face—in class meetings and during office hours. Computer technology has, however, opened other communication venues in academia for which rules of interaction are less clearly defined, such as electronic mailing lists, discussion boards, chats, and electronic mail. While the former principally serve to enhance information distribution and unconventional course content delivery, e-mail has become a major alternative for students to consult with their professors (Biesenbach-Lucas 2005; Martin, Myers, and Mottet 1999). While Americans in general place value on egalitarianism, relationships between students and faculty in academic institutions are nevertheless hierarchical: Faculty are in the higher-up position, which needs to be appropriately acknowledged in status-congruent ways by students (Bardovi-Harlig and Hartford 1990). E-mail, as a medium where visual and paralinguistic clues between interlocutors are lacking (Lea and Spears 1992), is often perceived as promoting informal language where the politeness requirements of face-to-face interaction do not so stringently apply. However, there is evidence that students in e-mail communication with faculty do attempt to observe relational hierarchies by crafting messages that are status congruent and polite; but the text-only context of e-mail presents linguistic challenges to native speakers (NSs) as well as non-native speakers (NNSs) of English, resulting in a range of linguistic choices that evidence not only status-inappropriate linguistic forms but also new, emerging e-mail conventions (Biesenbach-Lucas 2007).

One aspect in which e-mail writers can signal their understanding of the perceived relationship between themselves and their addressee is in the opening salutation. While the conventional business letter template *Dear* + name signals appropriate deference when addressing a higher-up, examinations of e-mail greetings have shown that this opening move is not perceived as necessary by many e-mail writers (Gains 1999; Y. Li 2000; Waldvogel 2007). Similarly, closing moves, such as *Regards* or *Sincerely yours,* and signatures, while a staple in conventional business letters, are seen by many e-mail writers as dispensable (Sherblom 1988; Waldvogel 2007), likely because that information is already included in the *from* line in the e-mail envelope information.

Recent investigations into e-mail greetings and closings suggest that they are, however, important politeness markers (Bunz and Campbell 2002), which set the tone for subsequent face-to-face and cyberspace interaction (Kankaaranta 2006; Waldvogel 2007) and also reflect e-mail writers' uncertainty about message greetings and closings they send (TechScribe 2006). Clearly e-mail writers do need specific advice on "little words" such as greetings and closings, as is evident in numerous online references and blogs on e-mail etiquette (e.g., E-variations in email salutations 2006; Gaertner-Johnston 2006).

Waldvogel (2007, 1–2) maintains that "the [e-mail] greeting is one means by which the writer constructs his or her social and professional identity and relationship with the addressee(s). A closing can help consolidate the relationship and establish a relational basis for future encounters." However, little research has investigated the use of greetings and closings in e-mails sent from university students to their professors. The student–professor relationship is marked by professors' higher institutional status over students and by relatively low social distance between them due to regular face-to-face contact in the classroom. In addition, while some research has compared student–professor e-mail messages from NSs with those from NNSs within the context of request speech acts (Biesenbach-Lucas 2005, 2006; Hartford and Bardovi-Harlig 1996), a systematic comparison of NS and NNS e-mail greetings and closings is missing. The present study examines the impact of faculty's higher status and relative social distance on the use of greetings and closings in student–professor e-mail communication, as it is in students' best interest to project a positive image of themselves and to maintain a positive relationship with their professor (Boxer 2002). The study conducts an analysis of linguistic realizations of greetings and closings and compares the linguistic patterns used by NS and NNS students. Findings can shed light on whether the e-mail medium might develop conventions different from those associated with traditional business letter templates and how this might affect the impressions that students' e-mail messages leave on faculty recipients.

Background
Background is provided on two relevant research areas: how one's impression on others is formed in online environments and existing research on greetings and closings in e-mail.

Online Impression Formation
There is evidence that linguistic and paralinguistic choices impact one's impression on others in face-to-face encounters (e.g., Bradac 1989). Accents, dialects, and concomitant choices of syntax, semantics, and vocabulary lead to positive or negative evaluations of speakers by their interlocutors. While inappropriate, or nonconventional, linguistic and paralinguistic choices can cause communicative stumbling blocks and miscommunication in any type of communicative domain among NSs of English (Boxer 2002), lexical and grammatical selections are often particularly prob-

lematic for NNSs of English and can lead to speakers' perception as being either rude or far too polite (Bardovi-Harlig and Hartford 1990; Bodman and Eisenstein 1988).

Communication in cyberspace presents yet another communicative hurdle because conventions long established for oral interaction may or may not be transferred to the electronic medium, in which a lack of visible context clues further exacerbates negotiation of self-image (Lea and Spears 1992; Walther 1996). Due to the absence of visible clues, words on the screen convey more than just a message through typographical features, use of upper/lower case letters, punctuation, typing errors, and emoticons—they also leave an impression about the sender, and recipients of online messages are quick to judge not only the sender's imagined physical appearance but also his or her character (Jacobson 1999; Lea and Spears 1992). In addition, the way in which message content is phrased might be inappropriate given the relationship between message sender and receiver, and in hierarchical relationships, such as employees–supervisors and students–professors, status-incongruence is not likely received positively and can have negative consequences (Boxer 2002; Bardovi-Harlig and Hartford 1990; Hartford and Bardovi-Harlig 1996). In fact, numerous educators have complained about students' lack of e-mail composing abilities (Inside Higher Ed 2006).

Greetings and closings, those seemingly little words at the beginning and end of letters and e-mail messages, have received little attention from the point of view of how their presence or absence, or their wording, might contribute to impression formation or status congruence. Little words are often particularly troublesome for NNSs of English because instruction typically focuses on broader aspects and grammar structures rather than authentic interaction patterns (Nunan 1999). As a result, NNSs may not be familiar with typical greeting and closing patterns, especially not those in e-mail communication to their professors. However, research on the serial position effect in memory suggests that words at the beginning and the end of a text are more likely to be remembered than text in the middle, and words that are more salient than others are also more easily retained (Healy, Havas, and Parker 2000). One might argue then that, by extension, greetings and closings are also more likely to leave an impression on the recipient, particularly if they are salient due to status-incongruent formulations.

Greetings and Closings in E-mail

Greetings and closings have been a frequently examined feature in educational as well as corporate e-mail messages but only recently with intention to explore status (in)congruence. Because both greetings and closings are typically set off from the message body, they are easily identifiable and also easily countable. In an early study on signature files in e-mails of employees of a large organization, Sherblom (1988) found that signature use was influenced by e-mail senders' position in the organizational hierarchy: Messages sent downward did not contain signatures, but one-third of e-mail messages sent upward did. Even more strikingly, Waldvogel (1999) discovered that more than 90 percent of the hierarchically upward sent e-mails she examined contained closings/sign-off phrases and signatures. Gains (1999) compared e-mail messages sent among employees of an insurance company with those sent among members of educational institutions (sender–recipient constellations are, however, unclear). Gains found that all e-mail writers generally adhered to conventions of standard English, with conversational features occurring only in the educational e-mails. In addition, Gains observed that 92 percent of the insurance company e-mails and 63 percent of the academic e-mails lacked an opening greeting, but it is unclear how hierarchical relationships might have influenced those choices.

Waldvogel (2007, 6) examined e-mail greetings and closings in an educational organization, more specifically, messages "to and from members of the teaching staff" with a mix in directionality (hierarchically upward and downward). None of the messages examined were sent from students to teaching staff, however. Waldvogel observed that more than half the e-mail messages did not contain any greetings, and those that did typically began with the recipient's name. Interestingly, greeting words plus name (e.g., *Hi/Dear* + name) tended to be used if the e-mail "introduced a matter of a fairly delicate matter, made a major request of a higher status person, or expressed appreciation for a major request" (8). With respect to closings, Waldvogel found that two-thirds of the e-mails in the educational institution she examined contained some form of closing, but one-third did not. Another third ended with the sender's first name, and few messages contained any farewell formula, such as *Thanks*—used as a "ritual closing formula" (10–11)—and *Regards*. Waldvogel concludes that greetings and closings were more likely to be included in senders' e-mails if they were addressing a higher-status person, and thus both greetings and closings are "a way of doing deference or signaling respect and thus constructing the addressee as having status" (12).

Duthler (2006) conducted a study specifically investigating students' use of politeness features, including greetings and closings, in e-mail and voice mail messages to a faculty member. While he found that address phrases were not more formal in e-mail than in voice mail, he did observe that address phrases in low imposition e-mails were surprisingly more formal (using *Dear* + title + name) than address phrases in e-mails in which the writer was making a high imposition on the addressee (where *Hi* without formal name tended to be used). Duthler explains the less formal *Hi* in high imposition e-mails as students' strategic tactic to redefine the student–professor relationship in order to bolster feelings of solidarity; however, the messages in Duthler's study were *elicited* messages sent to an *imaginary* faculty member and not authentic messages. As a result, his participants' selection of greeting and closing formulae was not subject to real-life consequences and real-life impression formation.

Studies on e-mail greetings and closings suggest that there is variability in their use in different organizations and institutions, which is in fact reflected in widely differing advice on e-mail etiquette. Vincent (1999, 12) recommends "us[ing] an appropriate salutation . . . by using the receiver's name" as well as a detailed signature file. Danet (2001) feels that e-mails should follow a traditional business letter format including both openings and closings. In contrast, Y. Li (2000) assures writers that, in e-mail, "the greetings . . . of telephone calls or daily conversations can all be neglected" (33).

If use of social protocol is problematic and variable for NSs of English, it is no surprise that little words can present an even greater challenge for NNSs, but few studies have compared NSs' and NNSs' use of greetings and closings. In one study, L. Li (2000) found that NNSs used more conventional salutations but fewer closings than NSs in their e-mail messages; however, the institutional context for this research is unclear. In another study, Kankaaranta (2006) examined greetings and closings in the English written e-mail messages among the employees of a Scandinavian organization, but comparisons to messages sent by NSs of English are unavailable. Kankaanranta found that most of the e-mail messages sent within the organization contained greetings, typically consisting of *Hello* + first name in positive politeness efforts (cf. Brown and Levinson 1987) to maintain good social relations among employees. Closings and signatures also occurred in nearly all messages, partially accounted for by the e-mail writers' use of preprogrammed signature files. Kankaaranta concludes that the co-occurrence of greetings and closings in e-mail messages "seemed to provide a frame of positive tone for the message" and was "one of the ways to create a feeling of closeness and solidarity in the shared corporate environment" (224).

Focus of the Present Study and Research Questions
The present study examines e-mail messages from NS and NNS students sent to one professor at a major American university. It fills a gap in the research on e-mail greetings and closings by going beyond a simple count of presence or absence through examination of different greetings and closings realizations; it also examines closings for existence of closing moves, similar to those found for oral interaction (Bardovi-Harlig et al. 1991). In the student–professor interaction domain, the power dimension is stable, as the professor is in a position of higher status by virtue of the student–professor relationship at American institutions of higher education. As a result, the students' e-mail messages represent messages sent hierarchically upward and thus make the use of status-congruent linguistic choices necessary (cf. Bardovi-Harlig and Hartford's [1990] research on academic advising sessions). The social distance dimension is relatively stable: Among students and the professor in the present study, face-to-face contact in classes occurred only once a week, but class contact was regular over sixteen weeks of a semester and included occasional face-to-face office hour meetings; thus positive politeness features might not be surprising. The present study also fills the gap on comparative research on NSs and NNSs of English and their attempts at navigating the treacherous waters of e-mail correspondence with faculty, where it is crucial that students leave positive impressions of themselves.

The following research questions guided the study:

- Do university students e-mailing their professor use standard letter writing conventions in e-mail greetings and closings, such as *Dear* (title + last name) and *Sincerely/Regards*?
- How are greetings and closings realized linguistically by native and non-native English speakers? Do particular forms emerge as favorites, and are these status congruent?
- Might e-mail communication in academia develop its own conventions for greetings/closings?

Methods: Subjects and Data

The subject pool in the present study consisted of NSs and NNSs of English, all of whom were enrolled in graduate level TESOL courses at a major American university. The NNSs came from Asian backgrounds (Korea, Japan, Taiwan) and had had prior instruction in English in their native countries. They had been accepted into the graduate teacher training program based on their TOEFL scores.

The data consisted of naturalistic e-mail messages sent to one middle-aged female professor, who taught the TESOL courses in which the students were enrolled. Due to ethical and privacy reasons, messages sent to other professors could not be obtained. Students' e-mail messages were collected over six semesters; students gave consent to the collection of their messages under the provision that no identifying information other than NS and NNS status would be revealed. A total of 375 e-mail messages from NSs and 150 messages from NNSs were analyzed.

The first step in the analysis involved identification of greetings and closings. Greetings, always occurring at the beginning of the e-mail messages, were defined as simple greetings, such as *Hello,* and salutations, consisting of greetings and/or the addressee's title and/or name, such as *Hello Professor Smith.* Closings were defined as those elements that signal the end of the e-mail message, such as a signature (the sender's name) and any other linguistic/semantic formulae that are not part of the message body and occur near the end of a message. Because analyses of spoken interaction have found preclosing sequences by which speakers signal the end of a conversational exchange (Bardovi-Harlig et al. 1991; Schegloff and Sachs 1973), it was assumed that written e-mail communication might exhibit similar characteristics. The next step in the analysis involved tallying the occurrences of greeting and closing expressions, calculating percentages, and comparing results for NSs and NNSs.

Results and Discussion

Results are discussed with respect to quantitative similarities and qualitative differences that emerged in NS and NNS students' e-mail messages.

Greetings

A comparison of NSs and NNSs with respect to the proportion of messages *with* greetings versus messages *without* greetings reveals that both groups clearly preferred to send messages to their professor that included a greeting (NSs = 87% and NNSs = 93%). Among these, the vast majority were greetings + name salutations (83% and 91%, respectively), allowing both an acknowledgment of greeting and the perceived relationship with the professor recipient.

These findings are in contrast to greetingless e-mails found to be quite frequent in other organizational environments where NSs of English e-mailed each other (Gains 1999; Waldvogel 2007), but the findings are similar to the preponderance of greetings in messages to higher-ups (Waldvogel 1999) and NNSs' e-mail messages (Kankaaranta 2006). The predominance of greetings in the present study suggests that e-mail composition to a person higher up in the academic institutional hierarchy is influenced by the traditional business letter template (Danet 2001). In a study eliciting e-mail messages from students to an imagined female professor, Duthler (2006) also found that his student respondents supplied greetings, indicating awareness of and the need for social protocol in student–faculty electronic interaction.

More revealing of differences between NSs and NNSs than a simple count of presence/absence of greetings and salutations is an examination of the actual greeting realizations. Overall, thirty-one different greetings realizations were found, with NSs producing sixteen different variants and NNSs producing nineteen—evidence not only of the enormous variability within the opening move but also of both native and non-native e-mail writers' uncertainty as to which greeting might be the most acceptable. The great variation in linguistic realization of greetings stems from the multiple possibilities that are created when the different greeting elements are combined: The faculty recipient's name was prefaced by either *Dear, Hello, Hi,* a time-of-day acknowledgment (*Good evening*), or no element; her title was realized as either *Dr., Professor, Prof.,* or *Mrs.* (which includes abbreviations visible only in writing); her hyphenated last name appeared either in its full form, as one of the two name parts, or was omitted or replaced by her first name (the professor typically introduced herself to students with first name plus second part of her hyphenated last name and did not encourage first name basis with students).

Figures 16.1 and 16.2 depict the three most frequently used greeting/salutation patterns observed for NSs and NNSs, respectively. Despite the range of greeting realizations, most of these did not occur with great frequency; instead, for each group of students (NSs and NNSs), a clear favorite greeting form emerged, which was used in nearly one-third of all messages. In addition, the preferred forms indicate apparent differences between NSs and NNSs, which point to a greater influence of conventional business letter discourse in the mail messages sent by NNS, and an intriguing move toward more bare-bones greetings in the messages sent by NSs.

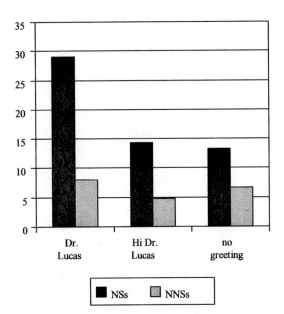

Figure 16.1 Most Frequently Used Greeting/Salutation Patterns for NSs

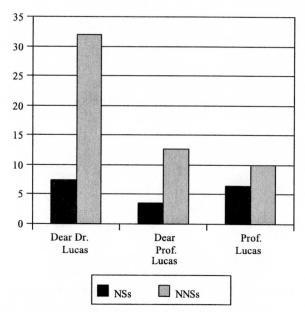

Figure 16.2 Most Frequently Used Greeting/Salutation Patterns for NNSs

Nearly one in three NSs chose to address the faculty recipient with *Dr. Lucas* (i.e., title + last name), a form that omits business letter formalities such as *Dear* but nevertheless acknowledges the recipient's institutional status by mentioning the proper academic title. The second most frequently used greeting pattern was *Hi Dr. Lucas,* which has a slightly more informal tone than *Dr. Lucas* by combining an informal greeting with a deferential naming practice; it might thus acknowledge the sender's attempt at building rapport with the professor, whom he or she sees regularly for classes and whom he or she might greet more informally if meeting face-to-face. The title + name combination serves to properly acknowledge the professor's status in a unique salutation combination, which students might not use if they were writing a conventional letter to their professor. Interestingly, the third most preferred pattern for NSs was not to use any greeting at all; this would most likely not be acceptable for conventional business letters but might signal that certain letter conventions are dispensable, or modifiable, in the e-mail medium (cf. Gains 1999; and Waldvogel 2007, for a high percentage of greetingless e-mails among NSs of English).

In contrast, nearly half the messages sent by NNSs begin with a conventional business letter salutation, *Dear,* followed by variants of the recipient's title plus last name, *Dr. Lucas* or *Prof. Lucas* (abbreviated form), indicating a heavy reliance on the letter template. In a recent survey on acceptable e-mail greetings and closings (TechScribe 2006), respondents felt that "using 'Dear' risked making the sender look older or inexperienced with email" (para. 4), suggesting that e-mail is indeed developing its own unique guidelines and conventions for norms of message creation and that NNSs are not in tune with current e-mail writing practices.

However, the third most frequently used greeting pattern used by NNSs was *Prof. Lucas,* a deferential title + name pattern that, even without other adornments and formalities, properly acknowledges the recipient's institutional status. Interestingly, NSs students used the title *Dr.* typically used in U.S. academic culture while NNSs preferred the abbreviated title *Prof.* The full title *Professor* was rarely used; apparently, not many students read the advice of e-mail etiquette experts who recommend that *Dr.* should never be spelled out but that *Professor* should always be spelled out (Gaertner-Johnston 2006).

Closings
Similar to greetings, closings were also found in most of the e-mail messages from both groups of students (NSs = 91% and NNSs = 89%), comparable to previous studies (Sherblom 1988; Waldvogel 1999, 2007). Apparently, presence of both greeting and closing is, at least at present, considered an important element in e-mail messages sent upward in the academic institutional hierarchy. However, what elements signal to the e-mail recipient that the body of the message is coming to an end? In spoken face-to-face interaction, preclosings are initiated by verbal discourse markers such as *well* and *okay* and nonverbally by breaking eye contact and glancing at one's watch (Bardovi-Harlig et al. 1991). Examination of the students' e-mail messages reveals closing sequences consisting of several elements, which differentiate clearly between NSs and NNSs.

Five moves occurred in a typical sequence in the e-mail messages of both groups of speakers but tended to be used predominantly by the NNSs: (a) a request for the professor's response (e.g., *Please let me know [what/when/if]*), which could be a move similar to a preclosing signal; this was followed by (b) an expression of gratitude (e.g., *Thank you*); then (c) a phatic oral leave-taking expression (e.g., *See you in class*); (d) a sign-off phrase (e.g., *Sincerely*); and (e) the student's name. Differences between NSs and NNSs surfaced in the presence or absence of these moves, as well as in the frequency with which individual moves occurred and the resulting typical message ending. Figure 16.3 indicates that, for both groups of students, the most frequently used

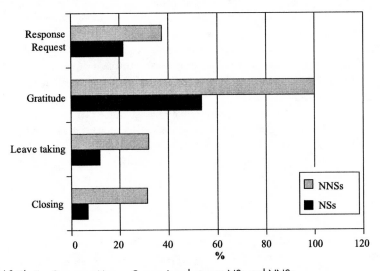

Figure 16.3 Closing Sequence Moves: Comparison between NSs and NNSs

closing move was an expression of gratitude; in fact, this verbal politeness marker (Bunz and Campbell 2002) occurred in all of the NNSs' messages (mostly the more formal variant *Thank you*) and in more than half of the NSs messages. A similar preference for *Thanks* has been noted by Waldvogel (2007, 10–11), who considers this move a "ritual closing formula" and not an expression "used genuinely to express thanks." At least one-third of NNSs' messages in the present study also contain requests for response, phatic oral leave-taking expressions (cf. Biesenbach-Lucas 2005 for observations on NNSs' use of phatic language in e-mail messages), and sign-off expressions, all of which occurred with much less frequency in the NSs' messages.

Similar to greetings and salutations, each of the closing sequence moves was realized through a variety of different surface structures, which reveal evidence of NNSs' close borrowing from conventional business letter templates but appear to be evidence of NSs' development of new e-mail conventions, reflecting that much of their daily communication is confined to writing on a keyboard and screen. In general, NNSs' message closings were characterized by slightly greater formality, deference, and concerns for phatic expressions, such as *Thank you very much, Sincerely,* and *See you next week;* in contrast, NSs tended to opt for a slightly more informal expression of gratitude, *Thanks,* as the only closing move (except for name), confirming Waldvogel's (2007) observation that *Thanks* might indeed be developing into a ritual closing move.

What emerges are two distinct e-mail formats that set NSs apart from NNSs in the former group's ability to produce brief openings and closings that do not detract from message content but are nevertheless appropriately status congruent given the faculty addressee. The NSs' truncated use of particularly the closing sequence reflects concerns for message clarity and brevity in e-mail (Biesenbach-Lucas 2006). This combination of status-acknowledging greeting and ritual gratitude expressing closing appears quite appropriate in a hierarchically upward e-mail and could reflect an emerging convention.

The NNSs in the present study use letter template greetings and at the end of their e-mail want to have assurance that their message is responded to; similarly, response requests are often included in business letters to ensure continuation of correspondence. In contrast, phatic leave-taking expressions, such as *see you tomorrow,* are more typical of oral interaction and informal, personal letters. Their inclusion by NNSs in the e-mails to faculty suggests that NNSs are unaware of blending formal business letter features with oral and informal personal letter attributes. In addition, it appears that NNSs are concerned with establishing and maintaining a positive relationship with the professor by adding phatics as positive politeness features. Further evidence for NNSs' mismatch of business and personal letter features surfaces in the very conventional sign-off phrase *Sincerely yours.* The blending of forms reflects NNSs' uncertainty about e-mailing higher-ups and, as a result, the borrowing from both formal and informal letter templates as well as oral interaction is an attempt at negotiating an appropriate level of solidarity and distance, or positive and negative politeness (Brown and Levinson 1987).

Conclusion and Suggestions for Future Research

The lack of *Dear* or *Hello* in NSs' e-mail greetings may suggest less formality but not necessarily greater informality or less deference; instead, the title + name greeting is neutral, status appropriate, and professional. The minimal closing sequence—*Thanks* + name—is short, very matter-of-fact, and reveals no extra attempt at deliberate positive image creation, but it also does not risk leaving a bad impression. In contrast, image creation is more at work in NNSs' messages through deliberate attempts at including negative and positive politeness features, that is, business letter template greetings and sign-offs, expressions of gratitude, and phatic leave-taking expressions, respectively.

While one can argue that greetings and closings are not what an e-mail message is about—the communicative purpose is expressed in the body of the message—the position of greetings and closings is nevertheless prominent in an e-mail message: They are the first and last words to be read by the recipient. Studies in psychology attest to the fact that items at the beginning and the end of text tend to be better recalled, particularly if they are salient or stand out. An e-mail that contains a status noncongruent (either too informal or overly polite) greeting or closing puts its sender at risk of leaving an unfavorable impression.

In conclusion, the developing convention in institutional e-mails calls for message brevity and neutrality, with minimal but proper status acknowledgment. For educators in the field of English as a second language, it is increasingly necessary to include the composition of appropriate e-mails with appropriate greetings and closings in their teaching syllabi, especially when the NNS students are planning to study at an American university where e-mail communication with faculty is becoming commonplace.

The present study had limitations in that only e-mail from graduate students in a particular field at a particular university, and sent to one faculty recipient, was examined. Future research should compare and examine greetings/closings in the following types of e-mail messages in academic institutional settings:

- Male versus female students, students in different age brackets, graduate versus undergraduate students, students in different fields and at different universities
- NNSs at advanced versus low proficiency levels in English
- Messages addressed to male versus female faculty, younger versus older faculty
- Messages with different communicative purposes (e.g., asking for clarification versus asking for an extension)
- Changes over extended message sequences, as well as over course of student–professor relationships

Conventions change with new communication media, and it takes time for conventions to become established. At present, e-mail writers do not receive clear guidance on message composition, as the varied advice on e-mail etiquette demonstrates (Gaertner-Johnston 2006; Vincent 1999). However, the need to communicate via e-mail exists, and writers need to make lexical, grammatical, and semantic choices. As they are navigating new communicative waters, they are also creating new norms and conventions. The present study suggests that e-mail from students to professors in an academic context is developing toward brevity and ritual formulae that differ from conventional business letters but nevertheless adhere to status-appropriate social protocol. Waldvogel's (2007) conclusion about e-mail greetings and closings in the workplace applies in the present study's academic context as well: "Greetings and closings [are] a means of reinforcing status relationships and underlining positional expectations" (3). NNS students need a little more help with these little words so that they convey a positive and professional image of themselves in academic e-mails.

REFERENCES

Bardovi-Harlig, Kathleen, and Beverly Hartford. 1990. Congruence in native and nonnative conversations: Status balance in the academic advising session. *Language Learning* 40:467–501.

Bardovi-Harlig, Beverly Hartford, Rebecca Mahan-Taylor, M. J. Morgan, and Dudley W. Reynolds. 1991. Developing pragmatic awareness: Closing the conversation. *ELT Journal* 44:92–94.

Biesenbach-Lucas, Sigrun. 2005. Communication topics and strategies in email consultation: Comparison between American and international university students. *Language Learning & Technology* 9 (2): 24–46.

———. 2006. Making requests in email: Do cyber-consultations entail directness? Toward conventions in a new medium. In *Pragmatics and language learning,* ed. Kathleen Bardovi-Harlig, Cesar Félix-Brasdefer, and Alwiya S. Omar, 81–108. Mānoa: Second Language Teaching and Curriculum Center, University of Hawai'i.

———. 2007. Students writing emails to faculty: An examination of e-politeness among native and nonnative speakers of English. *Language Learning & Technology* 11 (2): 51–81.

Bodman, Jean, and Miriam Eisenstein. 1988. May God increase our bounty: The expression of gratitude in English by native and non-native speakers. *Cross Currents* 15:1–21.

Boxer, Diana. 2002. *Applying sociolinguistics: Domains and face-to-face interaction.* Philadelphia: John Benjamins.

Bradac, James J., ed. 1989. *Message effects in communication science.* Newbury Park, CA: Sage.

Brown, Penelope, and Stephen Levinson. 1987. *Politeness: Some universals in language usage.* Cambridge: Cambridge University Press.

Bunz, Ulla, and Scott W. Campbell. 2002. Accommodating politeness indicators in personal electronic mail messages. Paper presented at the Association of Internet Researchers' 3rd annual conference, Maastricht, Netherlands. http://bunz.comm.fsu.edu/AoIR2002politeness.pdf (accessed April 11, 2007).

Danet, Brenda. 2001. *Cyberpl@y: Communicating online.* Oxford: Berg.

Duthler, Kirk W. 2006. The politeness of requests made via email and voicemail: Support for the hyperpersonal model. *Journal of Computer-Mediated Communication* 11. http://jcmc.indiana.edu/vol11/issue2/duthler.html (accessed November 9, 2006).

E-variations in email salutations. 2006. www.webmetricsguru.com/2006/11/evariations_in_email_salutatio.html (accessed April 11, 2007).

Gaertner-Johnston, Lynn. 2006. Salutations in letters and email. Business writing. www.businesswritingblog.com/business_writing/2006/01/greetings_and_s.html (accessed April 11, 2007).

Gains, Johnathan. 1999. Electronic mail: A new style of communication or just a new medium? An investigation into the text features of e-mail. *English for Specific Purposes* 18 (1): 81–101.

Hartford, Beverly, and Kathleen Bardovi-Harlig. 1996. "At your earliest convenience": A study of written student requests to faculty. In *Pragmatics and language learning,* ed. Lawrence F. Bouton, 55–69. Monograph Series, vol. 7. Urbana, IL: DEIL.

Healy, Alice F., David A. Havas, and James T. Parker. 2000. Comparing serial position effects in semantic and episodic memory using reconstruction of order tasks. *Journal of Memory and Language* 42:147–67.

Inside Higher Ed. 2006. Be polite, e-polite. http://insidehighered.com/news/2006/04/19/oregon (accessed May 4, 2006).

Jacobson, David. 1999. Impression formation in cyberspace: Online expectations and offline experiences in text-based virtual communities. *Journal of Computer Mediated Communication* 5. http://jcmc.indiana.edu/vol5/issue1/jacobson.html (accessed February 25, 2007).

Kankaaranta, Anne. 2006. "Hej, Seppo, could you pls comment on this!" Internal email communication in lingua franca English in a multinational company. *Business Communication Quarterly* 69:216–25.

Lea, Martin, and Russell Spears. 1992. Paralanguage and social perception in computer-mediated communication. *Journal of Organizational Computing* 2:321–41.

Li, Lan. 2000. Email: A challenge to standard English? *English Today* 16 (4): 23–29, 55.

Li, Yongyan. 2000. Surfing e-mails. *English Today* 16 (4): 30–34, 55.

Martin, Matthew M., Scott A. Myers, and Timothy P. Mottet. 1999. Students' motives for communicating with their instructors. *Communication Education* 48:157–64.

Nunan, David. 1999. *Second language teaching and learning.* Boston: Heinle and Heinle.

Schegloff, Emanuel A., and Harvey Sachs. 1973. Opening up closings. *Semiotica* 8:289–327.

Sherblom, John. 1988. Direction, function, and signature in electronic mail. *Journal of Business Communication* 25 (4): 39–54.

TechScribe. 2006. What to call your email recipient. www.techscribe.co.uk/ta/email-salutations.htm (accessed April 11, 2007).

Vincent, Annette. 1999. Business communication: Are the rules different for e-mail? *Supervision* 60 (9): 10–14.

Waldvogel, Joan. 1999. *Email: User perceptions and aspects of its role and impact in one workplace.* Master's thesis, School of Linguistics and Applied Language Studies, Victoria University of Wellington, New Zealand.

———. 2007. Greetings and closings in workplace email. *Journal of Computer-Mediated Communication* 12. http://jcmc.indiana.edu/vol12/issue2/waldvogel.html (accessed May 3, 2007).

Walther, Joseph B. 1996. Computer-mediated communication: Impersonal, interpersonal, and hyperpersonal interaction. *Communication Research* 23:3–43.

VI

Acquisition

17

Instructed L2 Acquisition of Differential Object Marking in Spanish

MELISSA BOWLES AND SILVINA MONTRUL
University of Illinois at Urbana-Champaign

IT IS WIDELY HELD that second language (L2) learners restructure their interlanguage grammars on the basis of input. But what form must input take to promote restructuring? Many studies find that input in the form of positive evidence is not sufficient for successful second language acquisition (SLA) and that some focus on language form is necessary to lead the learner to notice certain features of the input. That is, instructed L2 learners may benefit from some type of form-focused instruction, defined by Spada (1997, 73) as consisting of "events which occur within meaning-based approaches to L2 instruction in which a focus on language is provided in either spontaneous or predetermined ways." Form-focused instruction has been proven effective in many face-to-face classroom settings (Rod Ellis 2001, 2002; Lyster 2004a, 2004b), but many language programs have now begun to offer hybrid, or technology-enhanced, language courses, in which grammar instruction is offered via self-instructional units online. In such courses, face-to-face class meetings are reserved for learners to engage in communicative activities in the L2. But in these hybrid delivery contexts, how effective is grammar instruction that involves explicit rule presentation and practice with corrective feedback? This study seeks to answer this question, focusing on the instruction of one particularly problematic structure for native English-speaking L2 learners of Spanish, differential object marking, or *a-personal*.

Explicit Rule Presentation and Negative Evidence in L2 Acquisition

Researchers propose that first language (L1) acquisition is driven solely by positive evidence, or exemplars of possible utterances in the language, which are present in all grammatical speech. However, research on L2 acquisition (especially in immersion contexts) has suggested that positive evidence alone may not be sufficient for the acquisition of certain L1–L2 contrasts or structures that are not present in the L1 (Trahey and White 1993; White 1989, 1991; for discussion, see Lightbown 1998 and Long 1996). That is, learners may benefit from some type of form-focused instruction.

One way of delivering form-focused instruction is by providing learners with explicit information before or during exposure to L2 input, by means of either grammatical explanation or negative evidence in the form of corrective feedback (Sanz and Morgan-Short 2004). A substantial body of research investigating the role of explicit grammatical explanation or rule presentation in SLA has generally found it beneficial (Alanen 1995; Carroll and Swain 1993; de Graaf 1997; DeKeyser 1995; Nick Ellis 1993; Nagata 1993; Nagata and Swisher 1995; Robinson 1996, 1997; Rosa and Leow 2004a, 2004b). Furthermore, corrective feedback has been directly linked to the process of hypothesis formation and testing, which has been shown to facilitate restructuring and system learning (e.g., Rosa and O'Neill 1999; Rosa and Leow 2004a). Russell and Spada's (2006) meta-analysis synthesizes the research on corrective feedback to date, finding overall support for it for L2 acquisition of morphosyntax, as does Ellis, Loewen, and Erlam's (2006) review of studies. This finding suggests that even if negative evidence is not *crucial* for acquisition of some syntactic features of L2 grammar, it does *facilitate* SLA by speeding up the process of acquisition, as does explicit grammatical explanation or rule presentation.

Differential Object Marking

In Spanish, direct objects are marked differentially based on animacy, with inanimate objects being unmarked and animate objects being marked with the dative preposition *a* in a phenomenon referred to as differential object marking (DOM). In general, objects that are specific and animate are obligatorily marked with this preposition, as shown in (1), while other objects are obligatorily unmarked, as shown in (2) and (3):

(1) a. Marcelo vio *a* Mónica.   [+animate, +specific]
      Marcelo vio prep Mónica
      "Marcelo saw Mónica."

    b. *Marcelo vio Mónica.

(2) a. La crisis destruyó la moral del pueblo.   [-animate, +specific]
      "The crisis destroyed people's morale."

    b. *La crisis destruyó *a* la moral del pueblo.

(3) a. La bomba destruyó una iglesia.   [-animate, -specific]
      "The bomb destroyed a church."

    b. *La bomba destruyó *a* una iglesia.

In some contexts, grammatical sentences with indefinite determiners are possible with either a marked or an unmarked animate object, and the use of the preposition *a* determines whether a specific or nonspecific reading is possible, as shown in (4).

(4) a. José necesita un médico.   [+animate, -specific]
      "José needs a doctor." (any doctor)

    b. José necesita *a* un médico.   [+animate, +specific]
      José needs prep a doctor
      "José needs a doctor." (a particular doctor)

Sentence (4a), with an unmarked object, provides the [-specific] interpretation that José needs any doctor he can find, not one particular doctor. However, the preposition *a* must be used if a [+specific] interpretation, that José needs a *particular* doctor, is intended, as in the case of (4b).

The exact semantic and syntactic conditions regulating when objects should be marked with the dative preposition *a* are quite complex (Aissen 2003; Leonetti 2003; Torrego 1998; Zagona 2002). Current analyses of DOM maintain that semantic notions such as specificity, agentivity, telicity, and topicality seem to play a role in explaining the optionality of the preposition *a* with animate and inanimate objects. However, because this study focuses on L2 learners' acquisition of only the clearest, prototypical cases of DOM [those with human objects, as in (1)], the specific details of those analyses are not necessary. Crucially, following Torrego (1998) we assume that a specific functional category for DOM does not exist in English, the native language of the learners tested in our study.

Acquisition of Differential Object Marking

There is virtually no research on the L1 acquisition of DOM in Spanish, with the exception of a recent study by Rodríguez-Mondoñedo (2006). Rodríguez-Modoñedo conducted an analysis of the spontaneous production of four Spanish-speaking children (between the ages of 0;9 and 2;11) from the CHILDES database (López Ornat, Linaza, Montes, and Vila corpora). All sentences containing V-O structures were analyzed. From a total of 991 examples, the children made 17 errors (8 cases of *a* present but not required and 9 cases of *a* omitted when required with animate, specific objects). This amounts to a 98.38 percent accuracy rate with DOM before age three. Therefore this study suggests that Spanish-speaking children acquire the semantic constraints on the distribution of this preposition with direct objects easily and quickly, at least with the prototypical, clear uses of DOM.

The situation for L2 acquisition is different, however, especially when the native language the learners speak does not mark direct objects the way Spanish does. SLA research findings show that even the unambiguous cases of DOM, like those in (1), are difficult for English-speaking L2 learners of Spanish to acquire, despite their frequency in the L2 input (VanPatten and Cadierno 1993; Johnston 1995). Perhaps this difficulty is partially due to the polyfunctionality of the dative preposition *a,* which also appears with ditransitive verbs that take indirect objects (*Juan le dio un libro a Pedro,* "Juan gave a book to Pedro"), and with *gustar*-type psychological verbs that are inherently marked with dative case (*A Juan le gusta este libro,* "Juan likes this book").To date, there has been just one empirical SLA study to investigate the effects of instruction on DOM—Farley and McCollam (2004). At the outset of the study, participants were classified as either developmentally "ready" or "unready" to acquire DOM (Johnston 1995; Pienemann 1998). Twenty-nine adult learners of Spanish enrolled in a fifth-semester course were randomly assigned to either a control group or one of three instruction groups that provided varying degrees of explicitness and practice with DOM. Learners' knowledge of DOM was assessed based on their performance on a pretest and immediate posttest consisting of a grammaticality judgment task (GJT) and a picture description task. The study's results showed that readiness did not constrain learners' acquisition of the structure, as learners in all instruction groups improved in their ability to recognize and produce grammatical sentences on the posttest as compared with the control group that received no instruction on the form. However, the small number of participants who completed the pretest, instruction, and posttest (fewer than ten per group) limits the generalizability of the study's findings and necessitates further research on the L2 acquisition of DOM.

Research Questions

Given the limited research into the acquisition of DOM in Spanish, this study set out to answer the following research questions:

Does explicit instruction and practice (with corrective feedback)

- significantly affect intermediate-level L2 Spanish learners' ability to distinguish between grammatical and ungrammatical sentences involving DOM?
- significantly affect their ability to produce grammatical sentences with animate objects?

Theoretical Assumptions and Hypotheses

We assume the full transfer/full access hypothesis (Schwartz and Sprouse 1996), according to which the initial state of L2 acquisition is the entirety of the L1. That is, especially at the earliest stages of development, L2 learners impose the structural architecture of their L1 onto the L2 and may filter out relevant L2 input accordingly. Only when L2 learners realize that the L1 structure can no longer accommodate L2 input do they restructure their interlanguages accordingly and resort to other options (i.e., parameter values, features, functional categories) made available by universal grammar.

Based on this theoretical assumption, we hypothesize that, in general, low-intermediate proficiency L2 learners of Spanish will be quite inaccurate with DOM and will assume that Spanish, like English, does not mark animate, specific direct objects. If instruction helps them notice the presence of the object marker *a* in the input, they will restructure their interlanguages accordingly.

The Study

Participants

In this study, there was a native speaker baseline group consisting of twelve native Spanish speakers from a variety of countries. This group was included to verify that native speakers have clear, determinate judgments with respect to the grammaticality and distribution of DOM in sentences like (1). The original sample of experimental participants included 329 low-intermediate L2 learners of Spanish enrolled in a hybrid delivery fourth-semester language course. In the course, students review grammar concepts and complete practice exercises online prior to face-to-face class meetings, where they engage in communicative activities. Only native English speakers who completed all sessions (pretest, instruction, and both immediate and delayed posttests) were included in the final sample. These restrictions yielded a final experimental sample of 145 L2 learners.

During the period of the study, the *a*-personal was not formally presented in class, and related coursework did not focus on that structure. In fact, the *a*-personal is noticeably absent from the intermediate-level textbook used in the course. It is mentioned only briefly in the section on direct object pronouns, where just a two-line explanation is given.

Tests

Two different tests were used to elicit data from the participants in this study, as the research questions investigated both recognition and production of DOM in Spanish. A written grammaticality judgment test was used to determine whether learners could distinguish between grammatical and ungrammatical sentences involving DOM, and a controlled written production test was used to evaluate their ability to use DOM productively.

Grammaticality Judgment Test. The GJT contained seventy-five sentences, twenty of which targeted the *a*-personal. Of those sentences, ten were grammatical and ten were ungrammatical, and there were an equal number of sentences with animate and inanimate objects. The remaining fifty-five sentences in the GJT targeted the preposition *a* with ditransitive verbs and psych verbs, thereby functioning as distractors and simultaneously providing more information about participants' knowledge of the uses of *a* with other verbs requiring structural and inherent dative case. Due to scope limitations, only the results of sentences targeting DOM will be presented here. Participants were instructed to rate each sentence on a scale of 1 (incorrect) to 5 (correct).

Controlled written production test. In the controlled written production test, learners were instructed to use the words provided to form a complete, grammatical sentence in Spanish. Ten items included psych verbs (five with animate themes and five with inanimate themes), five included ditransitive verbs, and ten included transitive verbs (five with animate objects and five with inanimate objects). Because of space constraints, only the results of the transitive verb stimuli will be presented in this chapter.

Participants were instructed to use all of the words in the prompt to create grammatical sentences. They could combine the words in any way they wished; however, only those sentences for which transitive verbs were used were counted in the results. For instance, a student response of *El estudiante y la profesora se visitan,* "The student and the professor visit each other," although grammatical, would not be counted in the tallies because the student did not attempt to use the target structure.

The production data were scored for correct (non)use of the preposition *a*. Other errors, such as those having to do with verb inflection, were not taken into account. Therefore a student response of **Patricio visitaré el museo del Prado* would be scored correct for the purposes of this study because the target structure was used appropriately, even though the verb is incorrectly inflected.

One rater scored all of the production data, and a second rater independently scored 20 percent of the data. Interrater reliability, calculated using Cohen's kappa, was κ = .91.

Instructional intervention. The instructional intervention consisted of an explicit grammatical explanation of the *a*-personal, followed by a practice exercise in which corrective feedback was provided. The intervention contained both positive and negative evidence. Specifically, the grammatical explanation provided learners with positive evidence about *a*-personal in the form of grammatical sentences, which contained both animate and inanimate objects. In addition, it provided negative evidence, as it alerted learners to the contrast between Spanish, which requires the animacy marker *a*, and English, which does not differentially mark objects on the basis of animacy. An excerpt of the instructional intervention follows:

> From the perspective of an English speaker, the "a" appears to be an "extra" word. From the perspective of a Spanish speaker, the "a" is required, and to not use it is an error. So you could never say "Conozco María" in Spanish.

After reading the grammatical explanation, learners completed a twenty-item practice exercise online. Each item consisted of a sentence with a drop-down menu immediately preceding the object, from which the learners chose either *a* or —. Of the twenty items, ten had animate objects and ten had inanimate objects. Following each response, participants received feedback that indicated whether their response was correct and provided a grammatical explanation. Participants were allowed to review the explanation and complete the practice task as many times as necessary to achieve 90 percent accuracy. The participants were all familiar with the presentation of the explanation and practice activities (and with the 90% cutoff score), as this was standard practice for all of the online materials in the course.

Design. The study followed a classic pre-/post-test design. In week 1, both native speakers and L2 learners completed a language background questionnaire, followed by the written production and GJT pretests. Then, in week 2, the L2 learners completed the instructional module online, followed by the immediate posttests. Three weeks later, the L2 learners completed the delayed posttests.

Results
Research Question 1: GJT Results
To answer the first research question, mean grammaticality judgment scores from the native speaker baseline group were examined first. Native speakers performed as predicted, accepting grammatical DOM sentences (with the *a*-personal) ($M = 4.95, SD = .09$) and rejecting ungrammatical ones (without the *a*-personal) ($M = 1.1, SD = .35$).

Given this pattern of behavior by native speakers, the L2 learners' GJT data were then examined. On the pretest, the L2 learners' mean grammaticality judgment rating for ungrammatical DOM sentences (without the *a*-personal) was 3.92 ($SD = .89$). For grammatical DOM sentences (with the *a*-personal) their mean rating was lower, 3.76 ($SD = .62$), indicating that at the time of the pretest the L2 learners in fact found ungrammatical DOM sentences slightly more acceptable than grammatical ones. Nevertheless, the difference in their ratings for grammatical and ungrammatical DOM sentences did not reach statistical significance, $t(146) = -1.749, p = .08$.

The L2 learners' ability to distinguish between grammatical and ungrammatical DOM sentences improved markedly as a result of the instructional intervention, although certainly not to nativelike levels, as the graph in figure 17.1 shows.

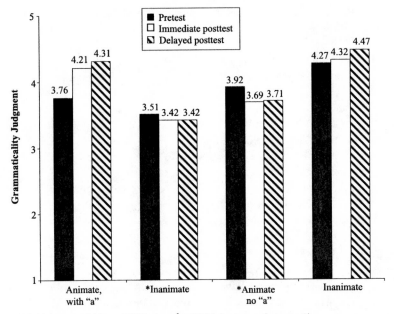

Figure 17.1 L2 Learners' Mean GJT Ratings for DOM Sentences (max = 5)

The L2 learners' mean GJT scores were analyzed using a factorial repeated-measures ANOVA with three within-subjects factors—time, grammaticality, and animacy. There were significant main effects for all three factors—time, $F(2,145)$ = 6.512, p = .002; grammaticality, $F(1,145)$ = 43.252, $p < .0001$; and animacy, $F(1,145)$ = 30.247, $p < .0001$. Specifically, the learners' scores differed significantly over time, and a post hoc Scheffé test indicated that pretest and immediate posttest scores were significantly different from each other, but immediate and delayed posttest scores were statistically similar. Furthermore, there were significant interactions between time and grammaticality, $F(2,290)$ = 52.012, $p < .0001$, and between time and animacy, $F(2,290)$ = 82.810, $p < .0001$. These interactions indicate that learners' sensitivity to grammaticality and animacy was a function of the point in the study when the test was taken. Specifically, learners behaved differently on the pretest than they did on both posttests. Whereas on both posttests learners rated grammatical sentences higher than ungrammatical sentences, on the pretest they did the opposite. Similarly, on both posttests learners rated animate sentences higher than inanimate sentences, but on the pretest they rated inanimate sentences higher. The interaction between grammaticality and animacy, $F(1,145)$ = 43.479, $p < .0001$, is a result of the fact that learners rated inanimate grammatical sentences higher than animate grammatical sentences and that they rated animate ungrammatical sentences higher than inanimate ungrammatical sentences. The significant interaction between time, grammaticality, and animacy, $F(2,290)$ = 10.631, $p < .0001$, indicates that whereas on the posttests, learners rated animate grammatical sentences higher than animate ungrammatical sentences, on the pretest they rated the animate ungrammaticals higher.

These patterns are to be expected, as they show that prior to instruction learners were treating animate and inanimate objects the same way, just as they do in their L1. The change in behavior after instruction and the durability of the effects (as evidenced by the similarity of scores on the two posttests) indicates that instruction was able to influence their ability to distinguish between grammatical and ungrammatical DOM sentences.

Further analysis of the individual sentence types shows that instruction had a significant effect on learners' ratings on all but the inanimate ungrammatical sentences (*Joaquín vio a la última película de Batman*). This result indicates that instruction was effective on the target structure, sentences with animate objects. Specifically, effect sizes were small for animate ungrammatical sentences ($d = .21–.25$) (*Jorge ama Carolina apasionadamente*) and large ($d = .67–.83$) for animate grammatical sentences (*El estudiante visita a la profesora*). Small effect sizes ($d = .29–.36$) were also observed for inanimate grammatical sentences (*Mi hermana vio una exposición de arte*).

Summary of GJT results. The first research question, whether instruction would enable learners to distinguish between grammatical and ungrammatical DOM sentences, was answered affirmatively—specifically, after instruction learners became more accepting of grammatical sentences and less accepting of ungrammatical ones. The largest effect sizes were found for animate ungrammatical sentences, indicating that instruction had the greatest impact on sentences that require DOM in Spanish.

Research Question 2: Written Production Results
To answer the second research question, participants' raw scores on the written production test were examined. Figure 17.2 represents the percentage of sentences for which the preposition *a* was used correctly.

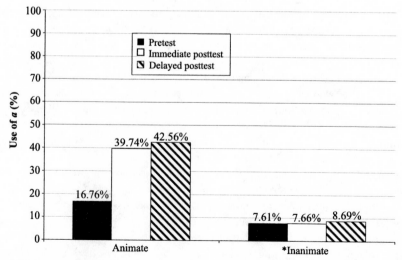

Figure 17.2 L2 Learners' Use of the Preposition *a* in Obligatory Contexts

The L2 learners' written production scores were then analyzed using a factorial repeated-measures ANOVA with two within-subjects factors—time and animacy. There were significant main effects for time, $F(2,292) = 28.757, p < .0001$, and for animacy, $F(1,146) = 460.705, p < .0001$, and a significant interaction between time and animacy, $F(2,292) = 23.715, p < .0001$. These results indicate that production scores increased over time, with a significant difference between the pretest and the immediate posttest, but no significant differences between scores on the two posttests. In addition, grammatical *inanimate* sentences were produced more frequently than grammatical *animate* sentences. Further analysis revealed that instruction had a significant effect on learners' ability to produce sentences with animate objects, $F(2,292) = 48.120, p < .0001, d = .71$, between the pretest and immediate posttest and .78 between the pretest and delayed posttest. However, instruction did not significantly affect learners' ability to produce sentences with inanimate objects, $F(2,292) = 1.190$, $p = .306$, although after the instruction there was evidence of slight overgeneralization, indicated by a slightly higher tendency for learners to use the preposition *a* with inanimate objects than before instruction.

Summary of results: Written production.   The second research question, whether instruction would enable learners to produce grammatical sentences involving animate and inanimate objects, was also answered affirmatively. As the effect sizes indicated, the gains were quite substantial, with learners averaging just 16.76 percent use of the *a*-personal in obligatory contexts on the pretest to between 39 percent and 42 percent use on the posttests. Furthermore, there was only a slight tendency to overgeneralize the rule, with 8.69 percent use of the *a*-personal with inanimate objects on the delayed posttest.

Discussion and Conclusion

Overall, the results of this study indicate that intermediate-level L2 learners of Spanish were able to improve in their ability to distinguish between grammatical and ungrammatical sentences involving DOM and to produce those sentences, after receiving explicit instruction and practice involving corrective feedback. Also, the online instruction in this study was modeled after the types of instructional modules used throughout a hybrid delivery Spanish course that uses online modules as a unit of grammar instruction, reserving face-to-face class time for communicative activities. Therefore the study found that students made gains with respect to the target structure from interacting with the self-instructional grammar unit. Although this study provides only written measures of learning and tests the efficacy of just one module of instruction, it seems to provide support for this type of hybrid instruction. Certainly further research in this area, and in the area of computer-assisted language learning (CALL) in general, is warranted to determine precisely which aspects of technology-enhanced instruction are most effective on which grammatical targets.

Despite the effects found for instruction in this study, it is important to note that the instructed L2 learners' posttest GJT ratings and production rates for DOM sentences were still significantly different from those of the native speakers. That is, although the instruction substantially improved learners' ability to distinguish between grammatical and ungrammatical sentences involving DOM, it did not make them perform like native speakers. Similarly, although the instruction caused them to supply the *a*-personal in obligatory contexts (with animate objects), their posttest percentages of use near 40 percent do not make them comparable to native speakers. These results should not be unexpected given the short duration of the instructional treatment and the difficulty of the structure for L1 English speakers, evidenced anecdotally by language instructors and in previous SLA research (VanPatten and Cadierno 1993; Johnston 1995).

Because the participants in this study received instruction that included explicit rule presentation, positive evidence, and negative evidence in the form of corrective feedback, our data do not allow us to make claims about which particular aspect(s) of the instructional intervention led to the gains. Future research could investigate the relative effects of each aspect, as Sanz and Morgan-Short (2004) did in their study on the acquisition of clitics in L2 Spanish.

Overall, results support the claim that L2 learners can restructure their interlanguages and overcome the structure imposed by their L1 (Schwartz and Sprouse 1996). Nevertheless, it is clear that these low-intermediate learners have not yet completely learned the rules for DOM and do not have nativelike grammars in this respect. Because of this, the data from the present study are not sufficient to determine whether full access is entirely possible in this grammatical domain. However, future research could weigh in on the issue by testing advanced and near-native L2 learners' ability to distinguish grammatical and ungrammatical sentences involving DOM. Such tests with advanced learners would reveal whether the problems attested here with low-intermediate level learners persist and whether instruction would be beneficial for learners at these levels as well. Perhaps most important, such tests would reveal whether learners' knowledge of DOM fossilizes.

REFERENCES

Aissen, Judith. 2003. Differential object marking: Iconicity vs. economy. *Natural Language and Linguistic Theory* 213:435–48.

Alanen, Riikka. 1995. Input enhancement and rule presentation in second language acquisition. In *Attention and awareness in foreign language learning,* ed. Richard Schmidt, 259–302. Honolulu: University of Hawai'i Press.

Carroll, Susanne, and Merrill Swain. 1993. Explicit and implicit negative feedback: An empirical study of the learning of linguistic generalizations. *Studies in Second Language Acquisition* 15:357–86.

de Graaf, Rick. 1997. The eXperanto experiment: Effects of explicit instruction on second language acquisition. *Studies in Second Language Acquisition* 19:249–97.

DeKeyser, Robert. 1995. Learning second language grammar rules: An experiment with a miniature linguistic system. *Studies in Second Language Acquisition* 17:379–410.

Ellis, Nick. 1993. Rules and instances in foreign language learning: Interactions of explicit and implicit knowledge. *European Journal of Cognitive Psychology* 5 (3): 289–318.

Ellis, Rod. 2001. Introduction: Investigating form-focused instruction. *Language Learning* 51, suppl. no. 1:1–46.

———. 2002. Does form-focused instruction affect the acquisition of implicit knowledge? *Studies in Second Language Acquisition* 24 (2): 223–36.

Ellis, Rod, Shawn Loewen, and Rosemary Erlam. 2006. Implicit and explicit corrective feedback and the acquisition of L2 grammar. *Studies in Second Language Acquisition* 28:339–68.

Farley, Andrew P., and Kristina McCollam. 2004. Learner readiness and L2 production in Spanish: Processability theory on trial. *Estudios de Lingüística Aplicada* 22 (4): 47–69.

Johnston, Malcolm. 1995. *Stages of acquisition of Spanish as a second language.* University of Western Sydney, Macarthur: The National Languages and Literacy Institute of Australia, Language Acquisition Research Centre.

Leonetti, Manuel. 2003. Specificity and object marking: The case of Spanish *a*. In *Proceedings of the Workshop "Semantic and Syntactic Aspects of Specificity in Romance Languages,"* ed. Klaus von Heusinger and Georg. A. Kaiser, 67–101. Fachbereich Sprachwissenschaft: Universitat Konstanz.

Lightbown, Patsy M. 1998. The importance of timing in focus on form. In *Focus on form in classroom second language acquisition,* ed. Catherine Doughty and Jessica Williams, 177–96. New York: Cambridge University Press.

Long, Michael. 1996. The role of the linguistic environment in second language acquisition. In *Handbook of second language acquisition,* ed. William C. Ritchie and Tej K. Bhatia, 413–54. San Diego, CA: Academic Press.

Lyster, Roy. 2004a. Differential effects of prompts and recasts in form-focused instruction. *Studies in Second Language Acquisition* 26 (3): 399–432.

———. 2004b. Research on form-focused instruction in immersion classrooms: Implications for theory and practice. *Journal of French Language Studies* 14 (3): 321–41.

Nagata, Noriko. 1993. Intelligent computer feedback for second language instruction. *Modern Language Journal* 77:330–39.

Nagata, Noriko, and M. Virginia Swisher. 1995. A study of consciousness-raising by computer: The effect of metalinguistic feedback on SLA. *Foreign Language Annals* 28:336–47.

Pienemann, Manfred. 1998. *Language processing and second language development: Processability theory.* Philadelphia: John Benjamins.

Robinson, Peter. 1996. Learning simple and complex second language rules under implicit, incidental, rule-search, and instructed conditions. *Studies in Second Language Acquisition* 18 (1): 27–67.

———. 1997. Generalizability and automaticity of second language learning under implicit, incidental, enhanced, and instructed conditions. *Studies in Second Language Acquisition* 19 (2): 223–47.

Rodríguez-Mondoñedo, Miguel. 2006. The acquisition of differential object marking in Spanish. Unpublished ms., Department of Linguistics, University of Connecticut.

Rosa, Elena, and Ronald P. Leow. 2004a. Awareness, different learning conditions, and L2 development. *Applied Psycholinguistics* 25 (2): 269–92.

———. 2004b. Computerized task-based exposure, explicitness, type of feedback, and Spanish L2 development. *Modern Language Journal* 88 (2): 192–216.

Rosa, Elena, and Michael O'Neill. 1999. Explicitness, intake, and the issue of awareness. *Studies in Second Language Acquisition* 21 (4): 511–56.

Russell, Jane, and Nina Spada. 2006. The effectiveness of corrective feedback for the acquisition of L2 grammar: A meta-analysis of the research. In *Synthesizing research on language learning and teaching,* ed. John M. Norris and Lourdes Ortega, 133–64. Amsterdam: John Benjamins.

Sanz, Cristina, and Kara Morgan-Short. 2004. Positive evidence vs. explicit rule presentation and explicit negative feedback: A computer-assisted study. *Language Learning* 54 (1): 35–78.

Schwartz, Bonnie, and Rex Sprouse. 1996. L2 cognitive states and the full transfer/full access model. *Second Language Research* 12:40–72.

Spada, Nina. 1997. Form-focused instruction and second language acquisition: A review of classroom and laboratory research. *Language Teaching* 30 (2): 73–87.

Torrego, Esther. 1998. *The dependency of objects.* Cambridge, MA: MIT Press.

Trahey, Martha, and Lydia White. 1993. Positive evidence and preemption in the second language classroom. *Studies in Second Language Acquisition* 15:181–204.

VanPatten, Bill, and Teresa Cadierno. 1993. Explicit instruction and input processing. *Studies in Second Language Acquisition* 15 (2): 225–43.

White, Lydia 1989. The principle of adjacency in second language acquisition: Do learners observe the subset principle? In *Linguistic perspectives on second language acquisition,* ed. Susan Gass and Jacquelyn Schachter, 134–58. New York: Cambridge University Press.

———. 1991. Adverb placement in second language acquisition: Some positive and negative evidence in the classroom. *Second Language Research* 7 (2): 133–61.

Zagona, Karen. 2002. *The syntax of Spanish.* Cambridge: Cambridge University Press.

18

The Role of Pedagogical Tasks and Focus on Form in Acquisition of Discourse Markers by Advanced Language Learners

MARÍA JOSÉ DE LA FUENTE
George Washington University

RECENT LITERATURE has pointed to the inherent difficulty in reaching an advanced level of proficiency in a language in a classroom environment (see Byrnes and Maxim 2003; Byrnes, Weger-Guntharp, and Sprang 2006). One of the characteristics that defines advanced proficiency in a second/foreign language (L2) is the ability to produce speech/text at the discourse level, which involves a mastery of the cohesive devices inherent to discourse. Constructing L2 discourse involves the use of cohesive resources or *discourse markers,* both lexical (e.g., deictic markers such as *all of this, that,* etc.) and grammatical (e.g., conjunctions). Discourse markers are words or phrases that signal a relationship between the segment they introduce and the prior segment, with their contribution to the meaning of the message being procedural rather than conceptual (Fraser 1999). Some examples of discourse markers in English are *moreover, in other words, however, on the contrary, therefore,* and *as a result.* Observational data from third- and fourth-year foreign language classes—years when students are expected to reach an advanced level of language ability—show that learners' speech and writing is phrasal or clausal rather than sentential and lacks cohesive mechanisms in the target language, even with several semesters of exposure to rich, content-oriented models of classroom L2 instruction. Despite the fact that these cohesive markers are certainly frequent in naturalistic L2 input, they still seem to lack salience for learners in an instructed environment, and instructional materials seem to offer little explicit instruction that would call their attention to these forms.

Review of Literature

Based on the theoretical premises that attention is needed for second language acquisition (SLA) (Schmidt 1990, 1993) and that for acquisition to take place learners must consciously notice forms in the input (and the meanings these forms realize) so they can process them in their short-term memory (Skehan 1996), some researchers advocate a type of classroom pedagogical approach that addresses the learner's need to attend to form (Doughty and Williams 1998a, 1998b; Ellis 2000; Harley 1998; Lightbown and Spada 1990; Long and Robinson 1998). According to Leow (1997 and elsewhere), awareness and noticing contribute to learning and retention; thus some type of form-focused instruction (incidental or planned) that induces noticing must be beneficial/needed for acquisition of certain L2 features. This attention to form can range from the unobtrusive view of Long and Robinson (1998), a reactive and unplanned approach where learners' attention is drawn to form as it happens incidentally, to the more proactive, planned approach proposed by Spada (1997) or Doughty and Williams (1998b),[1] which calls for planning of the elements where focus is desired.[2] In general, most researchers agree that, in the case of classroom L2 teaching, a teacher-generated, proactive focus on form may be more desirable (see Ellis 2003).

Two questions debated in the literature: Which forms are amenable to focus on form, and does the effectiveness of this type of instruction depend on the specific instructional treatment (i.e., what type[s] of focus on form technique[s] is/are used)? Regarding the first question, Doughty and Williams (1998b) point out that the term *form* can be applied not only to phonological and morphosyntactical features of an L2 but also to the lexicon, discourse, and pragmatics and that, aside from grammar, "other levels of linguistic form cannot be ignored as potential candidates for focus on form" (212). A review of the literature on focus on form reveals a focus of morphosyntactic (Jourdenais et al. 1995; Leeman et al. 1995; Williams and Evans 1998; Muranoi 1996) or lexical (de la Fuente 2006) features. However, and as Doughty and Williams (1998a) point out, there is little evidence in the literature of the efficacy of focus on form beyond the sentence level. Research that targets discourse markers as forms to focus on during pedagogical interventions is then needed. With respect to the second question, the type of focus on form (more or less explicit) is directly related to the implicit/explicit continuum; in other words, is language learning mostly an implicit, incidental process, or an explicit, intentional one? Examples of highly implicit focus on form techniques are *input flood,* based on the principle that the target structure should appear many times in the input so learners can notice it, and *input enhancement* (the input is made salient by highlighting it, for example).[3] A combination of input flood and input enhancement task is what Ellis (2003) calls *input enrichment* tasks. In these tasks, the L2 targeted features are frequent (input flood) and salient (input enhancement) in the input (Ellis 2003, 158).

Swain (1985, 1995) proposes that output also has a crucial role in noticing and paying attention to linguistic L2 features. According to Swain (1985), negotiation tasks can engage learners in *pushed output* that will attract feedback from the interlocutor. Explicitness of attention to form will increase if the task directs learners to reflect upon, discuss, and process linguistic form. Examples of an explicit technique are *consciousness-raising* (C-R) tasks (Ellis 2003). According to Ellis (2003, 163), C-R tasks are intended to create awareness of how an L2 feature works by having learners "talk meaningfully about a language point using their own linguistic resources." Fotos (1993, 1994) showed that learners are more likely to acquire explicit knowledge of targeted forms and notice them in subsequent tasks after completing C-R tasks than after unfocused, communicative tasks.

To be sure, the implicit–explicit continuum in focus on form needs to be further investigated with respect to classroom L2 instruction. Furthermore, there is a scarcity of studies directly or indirectly addressing the role of tasks with a focus on form—of either kind—in acquisition of discourse elements of the language. Pavlenko (2006, 114) observes that one aspect of advanced narrative competence, cohesion, is difficult to acquire, and may require noticing and C-R tasks. García Mayo (2002, 166) noted that learners in a group exposed to a dictogloss task seldom discussed any of the targeted features, among which were clausal connectors, and that they "seemed to be more concerned about the form and meaning of words than about the features targeted by the task."[4] Given the lack of research in this area, this study is certainly warranted.

Research Questions

This study explores whether and how two different types of interactive pedagogical tasks with a focus on form can promote learning of discourse markers by advanced learners of Spanish. The research questions of the study were the following: Are there differential effects in the immediate comprehension and in the retrieval of discourse markers between learners exposed to tasks with an explicit focus on form (C-R tasks) and those exposed to similar tasks with an implicit focus on form? During these tasks, do learners pay attention to and process target discourse markers? Do they negotiate target discourse markers?

Methodology

Participants

The sample population of advanced language learners was comprised of two groups of undergraduate students enrolled at the time of the research at the investigator's institution. The participants were twenty-four adult college learners of Spanish (eight male, sixteen female) enrolled in a class corresponding to a fifth semester of language study. Their mean length of exposure to the Spanish language in a classroom setting was 7.2 years. All participants selected met the following criteria: English was their first language, they were not heritage speakers of Spanish, and they did not know any other foreign language.

Procedure

A quasi-experimental comparison group design was used to address the first research question, utilizing a pretest, a treatment, and a posttest. A written recognition pretest including twelve isolated Spanish discourse markers was administered one day prior to the treatment. Participants were asked to provide an English translation for each connector and then write a paragraph in Spanish that incorporated the connector. After scoring the pretests, four Spanish discourse markers, unknown by all participants, were selected: *o sea* (that is), *entre tanto* (meanwhile), *en cuanto a* (regarding, in reference to), and *puesto que* (because). Two planned focus on form tasks were designed, each of them situated at opposite ends of the implicit–explicit continuum.

■ Consciousness-raising task. The task was intended to raise students' awareness and elicit conscious reflection through a focus on the form of the four Spanish discourse markers selected (see appendix). The input data was a written text containing examples of the four targeted structures, making them salient (enhanced in bold) for learners. The task focused learners' attention on these forms by making it necessary to process their meanings.

▥ Input enrichment task. This task was designed to induce learners' noticing of the target items while performing a meaning (content)-focused activity. The input data were the same text used for the other condition with the enhanced targeted forms (see appendix). The task required learners to respond to content questions and, at the same time, induce noticing of the forms.

Participants were randomly assigned to one of two groups: Consciousness-Raising (C-R), and Input Enrichment (I-E), each comprised of six pairs of students who had to work collaboratively to solve the assigned task. Every pair was given the same amount of time to complete the task. All in-task interactions were video recorded. After each pair completed the task, they participated in an introspective review session—stimulated recall[5]—with the investigator. The researcher replayed and reviewed with each pair of students the video containing their interaction during the task. The researcher addressed questions to the students that were pertinent to the study and had to do with levels of attention, items paid attention to while completing the task, items that were negotiated or not and why, and so on. These sessions were also recorded. Following the thirty-minute stimulated recall session, each participant received the first assessment task: a text in Spanish with eight blank spaces. Learners needed to read the text and then insert the four target items in the blanks (twice each). This assessment task measured gains in comprehension of the items. The following day they were given the second assessment task, a text in English with four discourse markers, equivalent to the four Spanish ones, underlined. Learners had to translate each of them into Spanish, avoiding several other options. In this way we would observe if learners could retrieve the forms as well as the meaning they conveyed.

Results and Discussion
Data were analyzed in two stages. First, the results of the two assessment posttasks, showing learners' gains in comprehension and retrieval of targeted discourse markers, were computed and submitted to statistical analysis; second, the in-task recorded interactions were transcribed for further analysis, and the videos of the stimulated recall sessions were reviewed.

1. Effects in Immediate Comprehension and Retrieval (Production) of Discourse Markers (Research Question 1)
In order to investigate differential effects in the immediate comprehension of the target items mean scores and standard deviations (*SD*) for assessment 1 were statistically analyzed using a *t* test. This between-group comparison showed a significant main effect of group ($p = <.001$). Results are shown in table 18.1.

In order to investigate differential effects in retrieval or production of the targeted items between groups, mean scores, and standard deviations (*SD*) for assessment 2 were statistically analyzed using a *t* test. This comparison also showed a significant main effect of group ($p = <.007$). Results are shown in table 18.2.

Table 18.1
Assessment Task 1: t test between-Group Comparisons

	N	Mean	SD	t	df
Group A	12	3.66	0.74	5.07	21
Group B	12	2.20	0.65		

p = <.001

Table 18.2
Assessment Task 2: t test between-Group Comparisons

	N	Mean	SD	t	df
Group A	12	2.25	0.96	3.01	18
Group B	12	1.25	0.62		

p = <.007

Although gains were observed for both groups, these results show that learners exposed to a more explicit focus on form task (C-R) were able to show more immediate comprehension of the newly introduced discourse markers than those exposed to a more implicit focus on form task (I-E). They also show that the first group was more successful at retrieving the discourse markers in order to complete a translation task. The results suggest that the C-R task was more effective at promoting attention to and noticing of discourse markers, as shown by the higher levels of both comprehension (meaning, function) and production (form) of the items. The gains observed in the learners under the IE condition indicate that some level of attention and awareness was present while these learners performed the tasks; however, further processing in short-term memory may have been more effective under the C-R task condition, which would explain the higher level of immediate comprehension and short-term retention. These results appear to confirm similar results of other studies investigating differences between implicit and explicit focus on form instruction (DeKeyser 1995; Robinson 1996).

2. Analysis of In-Task Interactions and Stimulated Recall
Protocols (Research Question 2)

The analysis of the transcriptions of *in-task interactions* showed that all interactions in the C-R group contained substantial amounts of *metatalk* (talking about the L2); this metatalk was a result of the task itself, which required students to figure out collaboratively the meaning of the discourse markers by using contextual clues and other strategies available to them. Dialogue between participants in all dyads was collaborative, balanced, and conducted in the L2 but with frequent code switching to the first language (L1), caused by the difficulty of producing metatalk in the L2.[6] Four dyads solved the task successfully, that is, they provided the right translation for each target item. One dyad translated three correctly, and one dyad gave a correct answer for two. For all six dyads, however, the nature of the task made it successful to focus attention on the target L2 features, and meaning negotiation of each item took place. Interactions and episodes of meaning negotiation always revolved around the target items. The most common strategy used to figure out meaning was hypothesis testing via translation, as reported in subsequent stimulated recall protocols, and as exemplified in (1):

(1) (dyad in C-R group)

STUDENT A: *"**En cuanto a** . . . [long pause]"*

STUDENT B: "[long pause] *it's kind of like 'regarding'*, [translating text] *regarding its importance, it's used . . . I don't know if that's what it's trying to say."*

STUDENT A: *"It would be like 'in relation to.'"*

STUDENT B: "Yeah, that would work too."

Several long pauses were observed during which students would reread parts of the text (and test hypotheses by translating into the L1 in their heads). Then they offered their solution to the other student who would agree or disagree. Once they agreed on a translation, they moved to the next item. The analysis of the interactions of the I-E dyads showed similarities as well as differences with respect to the C-R group. Dialogue between participants in all I-E dyads was also balanced and collaborative. Three I-E dyads solved the task successfully, that is, they answered all content questions. For these dyads, overt negotiation of the enhanced discourse markers was observed on just a few occasions. In most instances, they used strategies to answer the questions correctly that did not involve overt negotiation of the markers. All cases of incorrect answers to the content questions corresponded with a lack of noticing and processing of the discourse markers, as revealed by the in-task interaction transcripts. In other words, students exhibited poor comprehension when understanding of the discourse markers was crucial to answer the question. A substantially lower amount of code switching was observed: While interactions in the C-R group contained substantial amounts of metatalk, only six cases of metatalk in all six interactions of the I-E group were found. That is, talking about content in the L2 was easier than talking about the L2 itself. The interactions and negotiations that took place in the IE group revolved around the content of the text and, despite the fact that learners read through the enhanced target forms, in some cases several times, in order to look for answers to the questions, only four cases of negotiation of meaning of discourse markers were found. It is clear that the nature of the task had an effect on how learners used their attentional resources. This evident lack of awareness and noticing of target items seems to have been the cause of the differential effects found in posttests. Further evidence is provided by the answers that learners gave to the question following the first posttest: "Was the previous task helpful to you in order solve this one? How? Please explain." While learners in the C-R group clearly noted that they focused their attention on the target items, learners in the I-E group reported not paying attention to the boldfaced, enhanced items in the text.

(2) (student in an I-E dyad)

"I didn't even know that [the marker o sea] was there."

Others reported paying attention in a very brief manner but felt no need to negotiate and find out what their meaning/function was. In other words, they were perceptually salient but considered not needed for successful resolution of the task at hand.

(3) *"I saw a couple of them* [markers] *in that text but still I did not understand what they meant so they were difficult to place."*

(4) *"I remember these were used in the other text, but I have a tendency to skip over things like these, and then I never fully understand what they mean."*

Unlike in the case of the C-R group, several cases of negotiation of forms not targeted by the task were found in the transcripts of the I-E group. This means that lexical items, and not the enhanced forms, were the focus of meaning negotiation and that learners noticed those more than they noticed the target markers. These results are similar to those found in Kowal and Swain (1994), Foster (1998), and Williams (1999), among others. With more implicit focus on form tasks, such as I-E tasks, it is hard to predict which L2 areas will attract learners' attention.

In order to further explore the differences observed in amount and quality of learners' declared attention to, and noticing of, target items, we analyzed the stimulated recall protocols for both groups. We grouped opinions of C-R and I-E group participants with respect to different topics, generalizing when eight or more participants expressed similar points of view.

(a) Learners consider discourse markers necessary for L2 text comprehension.

(b) Learners consider discourse markers particularly difficult aspects of the L2 to learn.

(c) C-R learners positively value C-R tasks because they involve "active learning" and help subsequent retrieval of the L2 features. However, they think they are most likely to retain these forms only with subsequent exposures and uses.

(d) C-R learners prefer to solve C-R tasks (metatalk) in English, while I-E learners, with the exception of a few occasions, did not need to codeswitch (use of L1) to interact.

Conclusions, Implications for Classroom Pedagogy, and Further Research

This study assumes that use of focused or planned pedagogical tasks is needed to foster learning of discourse markers, an important aspect of being an advanced L2 learner/user. Its results suggest, however, that not all focused tasks may be of equal effectiveness. Although input enrichment tasks (a type of planned, implicit focus on form) seem to promote some level of effective attention to, and noticing of discourse markers in the L2 input, C-R tasks seem more effective by focusing learners' attention on their forms, meanings, and uses, and consequently raising learners' awareness of such forms, and promoting explicit learning. All of this results in higher levels of immediate comprehension and retrieval of target forms. During C-R tasks, learners negotiate meaning of L2 forms: They notice and formulate and test hypotheses.

Given their lack of salience, explicit learning (via C-R tasks) and metalinguistic awareness may be necessary cognitive steps to learn L2 discourse markers.

C-R tasks are valuable classroom activities, and a needed element in task- and content-based instruction, to foster explicit learning of discourse markers. In combination with more implicit focus on form tasks, such as I-E tasks, they may facilitate acquisition of discourse markers by helping that initial stage of noticing and awareness. Teachers then may move to more implicit tasks to facilitate further internalization of L2 forms.

Indeed, further research should investigate the relationship between implicit and explicit focus on form tasks (i.e., if it is a combination of tasks rather than the exclusive use of one form or another, which aids acquisition of L2 features). Also further studies should address the long-term effects of C-R tasks (retention) and compare the effectiveness of C-R tasks with other types of explicit focus of form techniques. The lack of delayed posttests to measure delayed effects and the small number of participants are limitations of this small-scale study that need to be mentioned. However, the scarcity of research in the area of task-based methodology and focus on form in relation to discourse markers in particular, and to other aspects of the discourse level of an L2 in general, opens a new path worth pursuing.

NOTES

1. Doughty and Williams (1998b) use the term *"proactive" focus on form* to refer to planned (not incidental) interventions to provide focus on form during tasks.
2. See also Lightbown (1998); Loschky and Bley-Vroman (1993); and Swain (1998).
3. Jourdenais et al. (1995) observed that learners are more likely to notice visually enhanced input than unenhanced input. White (1998) concluded that these techniques seem to be ineffective and that more explicit mechanisms to attract learners' attention may have to be used. Similarly, Leow (2001) found no differences between enhanced and unenhanced input in amount of noticing or subsequent acquisition of targeted forms.
4. This concern for lexical meaning rather than other aspects of the L2 has been found in many studies on interactive tasks and focus on form (see, e.g., Foster 1998; Williams 1999).
5. Stimulated recall is a needed introspective methodology, along with think-aloud protocols, to operationalize attention and noticing as cognitive processes. See Gass and Mackey (2000) for an excellent introduction to stimulated recall methodology for SLA research.
6. This was reported by participants during the stimulated recall session. See Scott and de la Fuente (2008) for a study on the uses of the L1 by L2 learners during C-R pedagogical tasks.

REFERENCES

Byrnes, Heidi, and Hiram Maxim, eds. 2003. *Advanced foreign language learning: A challenge to college programs.* Boston: Thomson Heinle.

Byrnes, Heidi, Heather Weger-Guntharp, and Katherine Sprang, eds. 2006. *Educating for advanced foreign language capabilities.* Washington DC: Georgetown University Press.

DeKeyser, Robert M. 1995. Learning second language grammar rules: An experiment with a miniature linguistic system. *Studies in Second Language Acquisition* 17:379–410.

de la Fuente, María J. 2006. Classroom L2 vocabulary acquisition: Investigating the role of pedagogical tasks and form-focused instruction. *Language Teaching Research* 10:263–95.

Doughty, Catherine, and Jessica Williams, eds. 1998a. *Focus on form in classroom second language acquisition.* Cambridge: Cambridge University Press.

———. 1998b. Pedagogical choices in focus on form. In *Focus on form in classroom second language acquisition,* ed. Catherine Doughty and Jessica Williams, 197–261. Cambridge: Cambridge University Press.

Ellis, Rod. 2000. Focus on form in task-based language teaching. In *Language policy and pedagogy,* ed. Richard D. Lambert and Elana Shohamy. Amsterdam: John Benjamins.

———. 2003. *Task-based language learning and teaching.* Cambridge: Cambridge University Press.

Foster, Pauline. 1998. A classroom perspective on the negotiation of meaning. *Applied Linguistics* 19:1–23.

Fotos, Sandra. 1993. Consciousness-raising and noticing through focus on form: Grammar task performance vs. formal instruction. *Applied Linguistics* 14:385–407.

———. 1994. Integrating grammar instruction and communicative language use through grammar consciousness-raising tasks. *TESOL Quarterly* 28:323–51.

Fraser, Bruce. 1999. What are discourse markers? *Journal of Pragmatics* 31:931–52.

García Mayo, María del Pilar. 2002. The effectiveness of two form-focused tasks in advanced EFL pedagogy. *International Journal of Applied Linguistics* 12:156–75.

Gass, Susan, and Allison Mackey. 2000. *Stimulated recall methodology in second language research.* Mahwah, NJ: Lawrence Erlbaum Associates.

Harley, Birgit. 1998. The role of focus on form tasks in promoting child L2 acquisition. In *Focus on form in classroom second language acquisition,* ed. Catherine Doughty and Jessica Williams, 156–74. Cambridge: Cambridge University Press.

Jourdenais, René, Mitch Ota, Stephanie Stauffer, Barbara Boyson, and Catherine Doughty. 1995. Does textual enhancement promote noticing? A think-aloud protocol analysis. In *Attention and awareness in foreign language learning,* ed. Richard W. Schmidt, 183–216. Honolulu: University of Hawai'i Press.

Kowal, Maria, and Merrill Swain. 1994. Using collaborative language production tasks to promote students' language awareness. *Language Awareness* 3:72–93.

Leeman, Jennifer, Igone Arteagoitia, Boris Fridman, and Catherine Doughty. 1995. Integrating attention to form with meaning: Focus on form in content-based Spanish instruction. In *Attention and awareness in foreign language learning,* ed. Richard W. Schmidt, 217–58. Honolulu: University of Hawai'i Press.

Leow, Ronald P. 1997. Attention, awareness, and foreign language behavior. *Language Learning* 47:467–506.

———. 2001. Attention, awareness and foreign language behavior. *Language Learning* 51:113–55.

Lightbown, Patsy M. 1998. The importance of timing in focus on form. In *Focus on form in classroom second language acquisition,* ed. Catherine Doughty and Jessica Williams, 177–96. Cambridge: Cambridge University Press.

Lightbown, Patsy M., and Nina Spada. 1990. Focus on form and corrective feedback in communicative language teaching: Effects on second language learning. *Studies in Second Language Acquisition* 12:429–48.

Long, Michael, and Peter Robinson. 1998. Focus on form: Theory, research, and practice. In *Focus on form in classroom second language acquisition,* ed. Catherine Doughty and Jessica Williams, 15–41. Cambridge: Cambridge University Press.

Loschky, Lester, and Robert Bley-Vroman. 1993. Grammar and task-based methodology. In *Task and language learning,* vol. 1, ed. G. Crookes and Susan Gass, 123–67. Clevedon, Avon: Multilingual Matters.

Muranoi, Hitoshi. 1996. Effects of interaction enhancement on restructuring of interlanguage grammar: A cognitive approach to foreign language instruction. Unpublished PhD diss., Georgetown University.

Pavlenko, Aneta. 2006. Narrative competence in a second language. In *Educating for advanced foreign language capacities: Constructs, curriculum, instruction, assessment,* ed. Heidi Byrnes, Heather Weger-Guntharp, and Katherine Sprang, 105–17. Washington, DC: Georgetown University Press.

Robinson, Peter. 1996. Learning simple and complex second language rules under implicit, incidental, rule-search, and instructed conditions. *Studies in Second Language Acquisition* 18:27–68.

Schmidt, Richard. 1990. The role of consciousness in second language learning. *Applied Linguistics* 11:129–58.

———. 1993. Awareness and second language acquisition. *Annual Review of Applied Linguistics* 13:206–26.

Scott, Virginia, and María J. de la Fuente. 2008. What's the problem? L2 learners use of the L1 during consciousness-raising, form-focused tasks. *Modern Language Journal* 92:19–38.

Skehan, Peter. 1996. A framework for the implementation of task based instruction. *Applied Linguistics* 17:38–62.

Spada, Nina. 1997. Form-focused instruction and second language acquisition: a review of classroom and laboratory research. *Language Teaching* 30:73–87.

Swain, Merrill. 1985. Communicative competence: Some roles of comprehensible input and comprehensible output in its development. In *Input in second language acquisition,* ed. Susan Gass and Carolyn Madden. Rowley, MA: Newbury House.

———. 1995. Three functions of output in second language learning. In *For H. G. Widdowson: Principles and practice in the study of language,* ed. Guy Cook and Barbara Seidlhofer, 125–44. Oxford: Oxford University Press.

———. 1998. Focus on form through conscious reflection. In *Focus on form in classroom second language acquisition,* ed. Catherine Doughty and Jessica Williams, 64–82. Cambridge: Cambridge University Press.

White, Joanna. 1998. Getting the learners' attention. A typographical input enhancement study. In *Focus on form in classroom second language acquisition,* ed. Catherine Doughty and Jessica Williams, 85–113. Cambridge: Cambridge University Press.

Williams, Jessica. 1999. Learner-generated attention to form. *Language Learning* 49:583–625.

Williams, Jessica, and Jacqueline Evans. 1998. What kind of focus and on which forms? In *Focus on form in classroom second language acquisition,* ed. Catherine Doughty and Jessica Williams, 139–55. Cambridge: Cambridge University Press.

Appendix
C-R tasks vs. I-E tasks
[Excerpt from the input data]

La ampliación del Canal de Panamá

En este ensayo discutiré un tema de gran importancia para los panameños: si el pueblo panameño debe aprobar o rechazar mediante un referéndum la ampliación del Canal de Panamá.

La regla general es que, cuando se quiere un camino, lo paga quien lo quiere usar. Por ejemplo, los panameños pagamos impuestos por las calles que el gobierno construye por donde podemos transitar, lo que nos convierte en usuarios, *o sea,* personas que usan el camino [. . .]

C-R task
Working with your classmate, provide a translation in English that reflects the meaning of these expressions as they appear in the text.
1. o sea _____
2. puesto que _____
[. . .]

I-E task
Work with your classmate to provide an answer to the following questions.
1. What is being debated regarding the Panama Canal?
2. Why will the Panamanians have to pay for the canal's expansion?
3. What does the word *usuarios* (paragraph 2) mean? How do you know?
[. . .]

19

Article Acquisition in English, German, Norwegian, and Swedish

TANJA KUPISCH, MERETE ANDERSSEN,
UTE BOHNACKER, AND NEIL SNAPE

University of Calgary, University of Tromsø, Uppsala University, and Hokkaido University

ARTICLE OMISSION is a well-documented phenomenon in early child speech. Interestingly, children differ in terms of how extensively they omit articles depending on their age and what language(s) they are exposed to. Different accounts have been proposed to account for this cross-linguistic variation. One of the most widely discussed models is the *nominal mapping parameter* (NMP), originally proposed in Chierchia (1998), which relates variation in child language to the syntactic and semantic properties of noun phrases across languages (e.g., Chierchia, Guasti, and Gualmini 1999; Guasti and Gavarró 2003; Guasti et al. 2004). Other influential accounts of determiner omission have been formulated in prosody-oriented research (e.g., Gerken 1991, 1994; Lleó 1998, 2001; Lleó and Demuth 1999; Roark and Demuth 2000; Demuth, McCullough, and Adamo 2007). So far, no common agreement has been reached.

This chapter presents a study on article acquisition in English, German, Norwegian, and Swedish, where article use is subject to similar syntactic and semantic conditions. Hence the NMP predicts similar acquisition patterns. In terms of their metrical structure, noun phrases in these languages differ considerably. Accordingly, different acquisition patterns are expected.

The chapter is structured as follows: In the first section, we present an overview of articles and article use in the four languages under discussion. In the second section, we introduce the NMP and two prosodic accounts. The third section presents our results, discussing them in light of the aforementioned models. Our data suggest that the NMP should be discarded as empirically false, while supporting prosodic approaches to article acquisition. Nevertheless, as we conclude in the fourth section, even prosodic accounts do not provide an all-encompassing explanation for children's omission of articles.

Article acquisition in these four languages has been studied in previous work (for monolingual first language [L1] acquisition, see, e.g., Brown 1973; Radford 1990; Abu-Akel and Bailey 2000; Demuth, McCullough, and Adamo 2007, for English; Clahsen, Eisenbeiss, and Penke 1996; Penner and Weissenborn 1996; Lleó 1998, 2001; Eisenbeiss 2002; Kupisch 2006, 2007, for German; Anderssen 2005, for Norwegian;

Bohnacker 1997, 2004, 2007; Plunkett and Strömqvist 1992; Santelmann 1998; Svartholm 1978, for Swedish). However, no study has provided a systematic comparison of these languages.

Articles in English, German, Norwegian, and Swedish

The four languages all have definite and indefinite articles. Indefinite articles occur prenominally. Definite articles are prenominal in English and German but postnominal in Norwegian and Swedish. [The articles in (1) are marked by italics.]

(1) En. *a* house vs. *the* house   Ge. *ein* Haus vs. *das* Haus
    No. *et* hus   vs. hus-*e*   Sw. *ett* hus   vs. hus-*et*

Prosodically, articles in these languages differ in terms of whether they constitute clitics or feet. English articles represent free clitics (2a) (Selkirk 1996). In the two Scandinavian languages, the prenominal indefinite article is proclitic to the noun, while the postnominal definite article is enclitic. Traditionally, the suffixal article in Norwegian (and Swedish) is implicitly taken to be of the kind represented in (2b). However, recent research suggests that the suffixal article is an affixal clitic (2c) based on the fact that the addition of the suffixal article does not alter the pitch accent of monosyllabic nouns (Morén 2007). German articles may be reduced or unreduced. Nonreduced articles have been analyzed as phonological words on their own, that is, they form separate feet (2d) (Wiese 1996, p.c.). Reduced articles may be enclitic, being subsumed under the host, which can be a preceding verb (2b) or a preposition (2d). In sentence-initial position, reduced articles may be proclitic (2a).[1]

(2)   a. free clitic   b. internal clitic   c. affixal clitic   d. prosodic word

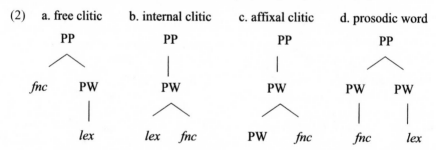

The four languages are largely similar in terms of the syntactic, semantic, and pragmatic conditions of article use. Generally articles are obligatory with singular count nouns, regardless of whether the reading is specific (as with the verb *see*) or generic (as with the verb *like*). The absence of an article (or any other determiner) results in ungrammaticality [cf. (3)].[2]

(3) En. *I see/like _ cat.   Ge. *Ich sehe/mag _ Katze.
    No. *Jeg ser/liker _ katt.   Sw. *Jag ser/gillar _ katt.

If the noun is plural or mass, it may appear bare. In this case, the noun phrase (NP) has a nonspecific or a generic reading, depending on the verb [cf. (4)]. Definite articles are allowed in these contexts, but they render the NP specific.

(4) En. I like/see _ cats.   Ge. Ich mag/sehe _ Katzen.

No. Jeg liker/ser _ katter.   Sw. Jag gillar/ser _ katter.

Besides these parallels, there are also some interesting differences. In fact, both Scandinavian languages sometimes allow bare singular count nouns whose meaning is slightly different from the corresponding indefinite marked nouns. The translation equivalents in English and German are ungrammatical. This point is usually not addressed in the linguistics literature and, despite its relevance, not mentioned in any papers dealing with the NMP (cf. Bohnacker 2004, 2007, 53–54, for details).

(5) En. *She has _ dog.   Ge. *Sie hat _ Hund.

No. Hun har _ hund.   Sw. Hon har _ hund.

Based on these observations, one may wonder whether it is still valid to test the NMP comparing these languages. We think it is, because according to Chierchia (1998, 356–57, 400–401) the Germanic languages pertain to one and the same parameter setting.

Prosodic Models versus Nominal Mapping Parameter and Predictions

In the following sections we summarize the basic ideas pertaining to the NMP and two prosodic approaches to article omission, and, based on those, we outline the predictions for article use in children acquiring the four Germanic languages under investigation.

The Nominal Mapping Parameter (NMP)

The NMP (Chierchia 1998) is concerned with the question of how semantic types of NPs are mapped onto syntax. Chierchia proposes that languages can be subdivided into three types according to what their nouns denote. Each of these types is representative of a parametric setting: In the Chinese-type language, all nouns are typically masslike. They come out of the lexicon as arguments and can be directly mapped onto syntax without projecting a determiner phrase (DP). In this type of language, nouns are always bare and there is no plural morphology. The Romance-type language represents the opposite case. Here, nouns are predicates, and D must be projected to convert them into arguments, which can then appear in argument positions. These languages have plural morphology and nouns must not be bare. In the third type of language, the Germanic type, languages can be either predicates or arguments, depending on whether they are count or mass. Only in the former case must D be projected. Nominals in all languages can be type-shifted (from predicates to arguments, and vice versa; see Chierchia 1998). This is necessary because nouns that are inherently count can sometimes be used as if they were mass, and vice versa.

Chierchia, Guasti, and Gualmini (1999) outline the predictions of the NMP for acquisition as follows: When acquiring articles, children pass through predetermined stages corresponding to parameter settings in the following way. The Chinese setting represents the default setting (stage 1). During this stage, children consistently omit determiners as if their target language were an articleless language. If this setting does not correspond to the target language, the discovery of plural morphology triggers resetting of the parameter to the Germanic setting where bare nouns and determiner-noun sequences appear to be in "free variation."[3] During this stage, children have to figure out which nouns are count and which are mass, and article omissions in obligatory contexts result from the misclassification of (particular) count nouns as mass. Children exposed to a Romance-type language have to reset the parameter again.[4] They can do so very quickly on the basis of positive evidence, that is, when discovering that nouns are consistently used with articles (rather than varying with bare nouns). The learning task is assumed to be more time-consuming in the Germanic-type languages, that is, it results in a more extended period of bare-noun use, because Germanic-learning children have to figure out for each noun separately whether it is mass or count. In Chierchia's typology, the Germanic languages are associated with one and the same parameter setting. Hence the NMP predicts that children acquiring English, German, Norwegian, and Swedish show similar patterns of article use and omission.

Prosodic Accounts

Prosody-oriented research has resulted in several different accounts on the acquisition of articles. We discuss two of them, which we refer to as *trochaic templates* and *bootstrapping via lexical models*.

Trochaic templates.   It is generally assumed that trochaic patterns, that is, words or phrases consisting of a strong syllable followed by a weak one (SW),[5] are unmarked as compared with iambic patterns, that is, words or phrases consisting of a weak followed by a strong syllable (WS). Experimental research has shown that nine-month-old American infants listen longer to lists of items that conform to the predominant strong-weak stress pattern of English than to lists that do not display this pattern (Jusczyk, Cutler, and Redanz 1993). Furthermore it has long been observed that children are less likely to preserve the initial syllable in the pronunciation of words like *baNAna* or *giRAFfe* than the final syllable of *CANdy* or *DONkey*, which also suggests that English children pay attention to SW structures. Gerken (1991) argues that the omission of various function words, including articles, should be explained in terms of a dispreference for iambic structures, as these elements are often prosodified as the pretonic syllables of an iamb. She provides empirical support from an imitation task: Children had to imitate utterances with weakly stressed syllables, including pronouns and articles. The children omitted extrametrical syllables from iambic structures, which led Gerken to suggest that child utterances have to fit what she referred to as a Trochaic Template.

English and most German NPs consisting of a determiner and a noun do not fit the trochaic template because the unstressed article precedes the noun, as in En. *a/the house* (WS), Ge. *(ei)n/das Haus* (WS) (and the majority of nouns are mono- or bisyllabic). The same is true for Norwegian and Swedish indefinite marked NPs, for example, No. *et hus* (WS) and Sw. *ett hus* (WS). By contrast, most Norwegian and Swedish NPs with a suffixed definite article fit the trochaic pattern, for example, No. *hus-e, katt-a* (SW) and Sw. *hus-et, katt-en* (SW).

If it is true that children show a preference for trochaic templates in acquisition, we would expect to see different acquisition patterns in the children acquiring English and German on the one hand, and children acquiring the Scandinavian languages on the other hand. More specifically, two predictions may be formulated: First, if children produce unstressed syllables more often in trochaic patterns than in iambic patterns, Swedish- and Norwegian-learning children should produce more articles than English- and German-learning children. Second, there should be an asymmetry in the Scandinavian languages between definite articles, which fit the trochaic patterns, and indefinite articles, which do not.[6]

Prosodic bootstrapping via lexical models.   According to Lleó and Demuth (1999), children's use of articles is bootstrapped through the presence of lexemes exhibiting an SWS structure in the input.[7] The authors compare Spanish-learning to German-learning children. As Spanish contains many trisyllabic WSW nouns, Spanish-speaking children are frequently exposed to WSW structures at the lexical level, that is, structures that are also required in the production of articles. German lexemes, by contrast, are mostly mono- or disyllabic, with the initial syllable being strong. The model is couched in terms of *optimality theory,* where WSW structures are assumed to require the violation of the *Exhaustivity Constraint* because they involve the production of an extrametrical syllable, that is, a syllable not immediately governed by a foot. Lleó and Demuth assume that because Spanish children have more evidence for the violation of Exhaustivity on the lexical level, they discover sooner than German children that violating Exhaustivity is a requirement in the production of utterances in their target language. Hence they produce articles earlier. This approach goes one step farther than the Trochaic Templates approach by motivating the early acquisition of articles in Spanish as opposed to German.

In the four languages we examine, the great majority of words have stressed initial syllables. An analysis of root nouns in Norwegian (facilitated by the Text Laboratory at Oslo University) indicated that only 648 (4.7%) of 13,848 nonderived nouns have initial weak syllables, the vast majority being loan words unlikely to occur in the input of small children. Because the four languages are typologically closely related, we do not expect their syllable structure to be noticeably different. Hence this model predicts that prenominal articles emerge late in all four languages, while definite articles should occur early in Norwegian and Swedish because they correspond to the predominant metric pattern in the target language.

The Study

Our analysis is based on longitudinal and cross-sectional data. For English and German, both cross-sectional and longitudinal data have been used. The English data represent different children at the ages of 1;10, 2;0, 2;1, and 2;5. For German, two children were examined longitudinally (1;6–2;5 and 1;8–3;0), and ten more children were studied at 1;10, 2;1, and 2;5. The English and German data were taken from the Manchester corpus and from the Szagun corpus, respectively, both available through CHILDES (Theakston et al. 2001; Szagun 2001; McWhinney and Snow 1990). For Norwegian and Swedish, where fewer data were available, we used only

▓ Table 19.1
Number of Recordings Analyzed and Total of Noun Phrases Requiring Articles (in brackets)

MLU	English	German	Norwegian	Swedish
1–1.49	7 (265)	26 (1,902)	0	14 (367)
1.5–1.99	13 (666)	10 (913)	7 (529)	5 (184)
2.0–2.49	8 (547)	10 (1,106)	3 (262)	3 (164)
2.5–2.99	7 (408)	6 (708)	4 (318)	3 (210)
3.0–4.0	3 (280)	3 (424)	13 (1,121)	1 (107)
Total	*35 (2,166)*	*48 (4,629)*	*27 (2,230)*	*26 (1,032)*

longitudinal corpora. The Norwegian data were collected by Merete Anderssen (Anderssen 2005). The Swedish corpus Markus was collected by Sven Strömqvist (Plunkett and Strömqvist 1992) and is available through CHILDES. The corpus Embla is from the Stockholm-based Swedish Child Language Syntax Project (Lange and Larsson 1973).

We compared the children in terms of mean length of utterances (MLU) rather than age to make our analysis comparable to others, particularly Chierchia et al. (1999). Our MLU is based on words rather than morphemes because the languages differ noticeably in the amount of bound morphology. An overview of the files analyzed is presented in table 19.1. We calculated the percentage of article use by determining the number of contexts in which an article was used from the total of contexts in which native speakers would use an article. We focus on the production of articles (rather than the whole class of determiners) to render our analysis comparable to previous ones testing the previously mentioned models. We ignored contexts in which bare nouns were used correctly, such as (4) through (5).

Figure 19.1 provides an overview of article omission in all four languages. To be able to run statistics, we also subdivided the data into MLU stages (MLU 1–1.49, MLU 1.5–1.99, etc.; figure 19.2). Between MLU 1 and MLU 2.5, there are statisti-

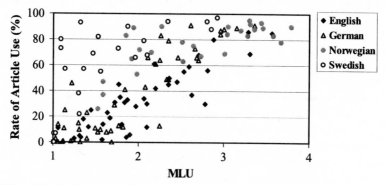

▓ Figure 19.1 Article Suppliance in English, German, Norwegian, and Swedish (stages)

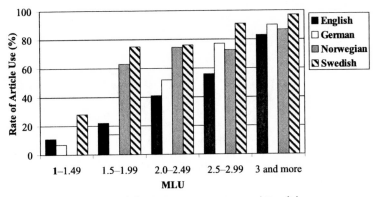

Figure 19.2 Article Suppliance in English, German, Norwegian, and Swedish

cally significant contrasts in the use of articles in obligatory contexts, between English and German on the one hand and Norwegian and Swedish on the other hand.[8] Between MLU 2.5 and MLU 3, the German children catch up with the children acquiring Norwegian and Swedish. Unexpectedly, the English children lag behind the German children here,[9] and so does the Norwegian child with respect to the Swedish children.[10] With an MLU above 3, children in all four languages use articles in more than 80 percent of all obligatory contexts.

Discussion

Our results falsify the NMP, which predicts similar acquisition patterns within Germanic languages. Furthermore, there is evidence against the assumption that article omissions in obligatory contexts in the free variation stage result from a misclassification of particular count nouns as mass, because article omission and realization sometimes occur within the same recording and even in parallel contexts of use. For example, at the age of 2;5.4, the English-speaking child Anne produced both *I want have a drink now* and *Want to have drink again*. At 2;1.21, the German child Martin produced both *Neemann*, "snowman," and *ein Neemann*, "a snowman," in two separate utterances, one right after the other. At 1;10.4, the Swedish child Markus produced the *bygga ett tåg*, "build a train," right after producing *bygga tåg*, "build train." At 1;10.4, Ina produced *en mann*, "a man," right after producing *mann*, "man." (See Cheng and Sybesma 1999; Munn and Schmitt 2001; Kupisch 2006, 103–4, for more counterevidence to the NMP, both theoretical and empirical.)

At the same time, the results lend support to the metrical template approach, which predicts lower rates of article omission in the Scandinavian languages. Moreover, in the Scandinavian languages, prenominal indefinite articles are omitted more than suffixal articles (figure 19.3). Again, this is exactly what the metrical templates approach predicts (see also Santelmann 1998). These results can also be captured by assuming that articles are bootstrapped via lexical models because Norwegian- and Swedish-learning children have lexical models for the metrical structure of nouns with definite articles, while German and English children do not. Figure 19.3 shows that the contrast between English/German and Swedish/Norwegian can largely be

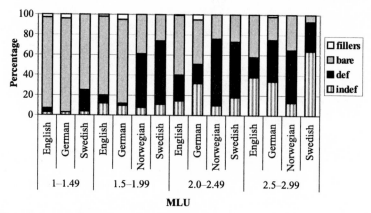

Figure 19.3 Article Type and Bare Nouns in Comparison

attributed to definite article use, while indefinite articles are used to similar extents and from the same age in all languages.

With regard to indefinite article use, it should be noted that although the idea of bootstrapping via lexical models is supported by our results with regard to the definite suffix in Norwegian and Swedish, it raises new issues. In fact, Lleó and Demuth's (1999) hypothesis that children start to produce articles earlier because their target languages contain many words with unfooted syllables cannot be applied to the languages under discussion here. First, all the children's utterances we analyzed show no production of any lexemes exhibiting WSW structures—this is not surprising given that the target languages exhibit few such lexemes. For example, none of the lexemes in the first Norwegian file involve an unfooted syllable (see Anderssen 2005, 277), but Ina already produces WSW structures in multiword utterances. The Swedish child Embla produces WSW utterances in the first file at 1;8.2, but she still omits articles in 26 percent of all obligatory contexts. Markus produces some WSW utterances between 1;7 and 1;9, for example, *de LAMpa*, "it-is lamp," at 1;9.3, while omitting 100 percent of all indefinite articles. This suggests that WSW lexemes in the input cannot be the factor that catalyzes prenominal article use, as extrametrical syllables occur in multiword utterances before they appear at the word level. In short, the idea of bootstrapping via lexical models predicts the early emergence of definite articles in the Scandinavian languages (many nouns having the metrical structure SW). However, it fails to explain how prenominal articles are acquired in these languages and why extrametrical syllables occur in multiword utterances while indefinite articles are omitted.

Does Input Frequency Provide an Alternative Solution?

We mentioned in the first section that indefinite articles appear to be more "optional" in the Scandinavian languages than in English and German. This raises the question whether the higher amount of definite as opposed to indefinite marked NPs in Norwegian and Swedish could result from different distributions in the adult input to the child. Similarly, the higher amount of bare nouns in English and German than in the

Table 19.2
Noun Phrases with a Definite Article versus Noun Phrases with an Indefinite Article in the Input (%)

	English	German	Norwegian	Swedish
Definite NPs	62	59	57	55
Indefinite NPs	38	41	43	45

Table 19.3
Bare Nouns from the Total of Noun Phrases in the Input (%)

	English	German	Norwegian	Swedish
Definite NPs	11	21	29	22

Scandinavian languages may result from respective distributions in the input. We conducted two analyses to test these possibilities, examining for each language the amount of definite as compared with indefinite articles and the amount of bare nouns from the total of NPs. Table 19.2 shows that NPs with definite articles are more frequent than NPs with indefinite articles in all four languages. However, only Norwegian and Swedish children show a higher use of definite articles in the onset of article use. Hence input frequency cannot provide an explanation for the early use of definite articles in Norwegian and Swedish.

Table 19.3 shows the amount of bare nouns from the total of NPs. A total of 894 noun phrases were analyzed in English, 643 in German, 552 in Norwegian, and 1,487 in Swedish. Proper names were excluded: Norwegian exhibits the highest amount of bare nouns, although articles in this language are acquired early. English exhibits the lowest amount, although articles in this language are acquired comparatively late. German and Swedish exhibit similar numbers, although children learning these languages show different patterns of article use. Hence input frequencies do not provide an alternative account for our findings.

Conclusions

Our analysis has shown that the NMP cannot account for the distribution of articles in child Germanic. It would only be tenable by adding to the original proposal auxiliary hypotheses to explain the variation attested across Germanic languages. However, auxiliary hypotheses would make the NMP lose much of its predictive force. Hence prosodic models, which can capture this variation without any additional assumptions, are preferable. The metrical template approach and the lexical bootstrapping approach correctly predict the early appearance of articles in the Scandinavian languages and the higher amount of definite as opposed to indefinite articles.

We have further shown that input frequencies do not provide an alternative solution to our findings because the distributions in the input do not match the acquisition patterns, either with regard to the amount of bare nouns found in the child data or with regard to the distribution of definite as opposed to indefinite articles. Overall we agree with Lleó and Demuth (1999), Lleó (2001), and Demuth, McCullough, and

Adamo (2007) that phonological patterns could be responsible for the variation we observe in the emergence of articles across languages. The fact that definite articles are part of trochees in Norwegian and Swedish seems to render them more salient, which can explain the children's early awareness of them.

Nevertheless, we admit that phonological approaches cannot provide an all-encompassing explanation of article acquisition. First, neither of the two prosodic models provides an account of why and how children acquire indefinite articles, which do not form trochees with the nouns they accompany and for which the languages provide no prosodic models in the domain of words (in the sense of Lleó and Demuth 1999). Second, neither prosodic model accounts for the (seemingly) optional use of articles at later stages of acquisition (especially MLU 2 to 3). Third, a closer look at the data from a qualitative perspective indicates that the distinction between Scandinavian definite articles (which fit the trochaic template and are acquired early) and indefinite articles (which do not fit the template and are acquired late) is too coarse. It makes a number of predictions that are not borne out: First, it leaves unexplained any omission of the definite article with monosyllabic nouns, for example, No. *hus-e,* Sw. *hus-et,* "house-the," *bil-n,* Sw. *bil-en,* "car-the." Such omissions are rare, but they do occur (see Bohnacker 2004; Anderssen 2005). Second, the trochaic template approach predicts the omission of the third syllable with nouns such as Sw. *ALbum-et,* "album-the," where the definite article adds a syllable to a trochee, as well as the omission of the third syllable in plural nouns, for example, Sw. HÄStar-na, "horses-the." Such (predicted) omissions are very rare (see Bohnacker 2004, 232–36 for a more detailed discussion). Third, while German children omit articles, they often produce combinations of deictic pronouns and nouns, for example, *da Messer,* "there knife," which have the same metrical structure as noun phrases with (unreduced) articles, for example, das Messer, "the knife." Hence there are some empirical data that metric approaches cannot capture. These need to be discussed in future research.

NOTES

1. According to Lleó (2001, 33), cliticized articles can never be initial in German. We think that there are exceptions. In High German, sentence-initial indefinite articles are often reduced, typically with topicalized noun phrases (NPs), e.g., *N'Haus kann ich jetzt nicht kaufen,* "A house I can't buy now."
2. We consider a NP to be *specific* if it refers to one or more particular entities and nonspecific if it does not refer to any particular entity.
3. As an anonymous reviewer pointed out to us, Aoun and Li (2003) show that, contrary to Chierchia's (1998) claims about Chinese, Mandarin does have a restricted (yet frequent) plural marker *–men,* which is obligatory on plural personal pronouns and optional on nouns denoting humans. The observation is problematic for the NMP, both because the NMP claims that articleless languages have no plural marking and because plural markings are supposed to trigger parameter resetting, from the Chinese to the Germanic setting.
4. The original order proposed was Chinese → Romance → Germanic. This ordering is problematic because "Romance" is a subset of "Germanic," if the Romance languages are defined as languages without any bare nouns. All nominals that Germanic-learning children in the Romance setting hear would be consistent with their grammar, and there would be no motivation to reset the parameter. This original proposal was revised in Chierchia, Guasti, and Gualmini (1999). Yet the fact that all Romance languages display some bare nouns raises the issue whether "Romance" and "Germanic" instantiate different parameters.

5. SW refers to the metric pattern, while Sw. refers to the language *Swedish*.

6. This is a simplification because it assumes that NPs always occur in isolation (which is not true for all cases). Articles may be prosodified with preceding material in the context of larger utterances, for example, if they follow a monosyllabic verb or preposition.

7. However, note that the "input" is determined through the children's utterances: The proportion of WSW structures is estimated based on the proportion of the children's vocabulary that involves a WSW structure (in the target language). A slightly different approach has been outlined in Roark and Demuth (2000).

8. We performed chi-square tests for comparing each language contrast in each MLU stage.

9. One reason may be our treatment of bare nouns after prepositions in German. German articles may fuse with preceding prepositions, for example, *in den Topf*, "into the pot" → *in 'Topf*. The bare noun structure *in Topf* only differs by a lack of lengthening on the final nasal of *in*. Because such acoustic differences are hard to perceive in child speech, we exclude such contexts from our counts, but they may be an area where variation is most persistent.

10. At the last MLU stage (figure 19.3), the Norwegian child Ina uses a surprisingly high number of illegitimate bare nouns as compared with the other children, particularly the two Swedish ones. Most likely this is the result of an individual characteristic of Ina. Studies of other grammatical domains suggest that Ina allows optionality for a prolonged period (Westergaard 2007).

REFERENCES

Abu-Akel, Ahmed, and Bailey, Alison L. 2000. Acquisition and use of "*a*" and "*the*" in English by young children. In *Proceedings of the twenty-fourth annual BUCLD*, ed. Catherine Howell, Sarah A. Fish, and Thea Keith-Lucas, 45–57, Somerville, MA: Cascadilla Press.

Anderssen, Merete. 2005. The acquisition of compositional definiteness in Norwegian. PhD diss., University of Tromsø.

Aoun, Joseph, and Yen-Hui Audrey Li. 2003. *Essays on the representational and derivational nature of grammar: The diversity of wh-constructions*. Cambridge, MA: MIT Press.

Bohnacker, Ute. 1997. Determiner phrases and the debate on functional categories in early child language. *Language Acquisition* 6:49–90.

———. 2004. Nominal phrases. In *The acquisition of Swedish grammar*, ed. Gunlög Josefsson, Christer Platzack, and Gisela Håkansson, 195–260. Amsterdam: John Benjamins.

———. 2007. The role of input frequency in article acquisition in early child Swedish. In *Frequency effects in language acquisition*, ed. Insa Gülzow and Natalia Gagarina, 51–82. Berlin: Mouton De Gruyter.

Brown, Roger. 1973. *First language acquisition: The early stages*. Cambridge, MA: Harvard University Press.

Cheng, Lisa Lai-Shen, and Rint Sybesma. 1999. Bare and not-so-bare nouns and the structure of NP. *Linguistic Inquiry* 30:509–42.

Chierchia, Gennaro. 1998. Reference to kinds across languages. *Natural Language Semantics* 6:339–405.

Chierchia, Gennaro, Maria Teresa Guasti, and Andrea Gualmini. 1999. Nouns and articles in child grammar and the syntax/semantics map. Presentation at GALA 1999, Potsdam.

Clahsen, Harald, Sonja Eisenbeiss, and Martina Penke. 1996. Lexical learning in early syntactic development. In *Generative perspectives on language acquisition*, ed. Harald Clahsen, 129–59. Amsterdam: John Benjamins.

Demuth, Katherine, Elizabeth McCullough, and Matthew Adamo. 2007. The prosodic (re)organization of determiners. In *Proceedings of the thirty-first annual BUCLD*, ed. David Bamman, Tatiana Magnitskaia, and Colleen Zaller, 196–205. Somerville, MA: Cascadilla Press.

Eisenbeiss, Sonja. 2002. Merkmalsgesteuerter Grammatikerwerb: Eine Untersuchung zum Erwerb der Struktur und Flexion der Nominalphrase. PhD diss., Heinrich Heine Universität Düsseldorf.

Gerken, Lou Ann. 1991. The metrical basis for children's subjectless sentences. *Journal of Memory and Language* 30:431–51.

———. 1994. A metrical template account of children's weak syllable omissions from multisyllabic words. *Journal of Child Language* 21:567–84.

Guasti, Maria Teresa, and Anna Gavarró. 2003. Catalan as a test for hypotheses concerning article omission. In *Proceedings of the twenty-fourth annual BUCLD*, ed. Barbara Beachley, Amanda Brown, and Frances Conlin, 288–98. Somerville, MA: Cascadilla Press.

Guasti, Maria Teresa, Joke De Lange, Anna Gavarró, and Claudia Caprin. 2004. Article omission: Across child languages and across special registers. In *Proceedings of GALA 2003*, ed. Jaqueline Van Kampen and Sergio Baauw, 199–210. Utrecht: LOT Occasional Series.

Jusczyk, Peter, Anne Cutler, and Nancy Redanz. 1993. Preference for the predominant stress patterns of English words. *Child Development* 64:675–87.

Kupisch, Tanja. 2006. *The acquisition of determiners in German-Italian and German-French children*. Munich: Lincom Europa.

———. 2007. Testing the effects of frequency on the rate of learning: Determiner use in early French, German and Italian. In *Frequency effects in language acquisition*, ed. Insa Gülzow and Natalia Gagarina, 83–113. Berlin: Mouton De Gruyter.

Lange, Sven, and Kenneth Larsson. 1973. Syntaxen i en 20-22 månader gammal flickas spontana tal. In *Svenskans beskrivning* 7, ed. C. Hummelstedt, 117–42. Åbo: Åbo akademi.

Lleó, Conxita. 1998. Proto-articles in the acquisition of Spanish: Interface between phonology and morphology. In *Models of inflection*, ed. Ray Fabri, Albert Ortmann, and Teresa Parodi, 175–95. Tübingen: Niemeyer.

———. 2001. The interface of phonology and syntax. The emergence of the article in the early acquisition of Spanish and German. In *Approaches to bootstrapping: Phonological, syntactic and neurophysiological aspects of early language acquisition*, vol. 2, ed. Jürgen Weissenborn and Barbara Höhle, 23–44. Amsterdam: John Benjamins.

Lleó, Conxita, and Katherine Demuth. 1999. Prosodic constraints on the emergence of grammatical morphemes: Cross-linguistic evidence from Germanic and Romance languages. In *Proceedings of the twenty-third annual BUCLD*, ed. Annabel Greenhill, Heather Littlefield, and Cheryl Tano, 407–18. Somerville, MA: Cascadilla Press.

McWhinney, Bryan, and Catherine Snow. 1990. The Child Language Data Exchange System: An update. *Journal of Child Language* 17:457–72.

Morén, Bruce. 2007. Central Swedish pitch accent: A retro approach. Old World Conference in Phonology 4, Rhodes, Greece.

Munn, Alan, and Cristina Schmitt. 2001. Bare nominals and the morpho-syntax of number. In *Current issues in Romance linguistics: Selected papers from the twenty-ninth Linguistic Symposium on Romance Languages*, ed. Diana Cresti, Teresa Satterfield, and Cristina Tortora, 217–31. Ann Arbor, Michigan, April. Amsterdam: John Benjamins.

Penner, Zvi, and Jürgen Weissenborn. 1996. Strong continuity, parameter setting and the trigger hierarchy: On the acquisition of the DP in Bernese Swiss German and High German. In *Generative perspectives on language acquisition*, ed. Harald Clahsen, 161–200. Amsterdam: John Benjamins.

Plunkett, Kim, and Sven Strömqvist. 1992. The acquisition of Scandinavian languages. In *The crosslinguistic study of language acquisition*, vol. 3, ed. Dan I. Slobin, 457–556. Hillsdale, NJ: Lawrence Erlbaum Associates.

Radford, Andrew. 1990. The syntax of nominal arguments in early child English. *Language Acquisition* 1:195–223.

Roark, Brian, and Katherine Demuth. 2000. Prosodic constraints and the learner's environment: A corpus study. In *Proceedings of the twenty-fourth annual BUCLD*, ed. S. Catherine Howell, Sarah A. Fish, and Thea Keith-Lucas, 597–608. Somerville, MA: Cascadilla Press.

Santelmann, Lynn. 1998. The acquisition of definite determiners in child Swedish: Metrical and discourse influences on functional morphology. In *Proceedings of the twenty-second annual BUCLD*, ed. Annabel Greenhill, Mary Hughes, and Heather Littlefield, 651–62. Somerville, MA: Cascadilla Press.

Selkirk, Elisabeth. 1996. The prosodic structure of function words. In *Signal to syntax: Bootstrapping from speech to grammar in early acquisition*, ed. James L. Morgan and Katherine Demuth, 187–213. Mahwah, NJ: Lawrence Erlbaum Associates.

Svartholm, Kristina. 1978. Svenskans artikelsystem: En genomgång av artikelbruket i vuxenspråket och en modell för analys i barnspråket. PhD diss., Stockholm University.

Szagun, Gisela. 2001. Learning different regularities: The acquisition of noun plurals by German-speaking children. *First Language* 21:109–41.

Theakston, Anna, Elena Lieven, Julian Pine, and Caroline Rowland. 2001. The role of performance limitations in the acquisition of verb-argument structure: An alternative account. *Journal of Child Language* 28:127–52.

Westergaard, Marit. 2007. Word order in subject- and object-shift constructions in early child language: Pragmatics or economy? Paper presented at Lund University.

Wiese, Richard. 1996. *The phonology of German.* Oxford: Clarendon Press.

20

A Continuum in French Children's Surface Realization of Auxiliaries

CRISTINA D. DYE
Georgetown University

A CENTRAL FOCUS of research in child language has been the acquisition of functional elements such as determiners and auxiliaries (see, e.g., Lust 2006, chap. 9, for a recent review). Early studies proposed that child speech is "telegraphic," that is, it consists mostly of content words such as verbs and nouns, which are essential to communication, while usually lacking function words (e.g., Brown 1973). The following two examples from child English illustrate what is usually referred to as telegraphic speech; in parentheses are possible functional elements that would render these utterances targetlike.

(1) (does) papa have it?   (Eve I, Brown 1973, 207)

(2) Adam (will) put it (in) (the) box.   (Adam I, Brown 1973, 205)

Telegraphic speech, or the ostensible absence of functional elements, has been widely discussed in the first language acquisition literature and has been claimed to be universal across languages (e.g., Brown 1973 and references therein). Specifically, the functional elements that are the focus of this chapter, that is, auxiliaries and modals (henceforth referred to as "auxiliaries"), have been claimed to be absent across child languages, for example, in early child English (e.g., Radford 1990), Dutch (e.g., Wijnen 1996/1997), or French (e.g., Schlyter 2003).

Numerous proposals have been offered to account for the ostensible absence of functional elements from early productions. Two major attempts to explain child "telegraphy" have consisted of proposing perceptual threshold limitations or deficient grammatical representations. The perceptual limitations view is based on the fact that, in contrast with content words, function words usually have shorter vowel duration and lower amplitude, fewer syllables, and simpler syllabic structure (e.g., Shi, Morgan, and Allopena 1998), and thus are less salient. Given this reduced acoustic phonetic salience, it has been proposed that children might simply fail to perceive or represent functional items in the speech they are exposed to (e.g., Gleitman and Wanner 1982; Echols 1993). Another attempted explanation is that the apparent absence of function words from early productions reflects a deficit in syntactic representations.

Here accounts range from proposals arguing for the complete absence of grammatical representations to proposals arguing for some specific grammatical deficit. For example, learner-based accounts such as Tomasello (1992) argue that young children lack grammar altogether. Some scholars suggest that children start out with a semantically based system and only later switch to a syntactically based one (e.g., Bowerman 1973; Gleitman 1981). Still others believe that the impoverished production of functional elements reflects a grammatical system that is radically different from adult grammar (e.g., Braine 1963). Within the generative paradigm, it has been proposed that early language is characterized by the general absence of functional categories and their projections (e.g., Radford 1990) or by the absence of specific functional categories (e.g., Hoekstra and Hyams 1999; Schlyter 2003; Schütze and Wexler 1996).

However, in spite of these long-standing views concerning functional items, a growing body of research argues that children's seemingly impoverished productions represent only an incomplete picture of their underlying grammatical competence. For example, examination of infants' and toddlers' comprehension indicates that they are sensitive to function words even before they produce these items (e.g., Gerken, Landau, and Remez 1990). Young children may in fact use functional elements to determine the syntactic category of the accompanying content words (e.g., Höhle et al. 2004; Kedar, Casasola, and Lust 2006). In a similar vein, a number of production studies reveal evidence for toddlers' knowledge of grammatical operations that depend on functional categories and their projections (e.g., Demuth 1992; Dye et al. 2004; Lust 1999, 2006; Whitman, Lee, and Lust 1991). Another growing line of studies argues that, at early ages, functional categories may be realized as "filler" vowels. Despite initial uncertainty regarding the status of filler vowels, more recent studies indicate that these behave as proto-functors[1] (e.g., Bottari, Cipriani, and Chilosi 1993/1994; Demuth and Tremblay 2007; Pepinsky, Demuth, and Roark 2001).[2] Fillers (or rather, proto-functors) occur in sentential slots where functional items are expected but have nontarget phonetic features, often taking the form of a reduced vowel (e.g., a schwa). Work on fillers suggests that functional categories may be present in syntactic representations early on, even though their initial overt realizations may diverge considerably from target forms. The status of functional elements in child language thus continues to pose a challenge to the field, and further investigation is needed to illuminate the way in which children acquire this fundamental part of the grammar.

The Present Study

This study, which is part of a larger investigation reported in Dye (2005), examines the status of one category of functional elements, namely auxiliaries, on the basis of a new corpus of child French. In contrast to much previous work, I argue that early productions are not as impoverished as typically assumed and that children might have greater grammatical knowledge than previously thought.

Data and Methods

The data for this study are from the Dye 2005 child French corpus. This consists of more than 5,000 child utterances based on cross-sectional natural speech samples containing 3,438 verb clauses; the high verb density provided for robust analyses. The participants were eighteen normally developing French monolingual children, with ages ranging from 1;11 to 2;11 (mean age = 2;5).[3] The children were recruited through day-care centers in Paris and Nancy, France, and were interviewed individually in a quiet room. Average interview length was thirty minutes.

My primary goals in compiling this new corpus were (a) to ensure the availability of discourse contexts for the linguistic structures under investigation, namely, verbs and auxiliaries, (b) to facilitate comparability among speech samples from different children, and (c) to ensure the audio quality necessary to capture functional items. To ensure that children had ample opportunity to produce the targeted items, I selected a set of activities, toys, and conversation topics that trigger utterances with verbs and auxiliaries. To render the speech samples obtained from different children more comparable, I attempted to standardize as much as possible several aspects of the interview process, namely, conversation topics, games, toys, interviewers, interviewer training, and interview location.

The sessions were videotaped. Also a separate audio-recording setup was used to ensure the audio quality necessary to capture functional items. A Sharp IM-MT880 digital minidisk recorder and Soundman OKM binaural stereo condenser microphones were used. The recorder attached to the interviewer's belt, and a pair of microphones was worn in the interviewer's ears, like headphones. This new audio-recording setup offered several advantages. First, it was mobile, allowing proximity to the child at all times. Second, it was unobtrusive, thus not distracting or intimidating the child. Third, the recorder quality made it possible to clearly capture children's voices even when they turned away or whispered. Fourth, the microphones were designed to capture sonic information in a manner similar to the human ear, thus producing very realistic recordings. Fifth, the microphones worked on phantom power from the recorder, thus eliminating the noise associated with a powered microphone.[4]

The recordings were digitally edited using Cool Edit to enhance the children's voices in relation to the background noise. The interviews were then transcribed with WAVpedal 5.0, transcription software that allows transcription directly from the computer, without going through analog and thus avoiding loss of quality. Audio samples were transcribed by trained native speakers and checked by the author, all of whom were present at the interviews. Transcription was carried out using French orthography. Where necessary, transcription and coding referred to spectrographic analyses carried out in Praat. Coding followed systematic procedures based on the Cornell University Virtual Linguistics Lab Research Methods Manual (Lust, Blume, and Ogden, forthcoming). In particular, utterances like *Spot va/veut partir* "Spot is gonna/wanna leave" were coded as consisting of a single verb clause. Although traditionally considered biclausal (e.g., Jones 1996), I treat strings like *va/faut/veut/peut* + infinitive "gonna/gotta/wanna/can + infinitive" as monoclausal because they are very common collocations in Colloquial French. Schlyter (2003, 21) makes a similar point based on the fact that "all these elements, in their most unmarked form (*a, e, va, veu, peu,* etc.) are used in very early stages both by children and adult learners, as markings of TMA (tense, modality, aspect)."[5]

Findings

The eighteen children studied produced a variety of auxiliary types and forms, as exemplified later. The specific types of auxiliaries observed in children's speech samples, in decreasing order of frequency, were the past tense auxiliaries *avoir/être* "have/be," the immediate future auxiliary *aller* "gonna," the modal auxiliaries *pouvoir* "can," *vouloir* "wanna," and *falloir* "gotta."

There was also a range in the surface realizations of auxiliaries. I begin by presenting examples with target auxiliary forms (i.e., child forms that match the target form in the adult language). Next I illustrate nontarget auxiliary forms and then filler auxiliaries. Before concluding, I also present utterances where the auxiliary is missing but that nevertheless evidence phonetic traces of the missing auxiliary.[6]

Target Auxiliaries

Examples of utterances with target auxiliaries are provided in (3) through (7).

(3) l'élépfant i **peut** pus, i **peut** pus tomber   (age 1;11)
    "the elephant he **can** no-longer, he **can** no-longer fall-INF"

(4) **vais** l'enver ça   (age 2;2)
    "am-gonna it remove-INF this"

(5) je **vais** mett' ça   (age 1;11)
    "I **am-gonna** put-INF this"

(6) oh, **a** perdu son pied   (age 1;11)
    "oh, **has** lose-PRT his foot"

(7) **veux** enver ss . . . euh . . . la saise   (age 2;1)
    "wanna remove-INF ss . . . ah . . . the chair"

Nontarget Auxiliaries

In addition to target auxiliaries, children also produced nontarget auxiliary forms. These may be forms including one or more inaccurate segments. For example, in (8) the child produced [po] for the target [pə] *peux* "can," combining the target consonant with a nontarget vowel.

(8) euh, **[po]** pas boire   (age 2;6)
    "oh, **can**not drink-INF"

Example (9) shows an auxiliary form with nontarget consonant and target vowel. Both the pragmatic and linguistic contexts support the interpretation of [ka] as the immediate future auxiliary [va] *va* "gonna." The child is in the process of deciding where to place a figurine (i.e., is holding the figurine in hand and is looking for a free spot), announces she is not going to place it in one spot, starts repeating this, and then suddenly notices the perfect spot:

(9) on **[ka]** pas mette là   (age 2;5)
    "we **are-gonna** not put-INF there"

    . . .

on [va] pas . . . , là!

"we are-gonna not . . . , there!"

In (10) the child is asking the adult to open the door for her. The linguistic and pragmatic context of (10) clearly suggests that the form [le] stands for the modal auxiliary [və] *veux*, "gonna" (here both the consonant and the vowel are nontarget).

(10) I qu'est-ce que tu veux faire?[7]   (age 1;11)

     "what is it that you wanna do-INF?"

   C **[le]** ouwrir la porte!   (asking the adult to open the door for her)

     "**wanna** open-INF the door."

   I tu veux ouvrir la porte?

     "you wanna open-INF the door?"

   C oui

     "yes"

Other nontarget forms involve reduced auxiliaries. The form *v'rait* in (11) represents a reduction of the auxiliary *voudrais* "would-like-to" and the form *vait* in (12) represents a reduction of the auxiliary *avait* "had":

(11) **v'rait** s'asseoir là la soris   (age 2;6)

     "**would-like-to** REFLEXIVE sit-INF there the mouse"

(12) **vait** fait la palle   (age 2;2)

     "**had** do-PRT the ball"

Some auxiliary forms are barely discernable. For example, in (13), the element immediately preceding the main verb was initially barely audible, having much lower intensity than the main verb.

(13) __rémonter (child is whining)   (age 2;1)

     "__go-up-INF"

Spectrographic analyses of (13) identified the first element in the utterance as the auxiliary *veux* "wanna" (figure 20.1). (13) is in fact (13'):

(13') **veux** rémonter (child is whining)   (age 2;1)

     '**wanna** go-up-INF'

Inspection of the linguistic and pragmatic context of (13') showed that it occurs in the context of the child's requesting to go upstairs to join the other children. Here the high quality of the digital audio recordings together with spectrographic inspection allowed for the identification of the auxiliary. It is possible that such auxiliary productions have been overlooked in studies based on older corpora collected with less sensitive equipment or not analyzed spectrographically.

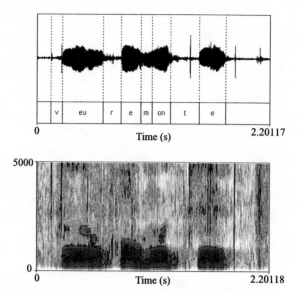

Figure 20.1 Spectogram of *veux rémonter,* "wanna go up"

Filler Auxiliaries

Besides target and nontarget forms, children produced filler auxiliaries as, for example, in (14). Here the element [e] may correspond to any of several possible auxiliaries (e.g., [pə] "can," [va] "gonna").

(14) I   bah oui, tu vois, on peut pas les enlever
         "well yes, you see, we cannot them remove-INF"

     C   Suilà, [e] l' enver? (asking if she can remove figurine)   (age 1;11)
         "that-one, FILLER AUX it remove-INF?"[8]

Quantitative results for auxiliaries are summarized in figure 20.2. Out of the total 3,438 verb clauses in the corpus, 785 contain auxiliaries.[9] Clauses with auxiliaries range from 3.1 percent (for a child age 2;1) to 35.6 percent (for a child age 2;6) of a participant's total verb clauses.

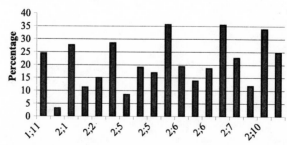

Figure 20.2 Clauses with Auxiliaries as a Proportion of Verb Clauses, by Individual Child and Age

As seen in figure 20.2, all children examined here produce auxiliaries, including the youngest child (age 1;11), whose percentage of clauses with auxiliaries (24.4%) resembles those of older children ages 2;7 and 2;11 (22.7% and 24.6%, respectively).

Phonetic Traces of Missing Auxiliaries

I now turn to utterances that, although not coded as containing an auxiliary, nevertheless appear to show evidence for an underlying auxiliary. This evidence consists of phonetic traces of the missing auxiliary. I illustrate two types of phonetic traces of missing auxiliaries.

One child tends to mark the syntactic slot of the auxiliary with a pause/breath, as, for example, in (15). This is consistent with Carter and Gerken's (2004) findings that English-speaking children tend to leave a prosodic/phonetic trace when omitting a weak syllable, that is, they have a longer pause between the item preceding and the item following the omitted syllable (compared with the pause between the preceding item and the weak syllable itself, when this is produced).

(15) qu'à haut, **(breath)** remonter   (age 2;1)

   "up there, **(breath)** go-back-up-INF"

   [ə] remonter

   "wanna go-back-up-INF"

   [və] rémonter

   "wanna go-back-up-INF"

The first utterance in the sequence in (15), where the position of the auxiliary is marked by a pause/breath, is immediately followed by two increasingly fuller productions of the target auxiliary [və] *veux* "wanna," a fact that supports the presence of an underlying auxiliary in the first utterance in this sequence.

Example (16) illustrates a second type of utterance in which the auxiliary is apparently missing. Here the child's production involves reduplication of the first syllable of the main verb.

(16) boum! **dar** darmir   (age 2;2)

   "boom! REDUPLICATION sleep-INF"

Although this type of production has not been discussed in relation to child French, it has been discussed for child Greek, where Christofidou and Kappa (1998) observed that prior to the productive use of the future and modal/subjunctive auxiliary particles (*tha, na*), children indicate these by reduplicating the first syllable of the main verb. The authors note that reduplications such as *pe petsume* for target *na peksume* MODAL PARTICLE play-PFV-NONPAST-1PL. "let's play," or *ka kani* for target *na kani* MODAL PARTICLE make-NONPAST-3SG. "she/he should do," are rather extensive in their data and systematically mark the function of modality or future, rendering the preverbal modal or future particles. The reduplicated syllable in the French example in (16) is therefore likely to represent an early realization of the missing auxiliary, which in this case is probably *va* "gonna" (the child throws the doll in the toy bed as she announces that the doll is going to sleep).

To summarize, we have seen that auxiliaries (including modals) are evidenced in all children from the earliest ages examined, contrary to what has been reported in many previous studies. The present results disconfirm previous claims that auxiliaries might be absent in young children's speech and, in particular, claims regarding the absence of auxiliaries in child French (e.g., Schlyter 2003).[10] These findings also contrast with previous reports that French-speaking children use the future auxiliary *aller* "gonna" from around the age of 3;0 on (Clark 1985, 723). As exemplified in the utterance in (4) (from a child age 2;2) and the utterance in (5) (from a child age 1;11), the children studied here produce the *aller* "gonna" auxiliary from much earlier ages. The eighteen French-speaking children evidence a range of auxiliary forms. Target auxiliaries, nontarget auxiliaries, and filler auxiliaries occur side by side, as illustrated in the sequence in (15) where the target [və] *veux* "gonna" has different realizations each time it is produced (by the same child during the same session). In addition, some of the utterances where the auxiliary seems to be missing show evidence for phonetic traces of the missing auxiliary. What these data show is a continuum in the surface realization of auxiliary forms.

Discussion

The current results provide evidence that auxiliaries are present in children's syntactic representations. The new French data reveal a continuum in the surface representation of auxiliaries: Target auxiliaries, nontarget auxiliaries, filler auxiliaries, and phonetic traces of auxiliaries occur side by side in children's productions.

The present findings call into question the traditional notion of telegraphic speech. As seen in the French examples, early child productions are not as impoverished as previously thought. The eighteen children studied here are not "telegraphic." Moreover, these data indicate that omissions in early speech do not simply reflect absence of function words. Rather early speech reflects a range in the degree of surface realization of auxiliaries and appears to be characterized by more gradation than usually assumed.

Furthermore, these findings challenge long-standing notions that children do not produce certain functional items (in this case, auxiliaries) because of deficient syntactic representations thereof or because of perceptual threshold limitations. Instead, the present results corroborate recent evidence of young children's sensitivity to function words (e.g., Gerken, Landau, and Remez 1990; Kedar, Casasola, and Lust 2006), as well as evidence of early competence for functional structure based on knowledge of operations dependent on functional structure (e.g., Demuth 1992; Dye et al. 2004; Lust 1999, 2006; Whitman, Lee, and Lust 1991).

Conclusion

The French child data do not support a simple present or absent analysis but rather reflect a continuum in surface realization, suggesting a need to revise the notion of what it means for the auxiliary to be "present." The study has uncovered new evidence supporting the continuous projection of auxiliaries in young children's grammatical representations, indicating that early productions are not as impoverished as previously thought. The present findings lend support to proposals for the primacy of syntax in child language acquisition; they cohere with the observation that "the building of syntax may actually precede the phonetic (or morpholexical) realization of functional heads themselves" (Demuth 1992, 84).

NOTES

My gratitude goes to Barbara Lust, Carol Rosen, Yashiro Shirai, John Whitman, Claire Foley, Yumiko Nishi, Réjane Frick, Marc Brunelle, Andrew Spencer, Yarden Kedar, and two anonymous reviewers. I also thank the parents and children who participated. This research was supported by a Sicca research grant and a Cognitive Studies Fellowship from Cornell University.

1. In fact, some studies refer to them as "proto-syntactic devices" (Bottari, Cipriani, and Chilosi 1993/1994).
2. But see Veneziano and Sinclair (2000), where fillers are argued to be prosodic placeholders.
3. I originally collected audio recordings from fifty subjects. For this study, I have transcribed only those for which I also have video recordings. Subjects who had problems participating in the task were excluded.
4. See Dye (2005) for more details about the recording setup.
5. See Dye (2005) for additional discussion of this point.
6. Further examples of the utterance types presented here are found in Dye (2005).
7. "I" stands for "interviewer," and "C" stands for "child."
8. One may wonder whether in (14) the filler syllable stands for the auxiliary or the subject clitic. Filler syllables do not occur with synthetic finite verbs. This suggest that fillers preceding nonfinite verbs as in (14) are unlikely to stand for a subject clitic (see Dye 2005).
9. The remaining 2,653 verb clauses included either synthetic finite verbs (2,496 clauses) or ostensibly nonfinite verbs occurring in matrix contexts (157 clauses).
10. Schlyter (2003, 27) reports that in the first recordings of three French (bilingual) children, when these children were ages 2;3, 2;0, and 2;2, respectively, auxiliaries and modals were absent.

REFERENCES

Bottari, Piero, Paolo Cipriani, and Ana Maria Chilosi. 1993/1994. Proto-syntactic devices in the acquisition of Italian free morphology. *Language Acquisition* 3:327–69.

Bowerman, Melissa. 1973. *Early syntactic development: A cross-linguistic study with special reference to Finnish*. New York: Cambridge University Press.

Braine, Martin. 1963. The ontogeny of English phrase structure: The first phase. *Language* 39:1–13.

Brown, Roger. 1973. *A first language: The early stages*. Cambridge, MA: Harvard University Press.

Carter, Allyson, and LouAnn Gerken. 2004. Do children's omissions leave traces? *Journal of Child Language* 31:561–86.

Christofidou, Anastasia, and Ionna Kappa 1998. Pre- and proto-morphological fillers in Greek language acquisition. *Studies in the acquisition of number and diminutive marking: Antwerp papers in linguistics* 95:193–214.

Clark, Eve. 1985. The acquisition of Romance with special reference to French. In *The Cross-linguistic study of language acquisition*, vol. 1, *The data*, ed. Dan I. Slobin, 687–782. Hillsdale, NJ: Lawrence Erlbaum Associates.

Demuth, Katherine. 1992. Accessing functional categories in Sesotho. In *The acquisition of verb placement: Functional categories and V2 phenomena in language acquisition*, ed. Jurgen Meisel, 83–107. Dordrecht: Kluwer.

Demuth, Katherine, and Annie Tremblay. 2007. Prosodically-conditioned variability in children's production of French determiners. *Journal of Child Language* 34:1–29.

Dye, Cristina D. 2005. Identifying auxiliaries in first language acquisition: Evidence from a new child French corpus. PhD diss., Cornell University.

Dye, Cristina D., Claire Foley, Maria Blume, and Barbara Lust. 2004. Mismatches between morphology and syntax in first language acquisition suggest a "syntax first" model. *Online Proceedings of BU-CLD 28*. www.bu.edu/linguistics/APPLIED/BUCLD/supp.html (accessed October 13, 2008).

Echols, Catharine H. 1993. A perceptually based model of children's earliest productions. *Cognition* 46:245–96.

Gerken, LouAnn, Barbara Landau, and Robert Remez. 1990. Function morphemes in young children's speech perception and production. *Developmental Psychology* 26 (2): 204–16.

Gleitman, Lila. 1981. Maturational determinants of language growth. *Cognition* 10:103–14.

Gleitman, Lila, and Eric Wanner. 1982. The state of the art. In *Language acquisition: The state of the art,* ed. Eric Wanner and Lila Gleitman, 3–48. Cambridge: Cambridge University Press.

Hoekstra, Teun, and Nina Hyams. 1999. The eventivity constraint and modal reference effects in root infinitives. *Proceedings of BUCLD* 23, 240–52. Somerville, MA: Cascadilla Press.

Höhle, Barbara, Jurgen Weisseborn, Dorothea Keifer, Antje Schultz, and Michaela Schmitz. 2004. Functional elements in infants' speech processing: The role of determiners in syntactic categorization of lexical elements. *Infancy* 5 (3): 341–53.

Jones, Michael A. 1996. *Foundations of French syntax.* Cambridge: Cambridge University Press.

Kedar, Yarden, Marianella Casasola, and Barbara Lust. 2006. Getting there faster: 18- and 24- month-old infants' use of function words to determine reference. *Child Development* 77 (2): 25–338.

Lust, Barbara. 1999. Universal grammar: The strong continuity hypothesis in first language acquisition. In *Handbook of child language acquisition,* ed. W. C. Ritchie and T. K. Bhatia, 111–56. New York: Academic Press.

———. 2006. *Child language: Acquisition and growth.* Cambridge: Cambridge University Press.

Lust, Barbara, Maria Blume, and Tina Ogden. Forthcoming. *Cornell University virtual linguistics lab research methods manual: Scientific methods for the study of language acquisition.* Cambridge, MA: MIT Press.

Pepinsky, Thomas, Katherine Demuth, and Brian Roark. 2001. The status of "filler syllables" in children's early speech. In *Proceedings of BUCLD 25,* 575–86. Somerville, MA: Cascadilla Press.

Radford, Andrew. 1990. *Syntactic theory and the acquisition of English syntax: The nature of early child grammars of English.* Cambridge, MA: Blackwell.

Schlyter, Suzanne. 2003. Development of verb morphology and finiteness in children and adults acquiring French. In *Information structure and the dynamics of language acquisition,* ed. Christine Dimroth and Marianne Starren, 15–44. Amsterdam: John Benjamins.

Schutze, Carson, and Ken Wexler. 1996. Subject case licensing and English root infinitives. In *Proceedings of BUCLD 20,* 670–81. Somerville, MA: Cascadilla Press.

Shi, Rushen, James Morgan, and Paul Allopena. 1998. Phonological and acoustic bases for earliest grammatical category assignment: A cross-linguistic perspective. *Journal of Child Language* 25:169–201.

Tomasello, Michael. 1992. *First verbs: A case study of early grammatical development.* Cambridge: Cambridge University Press.

Veneziano, Eddy, and Hermine Sinclair. 2000. The changing status of "filler syllables" on the way to grammatical morphemes. *Journal of Child Language* 27:461–500.

Whitman, John, Kwee-Ock Lee, and Barbara Lust. 1991. Continuity of the principles of universal grammar in first language acquisition: The issue of functional categories. In *Proceedings of NELS 21,* 383–97. Amherst: GLSA, University of Massachusetts, Amherst.

Wijnen, Frank. 1996/1997. Temporal reference and eventivity in root infinitives. *MIT Occasional Papers in Linguistics* 12:1–2.

WITHDRAWAL